Articulating the Elephant Man

Parallax 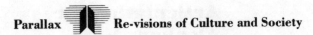 **Re-visions of Culture and Society**

Stephen G. Nichols, Gerald Prince, and Wendy Steiner,
Series Editors

Articulating the Elephant Man

Joseph Merrick and His Interpreters

PETER W. GRAHAM

FRITZ H. OEHLSCHLAEGER

The Johns Hopkins University Press
Baltimore and London

The Johns Hopkins University Press
701 West 40th Street
Baltimore, Maryland 21211-2190
The Johns Hopkins Press Ltd., London

Permission to quote from *Words for Elephant Man*, by
Kenneth Sherman, Copyright © Kenneth Sherman, 1983,
text, and Copyright © George Raab, 1983, illustrations,
is granted by Mosaic Press, P.O. Box 1032, Oakville,
Ontario L6J 5E9, Canada.

Library of Congress Cataloging-in-Publication Data
Graham, Peter W., 1951–
   Articulating the elephant man : Joseph Merrick and His
Interpreters / Peter W. Graham, Fritz H. Oehlschlaeger.
       p.   cm. — (Parallax)
   Includes bibliographical references and index.
   ISBN 0-8018-4357-X
   1. Pomerance, Bernard. Elephant man.   2. Merrick, Joseph Carey,
1862 or 3–1890, in fiction, drama, poetry, etc.   3. Treves, Frederick,
Sir, 1853–1923. Elephant man.   4. Drama—20th century—History
and criticism.   5. Merrick, Joseph Carey, 1862 or 3–1890.
6. Abnormalities, Human.   7. Neurofibromatosis.   I. Oehlschlaeger,
Fritz.   II. Title.   III. Series: Parallax (Baltimore, Md.).
PR6066.048E434   1992
822'.914—dc20   91-5106

Contents

Acknowledgments

This book is at all levels a collaborative effort—one that arose out of many conversations on matters related to medicine and the humanities and that was jointly researched and written. Accordingly, we both take responsibility for the assertions and interpretations offered here.

Those arguments and readings are, however, stronger than they might otherwise be thanks to the kind and resourceful help of a number of people who assisted us at various phases of the project. Fritz Oehlschlaeger began his work in medical ethics at James F. Childress's NEH-sponsored summer seminar "Principles and Metaphors in Biomedical Ethics." He would like to thank his fellow seminar members, Professor Childress, the University of Virginia, and the National Endowment for the Humanities. Once our research was under way, we were ably assisted by our Summer Research Assistant, Susan Gibson. The information we gathered about various representations of the Elephant Man story was more extensive and intensive thanks to the generous help of various people, especially Peter Bellerman, Ronald A. Carson, Roy Faudree, Jed Harris, George Hendrick, Anne Hudson Jones, Michael Roth, Sheena See, David J. Sleasman, John Stone, and the staff of the Carol Newman Library's Interlibrary Loan Department. Having written what we had to say, we were glad of the encouragement and insights offered by Joanne Trautmann Banks, Jacqueline Wehmueller of the Johns Hopkins University Press, and Grace Buonocore.

For continued support of various kinds, we are grateful to our colleagues in the English Department at Virginia Polytechnic Institute and State University and, as ever, to our families.

Articulating the
Elephant Man

1

Introduction

There are stories so compelling that they resist closure, so richly suggestive that they defy containment. Such stories continue to exist and develop independent of the individuals who have lived their facts or contrived their fictions—and though they may inspire enduring poetry, prose, music, and art, their own survival has comparatively little to do with the particular merits of the works presenting them. These stories live on in us because, in straightforward or indirect ways, we read ourselves in them. The truths they announce and the situations they explore are primordial, but each age adds a few figures and variants to the archetypal inventory—the evidence for such a claim being that, having burst the bounds of fiction or fact, they continue to evolve and to inspire, to renew themselves in creative minds of diverse sorts.

The most fascinating and enduring such stories from nineteenth-century England seem to center on doubles or divided selves. Victor Frankenstein and his unnamed monster and Dr. Henry Jekyll and Edward Hyde are fictional members of this immortal gallery. At the very time the stage version of Jekyll and Hyde was causing frenzy in the West End of London, two equally absorbing and enduring real stories were being enacted in the East End. In the dark streets and courts of Whitechapel, Jack the Ripper was pursuing his murderous course; and in the safe haven of the London Hospital, Joseph Merrick, the so-called Elephant Man and perhaps the most celebrated sufferer of the deforming disorder that has come to be known as the Proteus syndrome, was nearing the end of his life. The Elephant Man's existence was more thoroughly documented than Jack the Ripper's, but ultimately just as mysterious—and his presence has proven equally fascinating to popular, creative, and scholarly minds alike. Our goal in the following pages is to trace the story of the Elephant Man as it has evolved—to articulate, in all senses of the word and insofar as we are able, a story that shifts shape like Proteus himself and eludes the grasp of those who aspire to comprehend it.

This project rose out of our teaching Bernard Pomerance's play *The Elephant Man* and David Lynch's film of the same name. Both center on the life of Merrick. Both are crucially concerned with deformity and its various consequences, psychological and social. But the images the two texts present of their protagonist's character, medical condition, and circumstances are very different. The disparities between these two recent, popular, and critically acclaimed interpretations of a real-life situation intrigued us in several ways. Getting behind fictions to such facts as might be available was the immediate challenge, but even more compelling was a larger issue suggested by the variant stories— namely, that disease and deformity, even identity, are in part social constructs, arbitrary and mutable expressions of cultural and personal values. One of our main purposes in the following pages is to examine, in a chronological and critical way, how the phenomenon labeled "the Elephant Man" has been constructed and reconstructed—how Joseph Merrick has been transformed from a suffering individual to an exhibit, a shape-shifting curiosity whose different guises variously suit the needs of particular audiences, genres, and interpreters. The Elephant Man's successive presenters have included distinguished Victorian men of medicine (chief among them the surgeon Frederick Treves), a well-known social anthropologist (Ashley Montagu), and a diverse array of recent interpreters (best known among them the filmmaker Lynch and the playwright Pomerance). But preceding all these presenters is Merrick himself, no mere passive sufferer but the first mover in the process of creating the Elephant Man, an individual who bravely endured—and, when he had to, successfully exploited—his outrageously intractable bodily disorder.

Becoming the Elephant Man for the freak-show circuit may have started out as a modest bit of fiction making, but it proved to be a powerful figurative gesture, one that survived and subsumed the man who made it. Why should the Elephant Man be one of those characters defying containment? Why should his story resist closure? What made the myth of the Elephant Man so particularly compelling in Merrick's own time and place? What makes the story so fascinating today? All these questions proved important in our exploration of the Elephant Man narratives. It seems to us that Merrick's story has endured primarily because its deep truths are mythic. The story of the Elephant Man is, as successive interpreters have understood in their different ways, at once incredible and familiar. The real details of Merrick's life conform to a recognizable and perennially interesting pattern—one that, whether it be pared down to essentials or encrusted with elaborations, underpins many of our most ancient tales. As the epithet "Elephant Man" suggests, Merrick's is a story of metamorphosis. Imprisoned in a body being continuously and grotesquely remade through a process he could neither understand nor control, Merrick faced what every human being who grows old or falls ill must endure: the sense of exclusion from the world of the healthy and normal, the dilemma of whether to accept a blighted body as an attribute of essential identity or to reject it as a misleading mask, the sufferer's painful questions about cause and effect, about personal guilt or cosmic cruelty. His bodily condition, then, was extraordinary in degree, not in kind.

If Merrick's body experienced one sort of transformation, his personal status underwent another. The events of his life were such that they fit without much shaping into a social narrative we all find easily recognizable—that of the worthy but downtrodden being who overcomes unattractiveness, poverty, or some other handicap. As the stories of Cinderella, Dick Whittington, and Puss in Boots, to name a few of the more familiar archetypes, demonstrate, anecdotal evidence that the deserving but disenfranchised can rise in a world where the odds are against them has long been a mainstay of popular culture and will remain so until those who feel included greatly outnumber those who feel excluded. Things that actually happened to Merrick conform to this pattern. Patient, pious, and gentle, he was forced to make his way in an indifferent, even hostile, environment. He suffered indignities but enjoyed a dramatic change of fortune—through the sympathetic intervention of a young surgeon, not a fairy godmother or talking cat, and by means of public charity, not magic or chicanery. His life, like a folk hero's or heroine's, ended with a measure of comfort, a small portion of fame, and the courteous notice of the eminent, the beautiful, even the royal.

Such a sequence of events would prove interesting in any age; but the specific details of Merrick's rise in the world through the benevolent agency of Treves and the London Hospital strike us as especially well suited to interpretation by Merrick's Victorian contemporaries and in our own time. The Victorians were as complex as any group of people, and to boil down their collective ideology in a few phrases would be exceedingly simplistic. Even so, it is safe to generalize that they were inclined to be sentimental rather than cynical—that, though wide-ranging and eclectic, they tended to colonize diversity rather than to accept it on its own terms. Their cultural project of uplift extended from the imperial macrocosm, the "white man's burden" of "dominion over palm and pine," to the personal microcosm, where one might find a Treves attempting to normalize an extravagantly alien specimen such as the Elephant Man. This preoccupation with civilizing the barbarian and domesticating the savage coincided with the more basic uncertainties evoked by the work of Darwin and his fellow scientists. If the Victorians were, as cultural beings, engrossed in remaking the world in their own image, they were equally absorbed in trying to understand what distinguished them, as natural beings, from the rest of creation. Merrick's case, for all these reasons, was just right for inspiring both the compassion and the fears of his milieu. He was at once an ideal object of charity and a powerful reproach—an affirmation of cultural commonplaces and a challenge to the most basic assumptions about humanity.

A Victorian confrontation with the Elephant Man could result in true compassion or smug condescension. Similarly, our late twentieth-century encounters with the story have potential for expanding our sympathies or for pandering to our distinctive prejudices. Certain features of Merrick's story, some that attracted the Victorians and some that did not, make it ripe for retelling in our time. As the ultimate outsider, Merrick can represent all the categories of people whose worth we are striving to recognize even as we respect their difference: among others, women, minorities, the homeless, the unborn. Having seen the humanity in him, we might move on to cherishing it in the marginalized among us—a desirable consequence indeed. But the Elephant Man story also ministers to those largely unacknowledged cultural propensities that make us in some respects opposite and in other ways analogous to the Victorians, notably our suspicion of most kinds of authority and programs of improvement (particularly the patriarchal sorts that combined in "saving" Merrick) and our tendency to identify with the underdog rather than the top dog in power relations. If it was culturally convenient for the Victorians to patronize Merrick and congratulate his benefactors, it is as easy for us to exalt the former to a subversive hero and to debunk the latter as self-serving exploiters. No less than the Victorians, we are capable of learning about ourselves from the stories we tell about Merrick. No less than the Victorians, we are capable of schematizing and appropriating him.

The particular stories of the Elephant Man are interesting in and of themselves, but they also have a wider relevance. As scholars of diverse sorts—literary critics, medical ethicists, historians—have stressed, storytelling is seldom a simple matter of devising fictions or relating facts. Many genres, perhaps even most of them, involve intricately mixed modes of reportage: blends of description and creation, observation and self-revelation, selective recording, alteration, and suppression of details. Storytelling, whether it results in a drama, a film, a sequence of poems, or a medical case study, can show nearly as much about the observer as it does about the subject. The Elephant Man's presenters have distinctive personal, cultural, and generic biases that shape their perceptions of Merrick's character, circumstances, and medical condition. Thus, we examine not just the final texts but also, as far as possible, their paratextual circumstances. The first external fact to stress about these texts is that they do not exist in isolation from one another. The Elephant Man's story is, for most of its tellers, mediated through and thus modified by several previous versions of the story. For this reason, it might be best to begin with an informal genealogy of the texts to be examined in this articulation.

Frederick Treves's "The Elephant Man," first and title piece in the collection called *The Elephant Man and Other Reminiscences* (1923), provides a basis on which the major subsequent accounts have built. Treves's interest in Merrick, it hardly need be said, was far from simple. What began as a mere scientific transaction—his observation of a "freak of nature," followed by exhibition of this anomalous being before the Pathological Society of London and a written report on the disorder

("A Case of Congenital Deformity," published in the *Transactions of the Pathological Society of London* for 1885)—became, when Merrick re-entered his life in 1886, a personal commitment that cannot be fully understood in terms of a doctor's relationship to his or her patient. Writing from various perspectives, Treves is an eminent medical man looking back over his career, a man of letters making the most of his richest material, a confident and practical, yet sensitive, person meditating on what must have been one of the most mysterious and moving encounters of his life. The reminiscence has mythic overtones, with Treves casting himself as much as Pygmalion as Aesculapius. In the account, his chief end during the years of association with Merrick is not curing disease or even easing physical discomfort, but humanizing and socializing an outcast whose deepest sufferings, as he recognizes, are not necessarily bodily ones. Treves's reminiscence raises a host of fascinating issues both for those who have followed him in writing about Merrick and for us as students of medicine and literature: the role of selection, suppression, and shaping in the writing of medical reminiscence; the relationship between Merrick and women as objects of observation and the role of women in moving Merrick toward normality; the paradoxical relationship of physician and patient as the two develop in relation to each other, with Treves alternately perceiving his likeness to, and difference from, Merrick.

Ashley Montagu, who read Treves's account shortly after its publication, endeavored to bring Merrick and Treves back from oblivion in *The Elephant Man: A Study in Human Dignity* (1971). For Montagu, the story held triple appeal: "human nature, bones, and the London of Henry Mayhew." His monograph, which reprints Treves's reminiscence and then contextualizes it in various ways, is, like the Treves piece, multiple in its approaches. Montagu writes as an anatomist, as an anthropologist, as a medical educator, and, in a loosely speculative vein, as a student of the human condition. He amplifies upon, and sometimes corrects, Treves's reminiscence and, in the technical chapters devoted to neurofibromatosis, updates Treves's scientific writings on Merrick. But the Elephant Man story also interests Montagu because of its particular bearing on general issues he discusses in other of his books: the ways of becoming human and humane, the puzzles of heredity, the importance of love (especially maternal love in the formative years). Indeed, for Montagu, Merrick functions primarily as a hero of love, one who became a psychologically healthy adult able to love, work, and play despite his early socioeconomic deprivations and his terrible deformity. He thus enlists the gentle Merrick as a living refutation of theories of innate human aggressiveness and an exemplar of a way of being human free from the dominant male models of competition, conflict, and coercive power.

Montagu's book brought Merrick and Treves back into prominence—and the late Victorian story soon showed itself to be a richly suggestive tale for the times. In the years following the publication of Montagu's book, various film scripts and plays indebted to his and Treves's accounts were written. The most successful of the theatrical versions, Bernard Pomerance's *Elephant Man* (1979), is both a tour de force for the actor playing Merrick and a serious, thoughtful exploration of certain issues and problems raised by the Merrick-Treves relationship and not examined with much critical attention by Montagu. Pomerance is interested in such matters as the arbitrary tyranny of the "normal," the problems of medical paternalism, and the dance of attraction and repulsion acted out by Merrick and those who met him. The play explores both the narcissism of those who read versions of their own experience in Merrick and the ambiguities inherent in Merrick's development from exhibition, from being one paradoxically for others, to personal selfhood, being one with and among others. Because Pomerance's version of the Elephant Man story is, despite its substantial reliance on material from Treves and Montagu, ruled by generic conventions other than those prevailing for the medical man or the anthropologist, he is free explicitly to imagine and voice Merrick's side of things to a degree not possible in his predecessors' works. The result is a highly articulate, razor-witted Merrick who engages his healer-creator Treves on a wide range of problems implicit in relations where authority is of necessity present.

The preemptive success of Pomerance's play in London and on Broadway guaranteed that his would be, for a theatrical generation at least, the definitive stage version of Merrick's story—but in fact a number of other dramatists wrote Elephant Man plays contemporary with or previous to Pomerance's. In chapter 6 we examine the three best known, plays by Thomas Gibbons, William Turner, and Roy Faudree. Each dramatist brings a different interpretive framework to the story of Merrick and Treves. Each has a different way of using the source mate-

rials. Each is experimental in a different sense. Whereas Gibbons'
play is curiously noninteractive, a sequential splicing of monologues
sticking very close to published sources, Turner's gives free rein to
speculation, highlighting in a piquantly idiosyncratic way the parallels
between Merrick's lot and Princess Alexandra's. Chapter 6 gives particular attention to Faudree's carnival of transformations, in some ways
the most adventurous piece of theater devoted to Merrick's story. Exploiting the conventions of Victorian spectacular theater, the Ibsen
problem play, and Japanese Nō drama, Faudree playfully juxtaposes
period detail and blatant anachronism, facts from Merrick's life and
whimsical fancy drawn from the Parker Brothers board game Clue and
elsewhere. In his play, rigid class prejudices, repressive gender roles,
and constrictive fashions deform all the men and women surrounding
Merrick: Each character is a freak, and each actor has his or her turn to
play the Elephant Man.

Much better known than these latter plays is Lynch's film *The Elephant Man* (1979), which appeared shortly after the debut of the
Pomerance play and takes great pains to disavow any indebtedness to
its stage counterpart. A strenuous denial in some cases generates suspicion rather than allaying it; but in fact the film has objectives, preoccupations, and excellences clearly distinct from those of the play.
Where Pomerance demands that acting skill by itself convince the audience of Merrick's deformity, Lynch exploits the talents of the makeup
artist, to the extent that the presence of particular deformities chal-
lenged John Hurt (who plays Merrick in the film) in ways opposite but
perhaps equivalent to the difficulties that an absence of such features
presents to stage actors playing the role. We see the dreams but do not
hear the verbalized thoughts of Lynch's Merrick, who is less a creature—and master—of words than is Pomerance's. Unlike the stylized
sets of the play, the milieu in which Lynch's Treves and Merrick move is
realistic and richly particularized. In Lynch's grainy black-and-white
film, the foggy menace of 1880s Whitechapel and the grim realities of
late nineteenth-century hospitals become almost palpable. Specific
period images described in other Treves reminiscences from the *Elephant Man* volume, most notably "The Old Receiving Room," take on
form and presence in the film. Montagu's theories also inform Lynch's
vision, which presents Merrick's experience as a search for his lost
mother.

In *The True History of the Elephant Man* (1980), Michael Howell and Peter Ford correct misconceptions about Merrick and establish a reliable, though bare, narrative of his life, with helpful contextual material. It is Howell and Ford, for instance, who finally restore to Merrick his Christian name Joseph and correctly identify his parents. Their title, *The True History of the Elephant Man*, is richly significant: It has an appropriately Victorian sideshow sound, and at the same time it manages to suggest its own definitiveness and previous treatments' unreliability. If Howell and Ford's is a "true" history, earlier versions must, by implication, be more or less "false." Despite their title's claim, however, Howell and Ford's book is a mixed creature, one that blends myth and melodrama with factual detail to create what amounts to a Victorian novel featuring an urban Caliban and a descending surgeon-god in the person of Treves.

A number of texts exist outside the sequence traced above. These include such primary documents as the scientific narratives (Treves's and others) of Merrick's disorder; several letters written to the *Times* by F. C. Carr Gomm, chairman of the London Hospital's management committee; the recollections of several of Treves's medical contemporaries (Sir Wilfred Grenfell, D. G. Halsted, and Sir John Bland-Sutton) who formed their own firsthand impressions of Merrick; and, most crucially, *The Autobiography of Joseph Carey Merrick*, a pamphlet composed by Merrick or ghostwritten for him as publicity for his exhibitions. We have chosen to present these accounts—most, though not all, of which appeared prior to the publication of *The Elephant Man and Other Reminiscences*—together as a unit in our second chapter. Chapter 2 brings forward primary information that will be unfamiliar to most of our readers while also speculating on the contexts within which Merrick's contemporary observers situated the phenomenon of an Elephant Man.

Various scientific and imaginative works have appeared since Merrick's reemergence in the popular consciousness during the 1970s. Several of these works are grouped in the final chapter with Howell and Ford's *True History:* a biography of Treves by Stephen Trombley, a volume of poems by Kenneth Sherman, a rediagnosis of Merrick's disorder by Drs. J. A. R. Tibbles and M. M. Cohen, Jr., and children's books by Frederick Drimmer and by Howell and Ford themselves. In different ways, Howell and Ford's *True History* enables the various demystifications and remystifications of Merrick effected in these works. Other contemporary renditions of Merrick draw on popular perception rather than rediscovered details. Our afterword considers one such instance, entertainer Michael Jackson's highly publicized fascination with the Elephant Man—an interest literally acknowledged in his rock video *Moonwalking* (1988) but more subtly and organically evident in his autobiography *Moonwalk* (1988).

Our own part in this sequence of texts is to tell the story of the stories—but even with these modest goals, what we show and say depends in part on the nature of what we have seen and how we have been looking. Thus it seems worth mentioning that we each met Merrick and Treves through Pomerance. One of us first experienced the play in a 1980 stage version (London's National Theatre production, with David Schofield as Merrick and Peter McEnery as Treves), and the other read it. Next we saw Lynch's film, which took us to Montagu's book (containing, as it does, the Treves reminiscence along with a number of the miscellaneous primary documents), then to Treves's *Elephant Man and Other Reminiscences* itself, and then to Howell and Ford, where in appendix 1 we finally heard Merrick speak in what may be, and at any rate is meant to be taken for, his own voice. After our research was well under way, we read the lesser-known Elephant Man plays and viewed the Elephant Man according to Michael Jackson—though long before *Moonwalking* and *Moonwalk* came out, we, like other readers of the popular press, had been informed of and tantalized by Jackson's purported interest in purchasing Merrick's bones from the London Hospital.

We are not interested in purchasing Joseph Merrick's bones, either to preserve them from further exhibition or to exhibit them ourselves. What we propose instead is to re-member Joseph Merrick by gathering together and thinking about the accounts of his life. We do not seek to provide a true history of the Elephant Man, or of Joseph Merrick, or of Treves for that matter, for to do so would be to seek to impose closure on a story that has thus far refused to be closed. At two points in his own reminiscence of Merrick, Frederick Treves thinks that his relationship to Merrick has been completed. But on each occasion the relation opens again, at least in part because of actions taken by Merrick himself. Near the end of Bernard Pomerance's play, too, as Merrick puts the last piece of his model of Saint Phillip's church in place, he declares, "It is done" (a scene echoed in the David Lynch film, where the line is "It is finished"). But the manner of Merrick's death in that play and the influence he has on Treves again indicate that Merrick's story is not finished, at least in the ordinary sense of completeness. Pomerance's Carr Gomm would seek to have the last word about Merrick as well, but it is our contention that there is no last word about Merrick. While it is good to have the facts about him that Howell and Ford have unearthed, these do little to suggest the quality of his inner life or the character of his relationship to Treves, which can itself be understood only through the complex process of integrating the various accounts of it—from those presumably most factual, like Howell and Ford's, to those most clearly imaginative, like those of Pomerance, Faudree, or Lynch.

We think it no accident that Merrick's story has inspired so many theatrical productions, for it seems an inherently theatrical subject. Theater provides a space of relationship and interplay where, as Murray Schwartz puts it, "we do not ask whether our perceptions or actions create their objects or whether the world external to ourselves determines our perceptions; interplay means that each creates the others."[1] The story of the inarticulate, apparently inexpressive Elephant Man offers a particularly rich situation in which subject and interpreter create each other. Merrick's unclosed story has had the continuing power to create its interpreters, who find ways to talk about themselves while talking about Merrick. We want no last word about Merrick, and we recognize ourselves as interpreters who have found in Merrick ways to talk about ourselves as well. We recognize, too, that as a living, historical being, Merrick deserves the dignity of his own story, free of the constructions of others. We want to restore to him as much of that story as possible but believe that it can be recaptured only through consciously critical reflection on how others have constructed him—and themselves through him. In the introductory note to his play, Pomerance speaks of Merrick's building of the church as a "central metaphor" and observes that "the groping toward conditions where it can be built and the building of it are the actions of the play" (v). Our work here represents a further groping toward the conditions in which the church can be built, the church conceived of as a rich potential space in which Merrick's story can be heard with and among those of his interpreters, and in which no human voice speaks the last word.

2

Merrick at First Hand
Miscellaneous Accounts

Firsthand impressions of Joseph Merrick can be culled from the diverse group of narratives—scientific reports, letters, newspaper notices, memoirs—examined in this chapter. Our purposes are several. The first is simply to inform, to lay before the reader in some detail the earliest accounts of Merrick's condition—physical, existential, cultural—accounts on which his later interpreters draw. The second is to suggest something of the process by which he began to emerge from the shadowy status of phenomenon, the Elephant Man, and to acquire a specific history as Joseph Merrick. We begin here as well to suggest some of the cultural contexts within which Merrick's earliest interpreters framed his experience. We see him depicted variously as fairy tale hero, ideal object of Victorian charity, representative of the urban crowd, Darwinian metaphor. The accounts considered here are firsthand only in the sense that they were written by those who had known Merrick personally. As we will see, each is a mediated text, governed by its particular purpose, generic demands, and distinctive audience.

In all the major texts considered in this book, observers are to greater and lesser extents reading themselves through Merrick, and Merrick through Treves. Presumably things should be simpler in the case of *The Autobiography of Joseph Carey Merrick*, a seven-paragraph promotional pamphlet issued by Merrick's exhibitors, Mr. Sam Torr and Mr. J. Ellis. But even here the story is far from straightforward. The questions equal or outnumber the facts. The first question is one of authorship itself. Did Merrick write the pamphlet himself or was it the production of Mr. Torr or someone associated with him? Basing their position on the "authentic feeling" of the words and phrases, tone, and content, Howell and Ford, in their *True History of the Elephant Man*, opine, perhaps with a certain unresolved contradiction, that "Joseph most probably was its author, even if he did write it under the expert tutelage of Mr. Torr or his resident copywriter."[1] The question of authorship, then, remains a subjective matter. Our individual first impressions about who wrote the *Autobiography* were completely opposite, but these antithetical views curiously derived from identical phrases or observations in the text: "The deformity which I am now exhibiting"—"The face is such a sight that no one could describe it"—"My feet and legs are covered with thick lumpy skin, also my body, like that of an Elephant, and almost the same colour, in fact, no one would believe until they saw it, that such a thing could exist."[2] Detachment is the persistent effect of these and similar passages. But that detachment might plausibly be ascribed either to an external writer, Mr. Torr or his copywriter perhaps, or to Merrick's own distinguishing between his essence and the misshapen "thing" that was his body.

In any case, the *Autobiography* is a calculated account, not a mere transcription of facts or a mere fiction but a fictionalizing—a mixed utterance determined in certain ways by facts but in other ways by the demands and conventions of genre. The *Autobiography* is cast in a generic form likely to be familiar to Merrick, his exhibitors, and his audience alike: It resembles nothing so much as the folk tales by the Brothers Grimm, stories widely available and popular in the England of his childhood.[3] Like a Grimm story, "The Juniper Tree," for instance, Merrick's life begins happily enough: "I went to school like other children until I was about 11 or 12 years of age." Catastrophe intervenes—"the greatest misfortune of my life." As would be the case in Grimm, this misfortune is the mother's death and replacement by a cruel stepmother: "Henceforth I never had one moment's comfort, she having children of her own, and I not being so handsome as they, together with my deformity, she was the means of making my life a perfect misery." Abuse, exploitation, and failed attempts at escape follow.

As in the Grimm tales, the step-maternal cruelty is both extreme and habitual: "When I went home for my meals my step-mother used to say I had not been to seek for work. I was taunted and sneered at so that I would not go home to my meals, and used to stay in the streets with an hungry belly rather than return for anything to eat, what few half-meals I did have, I was taunted with the remark—'That's more than you have earned.' " Pushed beyond the limit, Merrick runs away and, after a series of misadventures, vows to make his living through self-exhibition. His tale, which exists to promote that exhibition, closes just as a Grimm tale would, with a deferential envoi to the reader and an edifying quotation, here a quatrain from Isaac Watts:

> Was I so tall, could reach the pole,
> Or grasp the ocean with a span;
> I would be measured by the soul,
> The mind's the standard of the man.

But Merrick's is a fairy tale with a difference, one taking place in the real and present world and one offering a tangible protagonist to the reader, who is enjoined not just to read but to come and see. Hence the specifics that would undercut a folk tale: a birthdate (though inaccurate), full addresses, precise body measurements, names and professions for the minor characters, authentically specified causes and effects.

Blending the elemental appeal of folk tale with prosaic detail, the *Autobiography* is a document effectively contrived to gain its end, namely, an audience for the spectacular Elephant Man. Whatever the extent of Merrick's participation in the making of this text, it is clear that he, from the start, was no helpless victim of exhibitors. Exhibition was for him an alternative to confinement in charitable institutions. The *Autobiography* presents him as the first to recognize that this thing, so unsatisfactory as a body, had a degree of use as a commodity: "So thought I I'll get my living by being exhibited about the country." This phrase perfectly captures the blend of agency and dependence that was to characterize Merrick's subsequent existence. Merrick's actual or impersonated voice here claims for him the resourcefulness and dignity of the free agent, but for him agency involves choosing on whom he will depend. In fairy tale terms, the boy must take on the role—Joseph

Carey Merrick, trusting himself to the promoters Torr and Ellis, must become the Elephant Man.

> Knowing Mr Sam Torr, Gladstone Vaults, Wharf Street, Leicester, went in for Novelties, I wrote to him, he came to see me, and soon arranged matters, recommending me to Mr Ellis, Bee-hive Inn, Nottingham, from whom I received the greatest kindness and attention.
>
> In making my first appearance before the public, who have treated me well—in fact I may say I am as comfortable now as I was uncomfortable before. I must now bid my kind readers adieu. (169)

The Elephant Man made his first appearance before the British medical establishment, specifically the Pathological Society of London, on December 2, 1884, an appearance briefly noted in the first of several articles that the *British Medical Journal* would devote to his condition and history in the years during which he was under Treves's care.[4] This first brief paragraph unintentionally casts Treves in the role of showman and emphasizes the Elephant Man's power as medical spectacle; it begins simply, "Mr. TREVES showed a man who presented an extraordinary appearance, owing to a series of deformities." The object of observation is allowed neither a name nor a history but is still cast exclusively in the role: "From the massive distortion of the head, and the extensive areas covered by papillomatous growth, the patient had been called 'the elephant-man' " (110). The *Journal* again contained notice of the Elephant Man when Treves gave a full description, illustrated by photographs, of a "Case of Congenital Deformity" to the society on March 17 of the following year. Now no longer immediately present, the Elephant Man had ceased to be a spectacle and had become a "case." This report of the society's meeting details some of the most extraordinary features of Merrick's condition: the increase in the subcutaneous cellular tissues, so extreme in some areas of the body, notably the right pectoral region and the buttocks, as to cause the formation of pendulous masses; the deformity and excessive growth of the skull, whose circumference was equal to that of the waist; the presence of papillomatous tumors on certain parts of the skin; the hypertrophic deformity of cranial and facial bones, the bones of the upper right limb, and the bones of the feet. On this occasion, too, the great skin specialist Dr. H. Radcliffe Crocker made one of the first attempts to

diagnose—to name—the disorder, doing so in the classic manner by
attempting to assimilate this case to other cases: He "thought that the
case belonged to the same class of cases as dermatolysis and pachydermatocoele," although the "occurrence of changes in the bones had
not, he believed been previously observed" in pachydermatocoele
(102).[5]

The Elephant Man is accorded something more of a history in
Treves's own first written description of him, the report published as "A
Case of Congenital Deformity" in the *Transactions of the Pathological
Society* for March 1885. Although Treves does not mention Merrick's
name, he does give his age, an explanation for his lameness (the childhood hip disease that caused the shortening of his left leg), and an
account of the removal of flesh from the upper jaw at the Leicester Infirmary.[6] He notes that the man "was a native of Leicester," incorrectly
states that he had no brothers or sisters, remarks that there was no
history of deformity in the family, and mentions, with some depreca-
tion, Merrick's "elaborate story" of a "fright his mother had received
shortly before his birth from having been knocked down by an elephant
in a circus" (107). From the patient himself, he has learned that the
head, right arm, and feet had "always been grossly deformed," but that
"as a child his skin was simply thickened, loose, and rough," without
the large papillary growths that Treves recognizes are "at present ex-
tending rapidly."

As most of Treves's report is a description of the Elephant Man's
disorder along the lines suggested above, we will not summarize it fully
here. Some features, however, are worthy of notice for the way they
relate to emphases of Treves's own later writing about Merrick or to
issues raised by Merrick's other interpreters. In general, Treves's description here relies much less heavily on metaphors and analogies
than does his reminiscence of 1923. Treves compares the remarkably
loose areas of Merrick's skin to "flaps" and indicates the size of the
rounded exostoses of the skull by saying they "were larger than a large
Tangerine orange" (106). But there is nothing like the elaborate description of Merrick's appearance in terms of one trope after another
that we find in the 1923 account. Neither is there any extended emphasis on Merrick's normal left arm and hand, through which he comes
to meet the world in Treves's reminiscence. In clear contrast with
the later account, too, is Treves's estimate of Merrick's intelligence.

Whereas Treves states in the reminiscence that he thought Merrick an "imbecile" after his initial examination, here he reports that "his intelligence was by no means of a low order." One final detail that has caught the imagination of several later interpreters is the "remarkable" fact that "the skin of the penis and scrotum was perfectly normal in every respect."

The task of describing Merrick presented Treves with difficulties. As a trained scientist might be expected to do, he proceeds analytically by breaking Merrick down into "parts," "regions," or "districts" and systematically describing the phenomena in each. But in some ways Merrick resists such schematic description. The "growths upon the skin followed no distinct areas of distribution" but "appeared to be scattered about casually or accidentally, and to be influenced by no specific anatomical arrangement" (105). When essaying to describe the skull, Treves himself confesses that its "surface . . . was so irregular as to render any detailed description very difficult" (105). Merrick seems at times almost a challenge to reason and science, to any orderly understanding of the body and its processes. His "whole head was ostentatiously unsymmetrical," while the surface of the skull, between the larger exostoses, "presented ridges and irregular upheavals of bone that disregarded sutures and were disposed in a perfectly chaotic manner" (106). Still, for the most part, Treves describes the symptoms of the Elephant Man's disorder confidently enough, almost totally sundering Merrick's physical self from his existential condition. Never is this separation more apparent than in Treves's closing of his account by saying that "the man enjoys good health" and "has suffered from no serious illnesses."

The accounts that we have looked at thus far, with the exception of Merrick's autobiography, all derive from Treves's first examination of Merrick in late 1884. Treves did not see Merrick again until late in 1886, when the latter arrived in England after a period of being exhibited in Belgium. Some of the details of Merrick's life after 1884 first became public in a letter to the London *Times* of December 4, 1886, written by the chairman of the hospital, Mr. F. C. Carr Gomm. Carr Gomm briefly tells the story of Treves's first finding Merrick, "in a room off the Whitechapel-road," where he was being exhibited. Hidden behind a curtain, Merrick would warm himself "over a brick which was heated by a lamp," until his manager had collected a sufficient number of pennies for a show, at which time "poor Merrick threw off his curtain and exhibited himself in all his deformity" (109). After the police stopped this exhibition in England, Merrick went to Belgium, "where he was taken in hand by an Austrian" who eventually stole his savings of fifty pounds, leaving him "alone and absolutely destitute" (110). At this point Merrick began a harrowing journey back to England, "for he felt that the only friend he had in the world was Mr. Treves, of the London Hospital." Carr Gomm concludes his history by announcing that Merrick has been taken in by the hospital, but that "there is, unfortunately, no hope of his cure." This announcement leads to the question that is the occasion for Carr Gomm's letter: "What is to be done with him in the future [?]" (110).

The London Hospital was an overcrowded general hospital and thus not the appropriate place for an incurable like Merrick. Yet Carr Gomm had received only refusals to his applications on Merrick's behalf to the established institutions for incurables. Thus Carr Gomm comes to the British public seeking advice and, more crucially, support for Joseph Merrick, whose Christian name he interestingly gets right, as opposed to Treves, who from the first insists on calling his patient John. In seeking support, Carr Gomm urges Merrick's need for privacy by stressing the dreadfulness of his appearance and the terror with which others respond to him. Now that Merrick is no longer exhibiting himself for a livelihood, the freakishness that had been a commodity becomes a constraint on him, though as Carr Gomm introduces him, he is still essentially a "sight": "There is now in a little room off one of our attic wards a man named Joseph Merrick, aged about 27, a native of Leicester, so dreadful a sight that he is unable to come out by daylight to the garden." While Carr Gomm unquestionably wants to protect Merrick from humiliation and debasement, the logic of his case for Merrick's privacy suggests that he, like the police, wants also to protect the public from something that should not be seen. Merrick must have privacy because "his appearance is such that all shrink from him"; more specifically, he cannot, "in justice to others, be put in the general ward of a workhouse, and from such, even if possible, he shrinks with the greatest horror" (110). Carr Gomm's language echoes itself, implicitly suggesting the possibilities for mirroring that seem to operate so powerfully in the story of Merrick. Merrick shrinks from others, others shrink from him; Merrick must be protected from others,

others must be protected from him. Apparently "women and nervous persons," who "fly in terror from the sight of him," particularly need such protection.

Carr Gomm was the first to describe some of the paradoxes that have become staples of Merrick's story. The *Times* letter stresses that despite the terror Merrick's outward appearance inspires in others, he "is superior in intelligence, can read and write, is quiet, gentle, not to say even refined in his mind" (111). Carr Gomm mentions Merrick's habit of making "little cardboard models" with his good hand and of sending these to people who had been kind to him: industry and benevolence persisting against great odds. He also mentions Merrick's carrying about with him "a painting of his mother," an icon that has received a great deal of attention from many of Merrick's interpreters, Treves being a major exception. Carr Gomm's version of why Merrick treasures the painting attributes to him a kind of genteel Victorian respectability; he carries the portrait "to show that she was a decent and presentable person, and as a memorial of the only one who was kind to him in life until he came under the kind care of the nursing staff of the London Hospital and the surgeon who has befriended him." The last part of this assertion by Carr Gomm is of particular importance, for it so directly contradicts Treves's own later strenuous denials that Merrick's mother had been kind to him.

The British public responded with such generosity to Carr Gomm's letter to the *Times* that Merrick was able to be supported at the London Hospital for the rest of his life. Howell and Ford have suggested that Merrick was the ideal object for Victorian charity (93). His inability to work could in no way be attributed to a deficiency in character; he could not be held responsible for his condition. Carr Gomm's letter goes to some lengths to stress both Merrick's inability to work and his blamelessness. In an oddly joined sentence from the letter's first paragraph, Merrick's one normal arm seems to define the limits of his social utility: "I will not shock your readers with any detailed description of his infirmities," Carr Gomm writes, "but only one arm is available for work." Later Merrick is described as "a case of singular affliction brought about through no fault of himself" (111).

In depicting him as the needy recipient of charity, Carr Gomm was the first to theologize Merrick's condition: "The Master of the Temple on Advent Sunday preached an eloquent sermon on the subject of our

Master's answer to the question, 'Who did sin, this man or his parents, that he was born blind?' showing how one of the Creator's objects in permitting men to be born to a life of hopeless and miserable disability was that the works of God should be manifested in evoking the sympathy and kindly aid of those on whom such a heavy cross is not laid" (112). In the passage in question, John 9:1–3, Jesus responds that "neither hath this man sinned, nor his parents," thus breaking the ancient connection between sin and disease, the habit of reading illness or deformity as punishment. Carr Gomm's theology picks up this freeing sense of the text, releasing Merrick and his parents from responsibility for Merrick's disorder—thus, in a curious way, accomplishing the same end as Merrick's story of his mother's being knocked down by the circus elephant. But Carr Gomm's theology also establishes a new polarization between objects and subjects, between those who receive and those who give charity, between those on whom the cross is laid and those on whom it is not. The Victorian Master of the Temple reads a pious justification for philanthropy into Jesus' saying further that the man has been born blind in order "that the works of God should be made manifest in him," a phrase that points most specifically to Jesus' own working of signs to stimulate faith in his divine mission. Though freed from guilt in this theology, Merrick has not yet become a full member of the church, conceived of as the community of all who obey the command to take up the cross and follow.

One week after the appearance of Carr Gomm's letter to the *Times,* the *British Medical Journal* published an updated account of "The 'Elephant-Man.' " It includes a brief summary of Merrick's life, based largely on Carr Gomm's letter, but adds some details relevant to his personal and medical history. Traveling in public conveyances, for instance, is added to the list of things that Merrick's condition prevents him from doing, the writer mentioning an experience of this kind, "acutely painful to his feelings," in which "a steamboat captain refused . . . to take him as a passenger." Readers of the *Journal* are also informed that the "disease has made great progress" since its last previous report in Treves's "Case of Congenital Deformity." Clearly the source for both the personal detail and the medical information is Treves himself. Even if he were not openly acknowledged in the article, as he is, one would know this because Merrick is referred to as John rather than Joseph.

The ostensible medical purpose of this piece is to clarify the diagnosis of the Elephant Man's condition. It is written primarily for "medical men" who may have read Carr Gomm's letter to the *Times* and concluded from it "that this unhappy man is the subject of elephantiasis." The writer does not advance any name for the disorder more specific than Treves's "case of congenital deformity," but he does make clear that the patient's stage name was "not meant to imply elephantiasis, but bestowed on him on account of the bony exostoses on his frontal bone. This, combined with a deformity of the superior maxilla which gives a trunklike appearance to the nose and upper lip, causes the profile of the face to remind the observer of the profile of an elephant's head." The dilemma of what to call Merrick, of how to classify him, continues here. On exhibition, his profile was seen as the profile of an elephant; in the medical theater, the question is what to see him as. What is clearer is what he should not be seen as, a case of elephantiasis.

Joseph Merrick's next appearances before the general and medical public occurred at the time of his death on April 11, 1890. Three pieces are of specific importance: another letter by Carr Gomm to the *Times*, April 16, 1890; a report of the inquest devoted to Merrick's death carried by the *Times* on the same day; and an article, called "Death of the 'Elephant Man,' " based on information from Treves and published in the *British Medical Journal* for April 19, 1890. Carr Gomm began his letter with what by this time had become the standard version of Merrick's history: his days as a freak in England; the closing of the show by the police; his venture abroad under the management of an "Austrian adventurer"; his abandonment in Belgium and the difficult passage back to England; his reception at the London Hospital, where he found at last a home through the care of Treves and the generosity of the British public. What was new in Carr Gomm's account were the details of Merrick's life in the hospital: his receiving "kindly visits from many, among them the highest in the land"; his becoming a great reader; his learning the art of basket making, through "the kindness of a lady, one of the brightest ornaments of the theatrical profession"; and his going "on more than one occasion" to the theater, "which he witnessed from the seclusion of a private box" (118). As he had in his earlier letter asking for charitable help in support of Merrick, Carr Gomm emphasizes the hopelessness of Merrick's existence. The cumulative effect of Carr Gomm's description of all the kindnesses done to Merrick is to deprive the latter of all agency or independent feeling. There could be no question of Merrick's feeling happiness or entertaining hope; his role was the purely passive one of having his wretchedness made more bearable: "The authorities of the hospital, the medical staff, the chaplain, the sisters, and nurses united to alleviate as far as possible the misery of his existence, and he learnt to speak of his rooms at the hospital as his home" (118).

Also new is the revelation of Merrick's religious life. Here again Carr Gomm has cast Merrick in the role of the passive recipient of good delivered from above. He does not mention—quite probably because he was not aware of—Merrick's background as a Baptist or his knowledge of the Bible, which Treves does remark in his 1923 reminiscence. Instead he mentions Merrick's "benefit[ing] much from the religious instruction of our chaplain" and records his private confirmation by Dr. Walsham How, Suffragan Bishop of Bedford. Just as Merrick could witness the theater "from the seclusion of a private box," he was able to take part in chapel services "by waiting in the vestry," something he had done twice on Easter, just five days before his death. Perhaps out of respect for the conventions of eulogy, Carr Gomm takes pains to express Merrick's reconciliation to life, citing his "last conversation" with Bishop How, in which he "had expressed his feeling of deep gratitude for all that had been done for him here, and his acknowledgment of the mercy of God in bringing him to this place" (119). Because a major purpose of Carr Gomm's letter is to account for his stewardship of the money given for Merrick's support, he stresses throughout Merrick's qualifications as the ideal object of public benevolence: "In spite of all this indulgence he was quiet and unassuming, very grateful for all that was done for him, and conformed himself readily to the restrictions which were necessary."

The *Times* report of the inquest and the *British Medical Journal* account of Merrick's death are of especial interest because that event has been subject to so much interpretation by the tellers of Merrick's story, from Frederick Treves onward. On the night before his death, Merrick had walked in the garden of the hospital, as was his custom, and on Friday, April 11, he seemed to be "perfectly well when the wardmaid brought him his dinner" at 1:30 P.M. He was found "lying across the bed dead" by Mr. Hodges, a house surgeon, who summoned another house surgeon, Mr. Ashe, at 3:30 P.M. The inquest report makes clear that "there were no marks of violence, and the death was quite natural." The doctor, coroner, and jury all concurred in their assessment of the cause of death: Merrick had been overcome by the weight of his grossly deformed head. While Merrick was "taking a natural sleep," the weight of the head had pressed upon the windpipe, causing suffocation. An inquest had been deemed "prudent," the coroner argued rather vaguely, because "the man had been sent round the shows as a curiosity."

The *British Medical Journal*, basing its information on Treves, first gave a slightly different explanation of the manner of Merrick's death and then included the inquest report from the *Times*. The *Journal* added detail on the last phases of Merrick's progressive disorder: The bony masses and the pendulous flaps of his skin grew steadily; the outgrowth of the upper jaw, the trunk, increased, making his speech more difficult to understand; and the "head grew so heavy that at length he had difficulty in holding it up." The continued growth of his head forced Merrick to sleep "in a sitting or crouching position, with his hands clasped over his legs, and his head on his knees," for "if he lay down the heavy head tended to fall back and produce a sense of suffocation." It was Treves's opinion, then, that Merrick's death had been caused not by his head's falling forward and pressing on the windpipe, but instead by its falling backward and dislocating his neck (123–24). Treves goes no further than this in accounting for Merrick's death here; he will leave a more speculative reading for his 1923 reminiscence.

Howell and Ford have noted one suggestive error of fact in the *British Medical Journal* article, which states that the "Committee of the London Hospital refused not only to permit a necropsy on the body of the 'elephant man,' but also declined to allow his body to be preserved" (125). Howell and Ford point out, however, that casts were made of Merrick's body and that Treves did a dissection, supervising as well the preservation of skin samples (lost during the Second World War) and the mounting of the skeleton (148–49). The skeleton continues to be on display in the London Hospital Museum, and photographs of it confront the reader of both Montagu's book and Howell and Ford's book. (Most recently the skeleton has come widely into public notice through the popular entertainer Michael Jackson's reported efforts to buy it.) Why Treves would want to conceal his dissection of Merrick from the British public remains a matter for speculation; on this matter, Howell and Ford's seems as good as any: "Perhaps he feared that it might create distress for those who had responded so compassionately in contributing to Joseph's happiness and welfare as well as, in many cases, cultivating his company" (148).

The ultimate disposition of his body seems to have been a subject of some humor to Joseph Merrick himself; at least it is reported so in *A Labrador Doctor: The Autobiography of Wilfred Thomason Grenfell*, whose brief memoir of Merrick predates Treves's reminiscence by four years (causing Howell and Ford to suggest that perhaps Grenfell's writing spurred Treves's imagination).[7] Grenfell, who came under Treves's tutelage while a member of the "walking class" at the London Hospital, remembered Merrick talking "freely of how he would look in a huge bottle of alcohol—an end to which in his imagination he was fated to come" (87). As a house surgeon under Treves, Grenfell took part in the care of the Elephant Man (his account does not use Merrick's name), whom he describes alternately as a figure of pathos and strangeness. For Grenfell, Merrick is a "poor fellow" who is "really exceedingly sensitive about his most extraordinary appearance." He stresses Merrick's "very cheerful disposition" and his "pathetic" pride in the left, or normal, side of his body. By minimizing the causal explanation of Merrick's death, even implying that such explanation is arbitrary assignment rather than objective recognition, Grenfell's account makes the event seem especially abrupt and mysterious: "Very suddenly one day he died—the reason assigned being that his head fell forward and choked him, being too heavy for him to lift up."

Merrick's strangeness is emphasized through Grenfell's insistence on the aptness of the animal metaphors used to define his patient. Grenfell calls Merrick's disorder "leontiasis," but he stresses primarily the resemblance to the elephant: "His head and face were so deformed as really to resemble a big animal's head with a trunk" (86). According to Grenfell, Merrick's room "was known as the 'elephant house,' " as a kind of zoo incorporated within the hospital. The zoo metaphor seems at least implicit, too, in Grenfell's own description of the Elephant Man's room and the restriction of his visitors' action to that of seeing him: "A special room in a yard was allotted to him, and several famous people came to see him—among them Queen Alexandra, then the Princess of Wales, who afterward sent him an autographed photograph of herself" (86). This photograph, kept in the "elephant house," "always suggested beauty and the beast" (87).

Wilfred Grenfell's brief account of the Elephant Man contains one other detail that is worthy of some attention, especially for the way it relates to the treatment of Merrick's initial journey from the place of exhibition to the hospital in Treves's 1923 reminiscence. Grenfell writes that Merrick "had been seen by some of the students, and invited over to be shown to and studied by our best physicians" (86). He places no particular emphasis on the difficulty of such a journey to the hospital, although he does go on immediately to note Merrick's extreme sensitivity about his appearance. In the reminiscence, Treves takes great pains, as we will see, with the difficulty both of his own approach to Merrick and of Merrick's crossing the road to the hospital. Grenfell seems altogether more casual both about going to see Merrick and about the possibility of his coming to be seen.

Grenfell's detached, matter-of-fact account of the Elephant Man offers a telling contrast to Treves's reminiscence, to which we turn in the next chapter; indeed, seeing the extent and nature of this doctor's response to Merrick shows that Treves's sympathetic blend of identification and paternalism was an extraordinary reaction instead of a typical one. Furthermore, Grenfell's remembering that Merrick's room had been called the "elephant house" may help point us to a way of understanding why people came to see the Elephant Man. In "Why Look at Animals?"—an essay devoted, among other things, to the inevitable disappointment many visitors feel in zoos—John Berger argues that the fascination animals have held for us lies in their role "as an *intercession* between man and his origin." Animals are capable of interceding in this way because they are "both like and unlike" human beings; the "parallelism of their similar/dissimilar lives" allows them "to provoke some of the first questions and offer answers."[8] The essential relation between human and animal is metaphoric: What the two terms share reveals what differentiates them. Berger places the development of public zoos in a period marked by "the disappearance of animals from daily life" and stresses the zoo's role in the nineteenth century as an "endorsement of modern colonial power," with the capturing of animals "a symbolic representation of the conquest of all distant and exotic lands." The word *zoo* became popular when, about 1867, a music hall artist in London sang a song titled "Walking in the Zoo is the OK Thing to Do."[9] Some twenty years later, going to see the Elephant Man became, at least for certain members of the ruling class, the "OK thing to do." And perhaps they went to the "elephant house" at the London Hospital for some of the same reasons they went to the zoo: to find in the Elephant Man, mysteriously like and unlike them, an intercession between themselves and their origin, an intercession perhaps particularly needed in a period when Darwinism was undercutting traditional religious explanations of an origin. Moreover, they went to see the Elephant Man at the London Hospital, an outpost of empire in the urban jungle of Whitechapel, an institution that at least promised the eventual conquest of the distant and exotic, the triumph of mind over the unruliness of nature.[10]

Merrick's position between the natural and the human, the wild and the civil, is interestingly suggested by the order in which Sir John Bland-Sutton gives his reminiscences of Treves and the Elephant Man in *The Story of a Surgeon*.[11] Although this autobiography was published seven years after Treves's reminiscence of Merrick, we consider it here because it derives, at least in part, from Bland-Sutton's own knowledge of Merrick and not simply from Treves's publication. Bland-Sutton begins his remembrance of Treves after describing some of his own studies in comparative anatomy and morphology, particularly those on ligaments, through which he gained "some light on the origin of the slings, loops, and pulleys, in the legs and wings of birds, and the arms and legs of beasts, as well as the flippers of whales, especially in relation to Man. It was to me a discovery of great interest that many ligaments and fibrous structures could be compelled to testify concerning Man's Mammalian Kinship and Descent" (136). After briefly mentioning several of the eminent men he had met while working in the prosectorium at the London Zoo, including Sir Harry Johnston, discoverer of the okapi, a beast that seemed half-zebra, half-giraffe, Bland-Sutton mentions that he was "also able to help Sir Frederick Treves, who wished to study what he facetiously called the bowels of Man and Mammals." Treves made "clever water-colour sketches" of the "arrangements of the small and large intestines from Marsupials to Man," basing his mammalian studies on specimens dissected by Bland-Sutton. As an example of Treves's "zeal" in these comparative studies, Bland-Sutton recalls one occasion in which Treves had the carcass of a young rhinoceros "conveyed from the Zoo to Whitechapel in order to dissect it leisurely." In addition to what Treves learned about anatomy from this experience, he also "soon learned how quickly the remains of huge mammals become offensive, and how difficult and expensive it is to dispose of them" (137).

After briefly sketching his friend Treves's personal and professional qualities—his "neatness, courage, quickness, and decision" as a surgeon—Bland-Sutton tells the story of Treves's operating for appendicitis on Edward, Prince of Wales, two days before his coronation in 1902. From Treves's triumph with the king, Bland-Sutton turns abruptly to the other end of the social spectrum: "The cosmopolitan crowd of patients at the London Hospital gave Treves an unusual insight into humanity and enabled him to manifest keen interest in men and women—poor, sick, maimed and malformed." For Bland-Sutton, Treves stands between the king and the poor, attending, on the one hand, to the mysterious eruptions of nature in the sovereign and, on the other, to the much more varied eruptions of the urban crowd. Treves's standing between is made explicit in Bland-Sutton's language of intercession: "In many tales he told of benefactions bestowed on his poor hospital patients, Treves was frequently the intercessor—often the benefactor." As one might expect, Bland-Sutton turns next to the poorest of the poor: the Elephant Man, whom he first saw in 1884 on one of his apparently frequent visits to "see dwarfs, giants, fat-women, and monstrosities at the freak-shows." Bland-Sutton provides nothing new in the way of factual information about Merrick, and, in fact, he seems somewhat vague on the sequence of events in Treves's and Merrick's association. There is no mention, for example, of Merrick's returning to exhibition, first in England and then in Belgium, after Treves's initial examination of him, or of Merrick's difficult journey back to London. Instead—and this is consistent with his sense of Treves's intercessory function—Bland-Sutton remarks that his friend's "interest did not end with the clinical and pathological aspects of the Elephant-Man" and then describes Treves's taking in the "outcast" Merrick, who appears metaphorically as one beyond the limits of ordinary community, either Christ child or wild beast: "None would give him lodging except in an outhouse, or a stable, as if he were a wild animal."

What is revealing, then, is Bland-Sutton's way of situating Treves and Merrick: his placing Treves between the king and the poor, represented above all by Merrick, and his placing of the whole story of physician, king, and Elephant Man just after the description of his and Treves's studies of "kinship and descent" in man and animal. The section is even graced with a plate showing an eminent Victorian sitting on a park bench next to a chimpanzee, the caption reading "Man and Chimpanzee," with a quotation from Tennyson: "Smile at the claims of long descent." It is appropriate, too, that the reminiscence closes with a long letter from the retired Treves dated March 28, 1918, a text rich in paradoxes of wildness and civility, nature and human order, the animal kingdom and royal power. Bland-Sutton prefaces the letter by explaining that "it was written in response to a query of mine concerning a statement that Sir Everard Home had been able to investigate the method of reproduction in opossums, as some of these animals were kept in a menagerie in Richmond Park." Treves, who as the recipient of royal hospitality was living at Thatched House Lodge in the park, begins his letter by saying he had "never heard of the Royal menagerie" and that "the idea, until at least the reign of Queen Victoria, was to keep the Park wild." He goes on to complain about some of the problems caused by animals introduced into the park—the gray squirrels have "become a plague," the badgers "are breeding out of all reason"—but, at least regarding the badgers, even here he shows a respect for the pure energy of nature: "It is wonderful what a hole they can make in an old oak fence and how quickly they dig. A couple tried to settle in my garden, and the hole they managed to dig in one night I kept untouched." Treves reveals himself to be aware of the irony of trying to keep a "wild" garden, in which the "pheasants will insist upon breeding," despite his "taking their eggs and hatching them out." But if his attempts to cultivate the wild are less than fully successful, the wild continues nonetheless, even amid the demonstrations of imperial power: "In spite of the war the nightingale has never left us. I still see the kingfisher; the Herons are as numerous as ever and the Crested Grebe still nests by the Pen Ponds." Though "few Londoners" will believe it, Treves continues, "I can nearly always show a long-tailed tit on Ham Common." The wild—nature uncolonized, uncivil, uncontrolled—could be seen and shown even in London, whether on Ham Common or in Whitechapel. Few Londoners would believe the Elephant Man either, at least at first, yet he too was there to be seen, evidence of nature's power and metaphor for Victorians trying to understand the kinship and descent of chimpanzee and king.

Londoners also had difficulty believing the outbreak of violence that took place in Whitechapel in 1888, the year of the murders of Jack the Ripper. Several remarkable coincidences juxtapose the Ripper and the Elephant Man. These invite a consideration of the two "cases" in terms of each other for what they suggest about the milieu in which they occurred. The first coincidence, of course, involves time and place: Merrick was a resident and something of a cause célèbre at the London Hospital at the very time, 1888, that the Ripper was terrorizing the streets of Whitechapel around the hospital. Second, because the Ripper's mutilation of his victims suggested a knowledge of anatomy, suspicion fell, for a time, upon members of the medical profession, some of them the doctors who were attending Merrick at the London. D. G. Halsted—whose account of Merrick in *Doctor in the Nineties* is the last we consider in this chapter—is a case in point.[12] As he put it, "no medical man, however high his character or reputation, could be exempted from suspicion, and naturally those of us at the London Hospital, right in the heart of Whitechapel, were in the limelight" (45). Thus, if the doctor could be seen, on the one hand, as a benefactor to the poor—as we have seen Bland-Sutton portray Treves, with his care of the Elephant Man especially in mind—he could also be seen as a potential malefactor, a being capable of preying on the poor in the foulest of ways. Doctors, however, were far from the only suspects in the Whitechapel murders, which were variously ascribed to a royal duke, supposed Jewish fanatics, dockland lascars, cork cutters, butchers, and shoemakers. Thus a third coincidence: Like Joseph Merrick, the mysterious East End killer proved to be a point of intersection for high and low, ruling class and underclass, cultural indigene and exotic import. Fourth, just as the Elephant Man had furnished horror and spectacle to the denizens of Whitechapel, the advent of the Ripper brought a new category of unseemly objects to light for both the purveyors and seekers of such experiences. In a remarkable coincidence noted by Howell and Ford, a wax museum on the theme of the Ripper murders flourished for a time on the site where the Elephant Man had previously been exhibited (38–39)—that is, until the police closed the museum down, as they had earlier closed down the Elephant Man, as one of the things that could not be allowed.

In remembering his years as a house surgeon under Treves at the London, Halsted takes up the Elephant Man and Jack the Ripper in succession, thus unintentionally reinforcing their linking as spectacular cultural phenomena. Halsted's memoir, published only in 1959, draws heavily on Treves's 1923 reminiscence, but does contain a pair of interesting perceptions that do not occur in other early accounts of Merrick. Halsted, whose duty it was to visit Merrick every day, confesses quite honestly, as no other figure does, that he "could never quite overcome a feeling of uneasiness in his presence" and that he "was always glad to get away from him." Despite noting Merrick's contentment with his lot, Halsted also suggests that Merrick was perhaps not as uniformly cheerful as some others have insisted. He remembers, for instance, his having a "word with him every day" and "cheer[ing] him up if he felt depressed" (40).

Writing so much closer to our own time, Halsted is able to bring a more modern perspective to his subject; he prefaces his account of Merrick, for instance, by saying "that the Elephant Man was the product of one of those ghastly genetic mutations which, once in a million times, results in some science-fictional monster instead of a normal human being. Generally such babies do not live long, or, if they do, they are hushed up, and quietly forgotten about." Only Treves's ministrations made it better that the "poor monster"—or alternatively, "poor creature"—lived rather than be "put out of his misery" (37–38). Halsted closes his treatment of service under Treves with an incident that seems somewhat parallel in his mind to attending the Elephant Man. That "great landmark in every doctor's career," his first confinement case, ends rather bizarrely when he delivers an "anencephaloid foetus." When he touches "the protruding top of the spinal cord," the "creature" gives a "violent convulsion" and goes on "giving sundry movements" for several minutes. In the same language he has used for the Elephant Man, Halsted describes the fetus as a "million-to-one rarity"; also like Merrick, the fetus, "on account of its great rarity . . . found its way into a medical museum" (44).

We hope it has become clear that all the texts presented above are mediated ones, not just the personal recollections and the pragmatically constructed *Autobiography*, but also the letters, newspaper accounts, and medical reports. Each account has its particular purpose, its generic demands, its distinctive audience. If Halsted, for instance, evoking the milieu of turn-of-the-century medicine for readers at the end of the 1950s, is obviously associative in his methods—juxtaposing celebrated phenomena and personal recollections of his day and revealing or creating meaning through that juxtaposition—Carr Gomm, writing in a position of public responsibility with an eye toward doing good to Merrick and serving the interests of the hospital he represents, also offers interpreted (that is, strategically selected and shaped) material. Even the scientific accounts, as we have shown, now display and then depart from conventions according to variable circumstances— for example, Merrick's physical presence or absence when his condition is under discussion in the *British Medical Journal* and Pathological Society pieces. Treves's own words acknowledge the inadequacy of those conventions to the task of adequately representing Merrick's physical condition. How much more difficult, then, to render faithfully the existential state of Merrick as he was, not Merrick in a role—as Elephant Man, cheerful accepter of fate, ideal object of charity, scientific curiosity, intercessor, Darwinian metaphor. In the account considered in the next chapter, we see further the process of Merrick's cultural construction, but we also see him paradoxically begin to emerge from, and perhaps even to consciously select among, the roles that would seem to take over his story.

3

Frederick Treves and the Art of Reminiscence

All of the accounts of Merrick's life described in the last chapter, including Merrick's own, paradoxically depend for their enduring interest on another account, Sir Frederick Treves's title piece from *The Elephant Man and Other Reminiscences* (1923). To reprint that reminiscence in full has become habitual for students of Merrick's story. Montagu, Howell and Ford, and Frederick Drimmer (author of *Very Special People*) all include Treves's piece in, or append it to, their own accounts.[1] We have made a specific choice not to follow the convention for at least two reasons. First, the Elephant Man reminiscence exists as but one of twelve pieces in a collection that itself is but a single book— the last—in a productive writer's career. To isolate "The Elephant Man" is to lose much of its enriching context and also to flatten out the achievement and sensibility of Treves. Our effort here is to recontextualize the reminiscence, allowing it to be seen with and against the depictions of late Victorian practice and patienthood that form its companion pieces. Second, while those who have reprinted Treves's reminiscence have questioned its particular details, they have tended to grant the narrative as a whole something like the status of an unmediated account. As such, the piece has been denied, or perhaps exempted from, interpretation as Treves's story of his and Merrick's story together: "The Elephant Man" thus becomes a source of facts about Merrick's life rather than a story of what Treves's mind has kept of Merrick. We want to look at the reminiscence as a reminiscence in the precise sense, as a place where Treves reinvokes his experience of Merrick, a place neither strictly "inside" nor "outside" but "between." What we observe on that middle ground is Treves understanding, thereby shaping, Merrick and being shaped in turn—the dynamics of Treves's evolving awareness and Merrick's developing personhood now relaxing and now reestablishing the differences between the two men.

Frederick Treves (1853–1923), born and raised in Thomas Hardy's Dorset, studied at University College London and trained in medicine at the London Hospital, his association with that institution beginning in 1871.[2] In 1877 he married Anne Elizabeth Mason. By the time he met Merrick, in 1884, he had risen to be lecturer on anatomy in the medical school attached to the London, and he had already published a number of medical works, among them *Surgical Applied Anatomy*, which for many years to come would remain an influential handbook for surgeons. Working in the early days of Listerian antisepsis, Treves enjoyed his most conspicuous surgical success with appendicitis. On this success he built an increasingly busy and prosperous West End private practice that frequently brought him the "100 guinea fee, then the upper limit." His most prominent patient was Edward, Prince of Wales, on whom he performed his most celebrated appendix surgery—two days before the appointed coronation in 1902. When Edward initially refused surgery despite his physicians' recommendations, saying he would go to the Abbey instead, Treves bluntly replied, "Then, Sir, you will go as a corpse." For his various medical services to the royal family, Treves was knighted in 1901 and created a baronet in 1902.

Treves held a belief that surgeons should not operate after the age of fifty. He retired from private practice in 1908, after which he had more time for writing, which had, even in his busiest years, been important to him. The wide range of his interests is indicated by such titles as *The Influence of Clothing on Health* (1886—centering on his well-known antipathy for corsets), *Tale of a Field Hospital* (1900—based upon his experiences in the Boer War), *The Other Side of the Lantern: An Account of a Commonplace Tour round the World* (1905), and *Highways and Byways of Dorset* (1906—Treves served as the first president of the Club of Dorset Men, his successor being Thomas Hardy). After retirement, most of his writing centered on his travels with Lady Treves. *The Cradle of the Deep* (1908) was followed by

Uganda for Holiday (1910), *The Riviera of the Corniche Road* (1921), and *The Lake of Geneva* (1922). The sequence of travel and writing was broken by World War I, during which Treves was president of the Headquarters Medical Board, "primary adviser on the higher personnel of the Force," and an active worker for the International Red Cross. During the war years Treves began to experience the heart problems that brought about his move abroad in 1920. Throughout his remaining years, Treves suffered a series of health problems including a severe attack of pneumonia in 1922. He died in December 1923, and his ashes were buried in Dorchester Cemetery. Thomas Hardy, who was among those at the grave side, wrote a lyric dialogue, "In the Evening: In Memoriam Frederici Treves, 1853–1923," paying tribute to Treves the man of medicine and Treves the man of Dorset.[3]

Toward the end of his life Treves, having begun and abandoned a recollection of his famous patients, including the late king, turned to writing reminiscences of his "queer unknown patients, from the great army of suffering men and women I've been mixed up with."[4] First among these in several senses was the Elephant Man. The fact that Treves looked back to Merrick's story in the last year of his life and as his health was greatly failing strikes us as testimony to the power and enduring effect of that story. Later interpreters of Treves, among them Montagu and Pomerance, have read his encounter with Merrick as a turning point in his personal history. We think that in so doing they have responded to authentic possibilities in the story and that the circumstances of composition constitute prima facie evidence that in coming to terms with Merrick Treves was, among other things, coming to terms with his own life. But before considering "The Elephant Man" in and of itself, it is worth considering the reminiscence in relation to the other pieces in the collection. This process will help us to understand its larger significances—what it reveals of Merrick, Treves, and the late Victorian world of which they were a part.

Treves's account of the Elephant Man in his reminiscence has remained interesting because it lies outside the narrowest boundaries of that amorphous narrative territory staked out as "case history" and because Treves's association with Merrick is never what can be characterized as a conventional "doctor-patient relationship." The account is radically different, both in selection of detail and in vocabulary, from Treves's published clinical reports on Merrick's condition. This reminiscence, like the others in the collection, concerns persons and stories more than complaints, literary elements of character and action more than medical specifics. The twelve vignettes (and that epic number itself signals the literary aspirations of the work) are loosely connected by their rising out of Treves's medical career, much as Sir Arthur Conan Doyle's *Round the Red Lamp* and Richard Selzer's various essays and short stories spring, to greater and lesser extents, from medical training or practice. Like Selzer's work, Treves's reminiscences occupy an interesting middle ground between reportage and fiction—they are the result of their author's understanding events and characters with professional expertise, then shaping them for artistic effect. It is important to recall that when Treves wrote these reminiscences his own status was not that of surgeon, teacher, or administrator, but that of medical exile, attempting, like many other prosperous invalids, to stave off death on the shore of Lake Geneva. Writing in the last year of his life and as his health was clearly failing might have shaped Treves's reminiscences in a number of ways. The powers of recollection might be impaired. Distance from home could have severely hampered the ability to verify details. The pressure of time might reduce the inclination to be meticulous in such matters of verification. With the end of life in view, the impulse to shape the raw materials of incident into something coherent and appropriate might be particularly strong, especially for someone with an artistic sensibility. For all these reasons, it is worth wondering how fact and invention might have combined in the individual reminiscences; it is well known that even works making claims to definitive or factual status (to take one example among many, the *Autobiography* of Treves's literary friend Thomas Hardy)[5] blend what actually happened with what might have happened, or what would have happened if life were art.

The reminiscences vary widely in nature and effectiveness. Some, such as "The Twenty-Krone Piece," "A Sea Lover," and "A Case of Heart Failure," are conventional anecdotes, stories Treves encountered in his medical career and retells here. Other works, mingling various recollected narratives with medical details that even in Treves's old age had become historical, show us more of the customs and values of the late Victorian age in which Treves practiced. "The Old Receiving Room," a picture of metropolitan emergency medicine as it existed in the days before anesthesia and antisepsis, is remarkable among the pieces for its avoidance of conventional posturing and its unflinching depiction of "the thing itself." Following immediately upon "The Elephant Man," the piece ironically contrasts the London Hospital's inaptly named "receiving room" with the room into which Treves admitted Merrick and where, once that room became Merrick's own place, Treves was received in turn. Here the room is "uninviting . . . very plain, and, like the outer hall, bears an aspect of callous unconcern"; here the "most repellent thing" is a "grim black couch," shiny with stain, where " 'the case' just carried into the hospital is placed" (43). It is worth noting Treves's self-awareness of his youthful pride in operating amid such conditions: "The surgeon operated in a slaughter-house-suggesting frock coat of black cloth. It was stiff with the blood and filth of years. The more sodden it was the more forcibly did it bear evidence of the surgeon's prowess. I, of course, commenced my surgical career in such a coat, of which I was quite proud" (57). To become conscious of the ironies inherent in this occupational affectation, Treves had to remove the blinders he had put on in becoming a surgeon—and one might imagine that Treves's experience of Merrick helped to restore or maintain his breadth of vision.

"Two Women" offers a pair of anecdotes affirming the courage of women in the face of physical suffering. Here, Treves juxtaposes the story of an ordinary London suburbanite, who gallantly conceals her mortal illness to soothe the husband whose life centers on her, with the Lamp Murder Case, a tale of the domestic brutality all too common in the East End districts surrounding the London Hospital. This piece, with its comparative discussion of male and female strength and its appraisal of lower-class and petit-bourgeois life from the standpoint of the eminent professional man, sometimes affirms and sometimes transcends the stereotypes current in Treves's day. Like "The Elephant Man," where identification with Merrick alternates with resistance to such loss of detachment, "Two Women" highlights the ambiguity of Treves's perspective. Everything he sees is colored by the specifics of his position—health, success, respectability, masculinity, medical training—but he is sometimes keenly aware of the limits imposed by that position.

Treves's most ambitious attempt to get beyond the constraints of his personal perspective is found in "A Cure for Nerves," a portrayal of the "idle rich" woman that completes the feminine triptych begun in "Two

Women." In this account, Treves not only enters the mind of his story's heroine, he also speaks in her voice. The result, an experiment in empathy along the lines of the dramatic monologues of Treves's hero Browning, is the collection's most accomplished piece of prose. This narrative perceptively explores the gap between internal experience and external understanding of illness, frequently by posing the woman's own description of her condition against various male constructions of it: that of a husband, who thinks she needs only to cheer up, rouse herself, and pull herself together; that of a patronizing physician who begins his addresses to her with "My dear lady" and tells her not to think about herself at all; and that of a more seemingly sensitive doctor, who secretly dismisses her in a note to a colleague as "a deplorable neurotic" who nevertheless "pays her fees" (78). The account of her recovery stresses her own sympathetic identification with a woman who is operated on in a room directly above hers in a rest home. The speaker has always had "a dread of operations which is beyond expression," likening them to assault or rape: "It must be as if a man knelt upon your chest and strangled you by gripping your throat with his hands" (80). As the operation goes on above her, she feels suffocated by the chloroform she knows the patient is receiving, and she can "picture the knife, the great cut, the cold callousness of it all" (85). Eventually a red patch of blood appears on her ceiling, drops to the "white coverlet" of her bed, and becomes a "red haze filling the room" and causing her to lose consciousness. Upon learning of the surgical patient's recovery, the narrator asks a nurse whether the woman had been frightened. The nurse's response curiously echoes the language Treves uses to describe the women who visit Merrick: "No; she walked into the room, erect and smiling, and said in a jesting voice, 'I hope I have not kept you waiting, gentlemen, as I know you cannot begin without me' " (88).

From this point begins the narrator's cure, effected by what she is able to identify with, and imagine, in the surgical patient's whole response to her situation, including violation by the strong male figure of the surgeon and the imminence of death. The narrator says simply, "It was absurd to say that I could not walk in the street when that brave woman had walked, smiling, into that place of gags and steel" (88). Treves, of course, is a master of the gags and steel, and thus what he has done in "A Cure for Nerves" is to find a way to enter into his patients' fears and doubts regarding his own vocation. The surgeon's voice remains "the one strong and confident thing" (84) in the upper room, but Treves can also give voice to the complaints of the suffering woman in the bed below. Ultimately, however, Treves the writer is also a master of gags, and, in the end, he silences those complaints by means of the narrator's consciously forced bravery. The mirroring actions so characteristic, as we shall see, of the Elephant Man reminiscence prevail here as well: Treves, the writer-surgeon, first sympathizes with his protagonist-patient by voicing her anxieties, and then stills the anxieties (or at least the voice) by causing her to sympathize with another female patient, more courageous or compliant.

Acknowledging his role in the suffering of one below is also central to the gruesome story laconically titled "A Restless Night," which imposes the "white man's burden" in nightmare form on Treves the pukka sahib and Treves the doctor. The tale is set in Rajputana, described in terms reminiscent of the nether realms with which he associates the Elephant Man: "So elemental was the landscape that it might have been a part of the primeval world before the green things came into being" (137). An officer in the Indian Medical Service tells Treves the story of a villager who blames the officer for the loss of both eyes. That night Treves—who has by accident or intention been assigned to the officer's room—finds his sleep disturbed by a visitation from the vengeful blind villager, who finds his way to the customary resting place of the man on whom he blames his blindness and assaults the occupant of that bed. This nightmare tale of deformity and diverse paternalisms (those determining the relations of medical professional and outsider, elite and outcast, Englishman and Indian, healthy and diseased) expresses in fantasy what might be seen as the sinister side of the association explored in "The Elephant Man." It acknowledges the deep resentments that the weak can feel for the strong, the disenfranchised for the privileged, the ill and impaired for the well and whole, the suffering patient for the healer whose aid has not sufficed— all grievances that might have seemed almost inevitable in Merrick's case but were notably missing from his character as Treves paints it.

Some of Treves's human and professional fears and guilts may be obliquely voiced in "A Restless Night," but other tales more directly reveal traits and qualities of the individual who more than anyone else

saved Merrick and preserved the Elephant Man. "The Idol with Hands
of Clay" is, like Hawthorne's "Birthmark," a vision of hubris enacted
by a scientific young man with a pretty, adoring wife. Here a fledgling
practitioner, confident of his untested powers, fatally botches a surgical procedure required by his wife, who insists that only he can per-
form the complex operation. A disconcerting blend of cloying senti-
ment and gory viscera, this story—supposedly told to Treves by the
vainglorious and bungling surgeon to whom it happened—might be
seen as an exemplary illustration of Oscar Wilde's words "each man
kills the thing he loves." It is also an incisive appraisal of the diverse
aptitudes and qualities that go into the making of a surgeon—perhaps
an imaginative meditation on what the ambitious Treves might have become had he remained, as he started out, in practice "in a humble
country town"—certainly a curious permutation of life in art, for
Treves, his age's expert on appendicitis, had lost a daughter to that very
disease, her case having advanced so far by the time it was discovered
that medical intervention would have been useless.[6]

The collection's last two pieces are yet more direct in presenting us
with insights into Treves himself, for unlike "The Idol with Hands of
Clay" they present him in the double role of narrator-actor. "Breaking
the News," an essay on the shifting blend of tact and candor needed for
telling patients the worst, explicitly demonstrates something implicit at
various points in "The Elephant Man"—Treves's ability (whether
innate or acquired as part of a long and successful career of serving
others) to face, and accept, at least some of his own mistakes. The
particular examples of ineptitude are carefully chosen. As verbal or
diplomatic false steps rather than professional miscalculations, they do
not call into question Treves's high status as surgeon and humanist.
Likewise, the volume's final story, an amusing little comedy of errors
called "A Question of Hats," shows that a great practitioner can also be
the sort of petty bumbler who confuses other people's property with his
own. Taken literally, this anecdote presents Treves as the preoccupied
sort of man who mistakenly appropriates another doctor's hat and then
leaves it in a West End vestibule, from whence it is worn by an equally
absentminded duke who confuses it with his own foul headgear. But "A
Question of Hats" also presents, in parable form, the deep need for
more than one arena of achievement and mode of self-definition sig-

naled by Treves's narrative and stylistic choices in *The Elephant Man and Other Reminiscences,* by the very existence of this book and others amid his medical achievements.

That metaphorical need to wear other hats, to go beyond the limits of his chosen career (glorious vocation though it may be), and to achieve this conquest of boundaries through the power of words unites Treves with such doctor-writers as William Osler, William Carlos Williams, Danny Abse, and Lewis Thomas. The literal image of the repulsive hat resting on a duke's table reinvokes the image of Merrick's bizarre headgear glimpsed early in the collection's first tale and, besides offering a deft means of literary closure, links Treves to Merrick, who also shares his desire for transcendence—as do many others of those minds who have found the story of the Elephant Man so fascinating. But such affinities are matters for later discussion. For now, let it be enough to say that the complex sensibility that presents in *The Elephant Man and Other Reminiscences* a narrative mixture of literary conventions and medical matters also seems to have made possible the extraordinary relationship between Treves and Merrick.

The story of that relationship does not begin at the London Hospital, but opposite it, across the Mile End Road. The territory is not the realm of medicine but that of commerce—"a line of small shops" (1), among them the "vacant greengrocer's" where Dr. Treves has gone in search of a living spectacle to which he gradually introduces his readers. Our first glimpse of the Elephant Man is a stylized sideshow announcement, a "life-size portrait," a "very crude production" in "primitive colours." In the nine pages that constitute a first section of the reminiscence, Treves goes on to give us the particular details of his encounter with this "creature," the sordid circumstances of exhibition, the repulsive physical particularities of the being exhibited, and his own credentials and circumstances as an observer. Treves is interested enough to arrange for a more detailed examination, this time on the other side of Mile End Road in his territory, the hospital. The final paragraphs of this first section show us what little Treves, on the basis of this interview, makes of "the man himself," the human sensibility that might or might not exist inside this "monstrous" object, the Merrick in the Elephant Man.

The persistent effect of the introductory details is to stress the geographic, sartorial, taxonomic, moral, and intellectual distance between Treves (here, the spectator rather than the doctor) and the Elephant Man (not yet Merrick), the object of his search. The Mile End Road may well be, as Montagu puts it, the very widest thoroughfare in London, but nonetheless it is not quite the gulf Treves makes of it in these paragraphs, where he stresses the apparent difficulty of passing from his territory to Merrick's or vice versa.[7] Advertised though the Elephant Man exhibit may be, Treves must make special arrangements for a viewing, through a "well-informed boy" who seeks out the "proprietor" in a public house. Transporting Merrick, who is said to be "as secluded from the world as the Man in the Iron Mask," across to London Hospital is presented as yet more difficult—perhaps more difficult than in fact it would have to be. "The Elephant Man could not show himself in the streets. He would have been mobbed by the crowd and seized by the police" (6). In the reminiscence Merrick manages the crossing only by means of a cab arranged for by Treves—and he crosses in "disguise," his traveling gear consisting of a long black cloak and a wide peaked cap complete with a gray flannel veil.

Treves's reading of Merrick's outerwear emphasizes the strangeness of this being who is transversing the Mile End Road. It is as if a longer journey were being undertaken by an exceedingly exotic traveler. The cloak's provenance is bizarre—"whence the cloak had been obtained I cannot imagine"—its like Treves had seen only "on the stage wrapped about the figure of a Venetian bravo." The "bag-like slippers" are clearly not shoes for the metropolis, and the cap "of a kind that never before was seen" is closest, in Treves's eye, to "a yachting cap." There are several ways of reading this "costume," one being to see it as an early instance of the dandiacal romanticism that later emerges as a key feature of Merrick's personality. But Treves's insistence on the costume's being "the most uncanny that has as yet been designed" (7) highlights, even exaggerates, the difference between Merrick and other crossers of the street. The adjective "uncanny" warrants particular notice, suggesting as it does a radical otherness of both intent and effect, an otherness that heightens Treves's self-consciousness.

What had troubled Treves in the grotesque advertisement that served as his preview of the Elephant Man was the uncanny nature of that representation—the ambiguity that resists classification as man or beast: "It was the figure of a man with the characteristics of an elephant. The transfiguration was not far advanced. There was still more of the man than of the beast. The fact—that it was still human—was the most repellent attribute of the creature" (1–2). The being exhibited under the name of the Elephant Man cannot be an Englishman like Treves. The fact that such a bias would be a cultural commonplace seems suggested by the displacements apparent in the "primitive colours" of the "very crude production" with its "palm trees in the background suggesting a jungle." Such a monster cannot belong among us, the representation seems to say, but instead must inhabit the realm of nightmare—and not the England of nightmare but some obscure, tropical corner of the empire. Recalling the sideshow announcement, Treves fears that the unskilled yet efficient daub might lead "the imaginative to assume that it was in this wild that the perverted object had roamed" (2). But the imagination he fears may be his own, if, as we are suggesting, the uncanny experience of observing Merrick calls into question Treves's own ways of, and categories for, understanding himself.

When Treves comes to describe the physical reality of the Elephant Man, he begins by returning to the "intensified painting," specifically to the misconception of gigantic stature suggested to his imagination by that representation. Treves's own words for the body displayed before him are similarly intensified and similarly distancing. A heightened version of the metaphoric language that is a convention of clinical reporting, Treves's account both denies any unified wholeness to the body he views and minimizes the humanity of the particular parts that obsessively engage his intention. The tropes of this passage come from the subhuman animals, vegetables, even tools. Among other grotesque particulars in the animated pastiche constituting the Elephant Man are "cauliflower" skin, a jaw protruding "like a pink stump," "a rudimentary trunk or tusk," a face "no more capable of expression than a block of gnarled wood," a "fin or paddle" of a hand whose thumb "had the appearance of a radish," its fingers the look of "thick tuberous roots," pendant flesh "like a dewlap suspended from the neck of a lizard." Describing the one unafflicted limb again pushes Treves to stress the Elephant Man's otherness. "Remarkable by contrast" is the left arm with which, as we shall see, Merrick comes to meet the world. "It was not only normal," Treves says, "but was, moreover, a delicately shaped limb covered with fine skin and provided with a beautiful hand which any woman might have envied" (4–5). Even the specific description of this "normal" arm stresses its incongruity, its peculiar inappropriateness for the body to which it is attached and also its unlikeness to the arms of other men—Treves among them.

The stylized sideshow portrait and Treves's word picture of the Elephant Man are both more metaphor than likeness. As such they exaggerate, but essentially correspond to, the misconception that denies Merrick's kinship with humankind and distances him from his species. The rhetoric of the account's opening pages takes a long time in granting straightforward human status to the Elephant Man: "A bent figure," "it" (2), "the creature," "a captive in a cavern," "a wizard watching for unholy manifestations," "the thing," "the most disgusting specimen of humanity that I have ever seen" (3)—through these referents Treves and his readers avoid coming to terms with the painful human reality before them, whether by disavowing or extrapolating from that humanity. These words express, and construct, illusions that must be entertained and rejected before one grants Merrick the minimally normal status implied by the ordinary third-person singular masculine pronoun "he" (3). Even after he has implicitly acknowledged Merrick's humanity, Treves retains the kind of moral description of disease that is one of our characteristic ways of setting distance between the sick and ourselves. "Degraded," "perverted," "repellent," "loathesome," "horrible" are some of the early words for Merrick. Each of these words is used with some degree of denotative precision, but all their connotations are unfortunate—unfortunate but perhaps unavoidable. Though Treves is certainly not blaming Merrick for his condition, the language available to him puts somatic conditions into categories identical to those ascribed to moral behaviors and distinguishes Merrick from the "sound" among his fellow creatures.

This male, being eventually allowed a nationality, a name, and an age, is examined, interviewed, and exhibited—the last of these behaviors not explicitly mentioned and in fact implicitly denied in the reminiscence. But even after such close scrutiny, Treves says that he "made little of the man himself" (7). Treves could make (in two senses) little of Merrick precisely because Merrick was being made or happening beyond any human making. Despite obtaining a good bit of information from Merrick on his origins, family, and progressive deformity, as the previously discussed report of "A Case of Congenital Deformity" suggests, and despite having concluded in that piece that Merrick's "intelligence was by no means of a low order," Treves remarkably claims to have "supposed that Merrick was imbecile and had been imbecile from birth" (8). This erroneous supposition has far more to do with the interpreter than with the evidence, as Treves acknowledges in avowing his conviction to be "encouraged by the hope that his intellect was the blank I imagined it to be" (8). Merrick's countenance may have been inexpressive and his voice inarticulate, but the basic obstacle was that the full humanity conferred by mental competence proved too painful a fact for Treves to face: "It was not until I came to know that Merrick was highly intelligent, that he possessed an acute sensibility and—worse than all—a romantic imagination that I realized the overwhelming tragedy of his life" (8–9). That "overwhelming tragedy" is something any kindhearted onlooker might resist seeing; but the truth must have been especially painful in retrospect to Treves, who had briefly brought Merrick in, then returned him to what from the vantage point of a successful Victorian professional man must appear to be a life of public degradation.

For all these strategies, the Elephant Man would not be distanced. Twice in the space of three paragraphs, Treves's rhetoric moves toward closure, without attaining it. "I assumed that I had seen the last of him," says Treves, who has returned Merrick "in a cab to the place of exhibition"—but his sentence directly turns on itself, continuing in another direction with the qualification "especially as I found next day that the show had been forbidden by the police and that the shop was empty" (8). Shortly thereafter, Treves opens the second phase of his essay with a mistaken declaration (and half-felt thwarted wish?) for the distance attainable through such closure: "The episode of the Elephant Man was, I imagined, closed; but I was fated to meet him again—two years later—under more dramatic conditions" (9). The three words "episode," "fated," and "dramatic," bringing back the notion of Merrick's life as tragedy in the classical sense, also serve to redirect the initiative that continues the association between the two men. In imagining a destined reunion thrust upon them from outside, Treves evades the recognition that he has laid himself open to the experience, indeed has actively promoted it by giving Merrick his card, a prop of great significance in the phase of the relationship and section of the reminiscence to which we now turn.

The middle part of the narrative, occupying roughly that section

between the introductory pages and the last section with its account of
Merrick's residence at the London Hospital, is different in tone from
what precedes and follows it. Perhaps because he was not part of the
story during the two-year period of wandering and public exhibition
that punctuates his acquaintance with Merrick, Treves largely effaces
his own voice and his explicit judgments from this section of the narrative. Instead we encounter an interesting blend of objectively stated
fact and empathetic projection into other minds than his own—a psychological and literary device superbly deployed by Treves's poet-hero
Browning in *The Ring and the Book*.[8]

The first paragraph of this interlude puts us within "the official
mind"—that collective Victorian entity that ruled on what would do
and what would not. The language earlier applied to Merrick's somatic
complaint returns, but here the moral connotations are primary rather
than secondary. Nonetheless, ambiguities pervade this pocket history
of Merrick's wanderings in England, which begins just prior to the exhibition in Whitechapel: "The showman and Merrick had been moved
on from place to place by the police, who considered the exhibition
degrading and among the things that could not be allowed" (13).[9] At
first we might want to agree with the judgment of the police here, but
the matter becomes more complicated when we recognize the un-
answered questions. In what way is the exhibit "degrading"? The moral
recognition that brutal exhibitions of this sort cheapen spectacle and
spectators alike is one possible way—but emotivist shrinking from
what is perceived as monstrous on the grounds that seeing such deformity threatens our sense of what constitutes humanity is an equally
possible and less worthy way. And if the exhibition "could not be allowed," what is the humane alternative? Clearly the "official mind" has
not come up with one—being "moved on," a usage later repeated (18),
is the fate visited on the outcast Jo in Dickens' *Bleak House*—and the
fact that Treves borrows Dickens' words stresses the parallel in the situations and encourages us to reach in Merrick's case the conclusion
laid out by the editorializing narrator in *Bleak House*, namely, that official policies and institutions are better at banishing social ills than at
curing them. The hypocrisy of such pretense to morality is clearly evident in the next sentence: "It was hoped that in the uncritical retreats
of Mile End a more abiding peace would be found" (13). Hoped by
whom? And abiding peace through what—continued exhibition, only

in a suitably squalid location? But the metropolitan official mind thinks like its provincial counterpart and "very properly decreed that the exposure of Merrick and his deformities transgressed the limits of decency" (13).

In the next paragraph the scene shifts to the Continent and ultimately Brussels, the city to which those transgressors of English morality—notably debtors or adulterous couples—who could not pass muster even in London traditionally fled for their sins. We now enter the consciousness of the showman, a speculator "in despair" because the stock in which he has invested has lost value. At this point it is worth noting that although Merrick had worked for more than one manager and that the Whitechapel impresario was not the Brussels one, Treves either did not know or did not choose to reflect the fact. If, as Treves suggests, being exhibited in freak shows denied the personhood of Merrick, being combined into one representative and villainous figure of exploitation does much the same thing to his real managers. Indeed, what contributes most powerfully to Treves's depiction of Merrick as victim is his complete denial, or ignorance, of Merrick's role as the instigating agent of his own exhibition.

Even Brussels decrees the exhibition of Merrick "brutal, indecent and immoral," not acceptable "within the confines of Belgium." The words of this verdict, embodying precisely the same judgment encountered on the other side of the Channel, widen the charge of hypocrisy to indict more than a single culture. The high pronouncements of officialdom (which essentially mean that "morally reprehensible" and "do it somewhere else" are synonyms) are shown as corrupt and made to seem the more so because the reasoning Treves projects upon the representative showman is that of a petty capitalist, someone connected, if tenuously, to the social structure that shuns his exhibit: "Merrick was thus no longer of value. He was no longer a source of profitable entertainment. He was a burden. He must be got rid of" (13–14). The remainder of this paragraph combines statement of fact with figurative language and supposition clearly intended to highlight the odious nature of the impresario's abandoning his charge. We see the helplessness of Merrick, "docile as a sick sheep," and the avarice and hatefulness of the showman, who stole Merrick's "paltry savings" and "no doubt in parting condemned him to perdition"—the last, one might expect, a superfluous imprecation. Interestingly, though such

interpretative touches clearly indicate Treves's intent of stressing the
showman's baseness, the details as related are less villainous and also
less accurate than those found in Carr Gomm's 1886 letter to the *Times*.
In Treves, the impresario at least gives Merrick a ticket to London and
puts him on the train; in Carr Gomm, Merrick is left "absolutely destitute" and alone in a foreign land. He must pawn some possession to
raise his fare and must make his own way to the station and the London
train, a matter of some difficulty for any stranded traveler, especially
one with his handicaps.

The details of Carr Gomm's account stress the specific inten-
tionality of Merrick's journey to London: "He felt that the only friend he
had in the world was Mr. Treves of the London Hospital" (Montagu,
110). Treves tells the story another way. His next two paragraphs, which
take Merrick himself as their center of consciousness, chronicle a trip
far more harrowing than what Carr Gomm presents. The brutality of the
curious crowds is comparable, but the terrible journey is worse for having no goal: "What was he to do when he reached London? He had not a
friend in the world" (10). Treves's account is consistent with his conception of Merrick as a figure in a tragedy—though it should be noted
that for Treves, as for his friend Thomas Hardy, tragedy implies less
heroic striving in the face of destiny and more pathetic endurance of
fate's rigors than a strictly classical sense of tragedy would allow. Merrick, like Tess Durbeyfield, for instance, suffers what happenstance
brings upon him. His self-sufficiency is minimized, especially at the
times when he must "move on": The Continental manager puts him on
the London train (in much the same way that Treves had arranged his
transport across the Mile End Road), and the benevolent London police
intervene in his behalf at Liverpool Station by summoning Treves,
whose card Merrick "produced with a ray of hope," and by dispatching
the two of them, in a cab, for London Hospital. Merrick's production of
the card marks a natural dividing point in the narrative: It reestablishes
his connection with Treves. The preservation of the card also suggests
that Merrick did not share Treves's earlier sense that the story between
them had closed. It is interesting to speculate about Merrick's motives
for keeping the card: Is Merrick casting Treves, as Carr Gomm's phrase
suggests, in the role of his "only friend in the world"? Even if he is not
doing so, Merrick is demonstrating himself a man capable of plans and
purposes. Having found his way to London, and to a particular person

whom he has actively retained in his life, Merrick is in fact more than a victim of happenstance, more than the "mere heap" or abandoned "bundle" Treves finds, collects, and carries to the attics of London Hospital. The transaction Treves thought he had closed two years before, Merrick has opened up.

About two-thirds of Treves's thirty-seven-page reminiscence is given over to Merrick's life at the London Hospital. His continued residence there is anomalous, for the hospital "was neither a refuge nor a home for incurables" but a place only "for those requiring active treatment" (12). In admitting and retaining Merrick, Treves had to commit an irregularity—not only in disregarding the forms of hospital bureaucracy but also in modifying his former, narrowly professional understanding of disease and his responsibility in ministering to it. Treves, no longer just a surgeon, has himself been opened up by this case that, he now understands, will not be closed. It is at this point that he applies to Carr Gomm for approval; and the "sympathetic chairman," himself understanding the situation in terms broader than his professional responsibilities would presuppose, addresses the English public through the *Times* and thereby obtains contributions adequate to support Merrick.

The early days of Merrick's hospital residence can be seen as diagnostic in so far as they involve the taking of a history, interpreting that narrative, and settling on an appropriate regimen (which in the reminiscence at least involves, among other things, reinventing the patient). Frequent baths, and presumably other attentions from "volunteer nurses," seem to be the only somatic component of the program of therapy. More important, at least to Treves, is therapeutic companionship, at first provided solely by Treves, who "saw him almost every day, and made a point of spending some two hours with him every Sunday morning" (14). As Treves and others became familiar with the patterns of Merrick's speech and Merrick gained the confidence that made him less diffident, Treves discovered his patient's intelligence and "passion for conversation." He became aware that Merrick was a "most voracious reader" who knew a limited number of works (the Bible, the Prayer Book) intimately and took delight in "romances."

Even so, Treves still held to his first assessment of Merrick as "an elemental being, so primitive that he might have spent the twenty-three years of his life immured in a cave" (15). The tenacity of this impression tells us much more about Treves's mind than it does about Merrick's. Joined with the capacity for unswerving adherence to a quickly reached decision (an ability for which Treves was noted, and one he attempted to instill in his students at the London)[10] is the capacity for associative intuition that set Treves apart from the many others who observed the Elephant Man and saw a disorder, not a person. Unlike the other admirable men whose contemporary accounts of Merrick we examined in the last chapter, Treves was keenly aware of Merrick the individual being. But even after becoming familiar with that person, Treves still sees him at least partially in terms of the literary situations his plight suggests to the play of fancy. Treves wearing his medical hat sees the connections between bone and skin disorders; Treves wearing his literary hat perceives (and in his prose implies) affinities between the suffering outcast Merrick and Caliban, Philoctetes, or the cave dwellers in Plato's allegory.

As Merrick remains in the hospital, Treves's goals for helping his patient become progressively ambitious. Recognizing and valuing Merrick's human potential, Treves no longer is content to provide refuge and physical comfort for a pitiful outcast. He wants to move Merrick toward the normal. The first step in doing so is to allay what Treves sees as Merrick's "two anxieties," the first centered on an assumption that he will eventually be moved on as before, the second, on his "fear of people's eyes, the dread of being always stared at, the lash of the cruel mutterings of the crowd" (19). Reassuring Merrick that he has a permanent place in his rooms on Bedstead Square is the first phase in what amounts to a transformation of Merrick. The second and crucial phase begins with reintroduction of humankind into Merrick's world: "To secure Merrick's recovery and to bring him, as it were, to life once more, it was necessary that he should make the acquaintance of men and women who would treat him as a normal and intelligent young man and not as a monster of deformity" (20). In Treves's view women were "more important than men in bringing about his transformation" because they his mind and enlarging his knowledge of the world," Merrick is "anxious to view the interior of what he called 'a real house' " (29), which prompts Treves to take him to his own "small house in Wimpole Street" among them the generalization that women who became nurses were coarsened, even unsexed, by their responsibilities.[11] More important than the nurses' professional (hence unwomanly) care would be the regard of such ladies as the "young and pretty widow" Treves asked to enter Merrick's room "with a smile, wish him good morning and shake him by the hand" (22). This woman "said she could and she did"— and she was the first of a "constant succession" of visitors, preeminent among them Alexandra, Princess of Wales, who in Treves's account does just what the young widow has done. Alexandra "entered Merrick's room smiling and shook him warmly by the hand" (24), thus setting a new convention for responding to this now "delighted creature who had been all his life despised and rejected of men" (25). A transformation indeed—and yet all these visits are, like Treves's first encounter with Merrick, private (inter)views, but with Treves in the role of agent.

Once the world has come to him and smiled, Merrick begins to think himself able to venture back into the world; and the last pages of Treves's narrative chronicle Merrick's series of attempts, all but one of them stage-managed on Treves's part but every one a sign of Merrick's imagination or courage, of his great wish to be like the people who have visited him. He asks that his Christmas present be "a silver-fitted dressing-bag," the accessories of "a dandy and a young man about town" (26, 27). With "modest ambitions in the direction of improving his mind and enlarging his knowledge of the world," Merrick is "anxious to view the interior of what he called 'a real house' " (29), which prompts Treves to take him to his own "small house in Wimpole Street" (30). A "more burning ambition" was to visit the theater, a more difficult excursion to arrange but one made possible by the assistance of "that kindest of women and most able of actresses—Mrs. Kendal" (31), who obtains a Drury Lane box from which Merrick, Treves, and three hospital sisters who " 'dress' the box," watch "a popular pantomime" (30, 31). The logistics of a visit to the country, inspired by Merrick's reading but also no doubt by his desire to emulate the migrations of his noble and gentle visitors, are yet more intricate. But again through a combination of Treves's resourcefulness and "the kindness and generosity of a lady—Lady Knightley—who offered Merrick a holiday home in a cottage on her estate" (33), Merrick's wish is granted, and richly so—the freedom of roaming amid scenes of natural beauty and the kindness of the country couple who receive him make possible "the one supreme holiday of his life" (34).

Treves's reminiscence rather abruptly shifts from the scene of Merrick's country idyll to his deathbed some six months later. But in a sense the transition is perfectly appropriate to Merrick's life as here written. From the "supreme holiday"—the ultimate approximation of the normal engineered by Treves and other well-disposed outsiders— Merrick goes to an independent venture into normal territory. Because of the weight of his skull, Merrick's practice had been to sleep sitting up in bed, his back supported by pillows, his knees drawn up, his arms clasped around his legs, his head resting on his knees. On Merrick's last night,[12] Treves theorizes, "he must, with some determination, have made the experiment" of lying down to sleep. His heavy head must have fallen backward, dislocating the neck. Acknowledging that "the method of his death was peculiar," Treves does not see accidental death or suicide as possibilities: Instead, Merrick's death "was due to the desire that had dominated his life—the pathetic but hopeless desire to be 'like other people' " (36).

The largest physical gap in the narrative intervenes between this death scene and the two-paragraph coda to Merrick's story, where Treves polarizes the "ignoble and repulsive" specimen of Merrick's outer self and the spirit that, if it could be seen, "would assume the figure of an upstanding and heroic man, smooth browed and clean of limb, and with eyes that flashed undaunted courage" (36–37). The last paragraph, weighed down with literary convention, replaces Hardy's suffering wayfarer with Bunyan's pilgrim—and, unintentionally perhaps, Treves's literary tastes give way to something far more characteristic of Merrick's temperament and milieu. Having been "plunged into the Slough of Despond," "Ill treated and reviled and bespattered with the Mud of Disdain," having escaped "the Giant Despair," Merrick has with "manly steps" gained the farther shore—"the 'Place of Deliverance' " (37). For Treves, he has crossed something much wider than the Mile End Road.

Much of the drama of the latter part of Treves's narrative involves the ambiguities of his transformation of Merrick. While Treves recognizes, for instance, that Merrick is not in somatic need of "active treatment," he nevertheless embarks on a very ambitious project of remaking his patient, one he compares quite specifically to bringing him to life, as if Merrick were a ready-made Frankenstein monster to be nurtured and cultured into civility. Thus while guilty, on one level, of violating the hospital's rules against admitting incurables, Treves acts in accordance with the spirit of those rules and his own professional self-understanding as a surgeon. His is no passive care of the patient; Treves sets out, in a real sense, to cure Merrick of what afflicts him: loneliness, suffering, lack of self. Paradoxically, to begin this process Treves must make a highly paternalistic decision about Merrick's future. He and Carr Gomm determine "that Merrick must not again be turned out into the world" (13). To give Merrick agency, he must first be deprived of it. Thus is the dilemma of medical paternalism focused very starkly here. We must certainly applaud the opening of the hospital to Merrick's perpetual residence, but we must also wonder how different Treves's sentiments are from those of the "official mind" in its London or Brussels incarnation. Must Merrick be kept in hospital because to turn him out would be indecent, obscene, one of the things that must not be allowed?

The delicate ambiguities of Treves's relationship to Merrick emerge from his account of coming to understand Merrick's speech. It is difficult to characterize Treves's role in this section of the narrative. At times he sounds as if he is Merrick's friend, come to converse for two hours every Sunday morning; at others, he is more clearly the professional observer, "endeavor[ing] to understand his mentality" in "a study of much interest" (13–14). This confusion of roles reflects the fundamental paradox of Merrick's being both like and unlike his physician, a paradox that Treves both recognizes and resists. In acquiring Merrick's language, Treves contributes to the development of Merrick's self, his sense of agency. Merrick now has someone to speak with, an audience for whom to put his experience into shape. Thus Treves makes a real contribution to the bettering of Merrick's existential condition, but not through the active intervention to which he has been trained. Instead he does so by learning to listen, by developing ears to hear. Treves is learning to give himself to Merrick, to be there for Merrick, to yield the difference between himself and Merrick. Meanwhile Merrick, through his passionate conversation, is becoming both more like and unlike Treves. On finding a hearer, he becomes a being capable of articulating a specific personal history as well as desires and projects of his own. In becoming more clearly a willing subject, he becomes more like Treves, yet his very ability to have his own history understood further distinguishes him from the physician. Treves's language reflects these paradoxes. While he enters freely into Merrick's passionate conversation, he also denigrates it as frequently being little more than a near ceaseless "chatter." Similarly, though amazed by Merrick's "remarkable" intelligence, he finds Merrick a "child" in his "outlook upon the world," an "elemental being."

It is no accident, then, that Treves turns next to giving an account of Merrick's history, an account that is as remarkable for what it omits as for what it contains. Treves makes no mention of Merrick's own characteristic explanation of his deformity, the story of the circus elephant's traumatizing his mother. As a scientific man, Treves no doubt found this story absurd, but it is nevertheless curious that he would omit such an important part of Merrick's self-understanding. While he notes Merrick's "favourite belief" in his mother's beauty, Treves also omits all mention of her miniature portrait, which Merrick seemed to cherish, at least according to Carr Gomm. Indeed Merrick's mother is the subject of major discrepancies between what seems to be "factual" and Treves's history of his patient. Whereas Howell and Ford maintain that Merrick's mother stayed with him until his early teens,[13] Treves says that she "basely deserted him when he was very small, so small that his earliest clear memories were of the workhouse to which he had been taken" (16). One might of course argue that Merrick failed to make his history clear to Treves and that such discrepancies should in no way be attributed to Treves's reinventing Merrick. Such may be the case. But on at least two occasions Treves directly sets his version in conflict with Merrick's. One of these contradictions involves Mrs. Merrick's beauty: "It was a favourite belief of his that his mother was beautiful. The fiction was, I am aware, one of his own making, but it was a great joy to him" (16). A second concerns her character, epitomized here by insistence that she abandoned her child: "Worthless and inhuman as she was, he spoke of her with pride and even with reverence" (16). Perhaps it is as well to mention here as elsewhere Treves's persistent habit of referring to Merrick as John rather than Joseph, as he is called in most other documents, from his autobiography to his obituary. It seems hardly likely that Treves was unaware of Merrick's actual Christian name. How, then, are we to understand his insistence on calling Merrick John? Did that name fulfill a need for Treves that Joseph could not? Was Treves somehow compelled to rename Merrick, to place himself in the role of father—must Treves become the giver of the true name, thereby supplanting those parents who, as he insists on seeing it, had abandoned their child?

Naming his patient, Treves implicitly acknowledges his own wish, in this reminiscence, to have authority over Merrick's story—to rewrite it in a fashion that he deems appropriate. The revisions of Merrick's biography point to a series of interrelated ways in which Merrick's version of his own life is unsatisfactory to Treves. All these matters reassert the gap between Treves and Merrick—and do so precisely by denying any potential normal relationship between Merrick and women. Unlike Treves, Merrick must not have an English mother (especially a beautiful one) to rear him with kindness and make him a person with a history instead of a phenomenon to be discovered. Similarly, Merrick must be denied any fatherly (or fathering) possibilities of his own, possibilities glimpsed, one might say, in the paternal-sounding "Joseph" but absent from the various biblical connotations of "John." The latter name, which means "the Lord is gracious" (no small irony in Merrick's case), suggests loving and beloved discipleship in the case of the Evangelist, supernatural intervention in human reproductive matters and leaping in utero in the case of the Baptist. Thus Treves's account of Merrick's life at the London is fraught with associations of the former Saint John, and Merrick's own account of his prenatal catastrophe displays congruences with the latter's miraculous origins. Father and son can reflect each other without mutual diminishment in the Gospel of John, but not in real life—certainly not in the relationship between Merrick and Treves. A sign of this state of affairs is Treves's persistently protective, even proprietary, attitude toward the women he introduces into his patient's life but keeps within strictly set limits once they are there.

Paternalism is clearly evident in the reminiscence's treatment of the nurses who were in fact Merrick's closest companions, day in and day out, during his life in the hospital. Treves stresses the way the first such attendant, a nurse who has not been "prepared" for the frightful particulars of Merrick's appearance, drops her tray and runs shrieking through the door (an episode consciously echoed later on when, "like the nurse at the hospital," the housewife who was to offer Merrick hospitality during his stay in the country throws her apron over her head and flees gasping to the fields). The reminiscence downplays the con-

stant care prepared nurses could and did provide. Acknowledging that
there were plenty of volunteers for such service, it elides the specifics
of the ministrations and characterizes the interactions as "somewhat
formal and constrained." Although it mentions in passing the baths
Merrick's malodorous skin condition made necessary "at least once a
day," Treves's account does not reflect the essential presence and
agency of the nurses on these intimate occasions, nor does it convey the
importance of these baths as the first step in overcoming Merrick's isolation, in making him presentable to a world beyond specially trained
professional caretakers. Treves is careful to suggest that the nurses,
while they minister to Merrick, leave behind the femininity that be-
longs to them in the real world—and he is equally careful to characterize that service as *his version of Merrick* understands it: "Merrick, no
doubt, was conscious that their service was purely official, that they
were merely doing what they were told to do and that they were acting
rather as automata than as women. They did not help him to feel that he
was of their kind. On the contrary they, without knowing it, made him
aware that the gulf of separation was immeasurable" (11–12).

As we have already seen, women (especially ladies) from the outside world were, as Treves saw it, crucial to Merrick's recovery. To
"bring him . . . to life once more," it was especially necessary that he
meet women, for they were "the more apt to give way to irrepressible
expressions of aversion when they came into his presence" (21). To be
brought to life suggests the conversion of Merrick's status from passive
object—a recipient of the gaze of others—to willing subject, one who
looks at others. Women, then, serve as the Other, against which Merrick's male self is to be defined. Moreover, Treves's gallery of women
visitors must not be allowed their own reactions, for these might be to
gasp and run. He first chooses a "young and pretty widow"—perhaps
because, twice wounded, she has already experienced the worst—and
asks her "if she thought she could enter Merrick's room with a smile,
wish him good morning and shake him by the hand" (22). Treves seems
to have carefully stage-managed the reactions of each of Merrick's visitors, even that of the Princess of Wales, later Queen Alexandra. Several times he recurs to close variations of the sentence "They were all
good enough to welcome him with a smile and shake hands with him"
(the "good" here perhaps connoting theatrical competence and courteous poise rather than moral worth). Thus the women are doubly de-

prived of agency in a transaction that reverses the roles of looking and exhibiting but perpetuates the "indecency" of the Elephant Man shows from which Treves has rescued Merrick. The women are ostensibly visitors, but Treves scripts their actions and reactions; because their freedom to respond has been constrained, Merrick does not "meet" but looks upon them. One might speculate that Treves's introducing of women to Merrick resolves the crisis in his own self-understanding caused by his confrontation with the ambiguously human in Merrick. In one regard at least, their difference from the female Other, Treves and Merrick are the same. What Treves is about, too, is the careful creation of Merrick's self-image. During his section on Merrick's lady visitors, he notes Merrick's lessening consciousness of his "unsightliness," brought about in part by "the circumstance" that Treves "would not allow a mirror of any kind in his room" (23). Merrick's lady visitors effectively substitute for this mirror; they provide the reflection through which Merrick is to understand himself.

Merrick's exposure to Treves's gallery of women brings about a subtle change in the relationship between the two men. Merrick begins to become more active in his own transformation, moving more toward the normal and Treves. On the other hand, Treves, originally the author of Merrick's transformation, now becomes more ambivalent about the process, increasingly emphasizing Merrick's limitations. An incident that illustrates the delicate, easily upset balance of dependence and independence, similarity and difference, between the men involves Treves's buying Merrick the Christmas gift mentioned earlier. Treves has been given money by "benevolent visitors" to "expend for the comfort of the *çi-devant* Elephant Man" (26). The phrase carries lingering overtones of condescension but also acknowledges a change in Merrick's status. And what Treves does with the money indicates that his relationship is no longer one of simple philanthropic paternalism toward an "Elephant Man": "When one Christmas was approaching I asked Merrick what he would like me to purchase as a Christmas present" (26). Here Treves diminishes his authority over the gift, allowing Merrick to control, for once, what is given to him. Merrick must still depend upon Treves, but he now has the chance to work through Treves to re-create himself. What he asks for, a "silver-fitted dressing-bag," seems hardly surprising. He is looking to acquire the kind of personal items essential to the sort of gentlemen who have been coming to call on him. In an entirely normal way, he is trying to become like his visitors; he has believed the illusions created for him by Treves in the faces of those women who have come through his door. But Treves is "startled" by Merrick's request (or perhaps by his own theatrical illusion's being so fully believed). He accordingly spends several paragraphs in stressing the impossibility of Merrick's self-transformation. One of these reveals Treves's new difficulties in placing Merrick, whose defiance of categories is here evident in the curious and condescending mix of gender descriptions: "I fathomed the mystery in time, for Merrick made little secret of the fancies that haunted his boyish brain. Just as a small girl with a tinsel coronet and a window curtain for a train will realize the conception of a countess on her way to court, so Merrick loved to imagine himself a dandy and a young man about town. Mentally, no doubt, he had frequently 'dressed up' for the part. He would 'make-believe' with great effect, but he wanted something to render his fancied character more realistic. Hence the jaunty bag which was to assume the function of the toy coronet and the window curtain that could transform a mite with a pigtail into a countess" (26–27).

For Treves, Merrick cannot be simply a rather ordinary man aspiring to be like the men who have come to see him and to be attractive to women who have smiled on him. Although he no longer plays the role of Elephant Man, he remains ambiguous to Treves. What the above description is clear on, though, is that Merrick, in his courting behavior, is the child, presexual. Perhaps he must remain so in order that Treves can avoid the unthinkable, Merrick as father, "John" as "Joseph," a role that would force Treves to revise or relinquish his own role as patriarchal creator. Merrick is more cooperative than malleable, and his life resists paternalistic molding. This point is implied through unintentionally ironic equivocations about the silver-fitted dressing bag mentioned above. "When I purchased the article I realized that as Merrick could never travel he could hardly want a dressing-bag," says Treves (28). Admittedly, the individual articles—silver brushes, razors, a shoehorn, a cigarette case Treves has taken care to fill— cannot be used for their intended functions. In that sense Merrick cannot want (in the sense of needing) them. But he can want (in the sense of desiring) them. He can put them to use: The daily act of laying out these luxuriously made necessities of ordinary life is vital to the fiction of Merrick's devising. Having these props makes him, as Treves puts it, "the real swell" and "the knockabout Don Juan of whom he had read" (28). So the articles are in fact wanted—and furthermore in the following pages of the reminiscence Merrick does little but travel: to Treves's "real house" in Wimpole Street, to the theater in Drury Lane, to the country lodgings loaned him by Lady Knightley.

The thing to notice about all these ambitions is that they are ordinary. Merrick, cast by life and circumstance, by his own needs to survive and the exploitative perceptions of others, in the monstrous role of Elephant Man, was able at the London Hospital and with the aid of Treves to revise himself. What that revision involves is Merrick, despite those somatic features that make him extraordinary, acting out perfectly ordinary aspirations. He takes on the role of any ambitious and romantic working-class youth assuming the role of gentleman when destiny draws him into higher circles than those in which he was born. Treves and the rest of us find it easier to make Merrick more or less than he is, Elephant Man or creative genius *manqué*, for to do so is to preserve distance and otherness. What the facts, though not the rhetoric, of Treves's reminiscence reveal is that desire to rise in the world shared by most people, from the Prince of Wales (who is not yet a monarch) on down.

The desire to be like others takes its most elemental shape at the end of Treves's account, as Merrick, compelled by his head's heaviness to sleep sitting up with back supported, knees drawn up, arms clasped, and head propped, lies down. To sleep or to die? Treves's account implies the former, though his speaking of the "method" of Merrick's death suggests that he did not utterly dismiss the latter possibility. But Treves's hypothesis is not suicide. "He often said to me that he wished he could lie down to sleep 'like other people.' I think on this last night he must, with some determination, have made the experiment. . . . Thus it came about that his death was due to the desire that had dominated his life—the pathetic but hopeless desire to be 'like other people' " (36). As we see later on, each reader of Merrick's life finds a different meaning in Merrick's death—a meaning that tells us more about that reader than it does about the event itself. Here, Treves reveals certain professional and personal biases. As a medical man, he is trained (and sworn) to preserve life. As friend and patron and impresario, he is accustomed to seeing himself as arranger of Merrick's comings and goings. His Merrick is not to play God or play Treves but to accept a less active role—the pathetic one of hopeless longing. What Treves resists stressing in the death is what he failed to see in the life: Merrick's agency and his common bond with all humanity. Wanting to be "like other people" is a universal, if intermittent, desire—as is the opposite impulse, to be unique. None of us succeeds in either aim, and in his failure Merrick is like us all. It is fitting, then, that in the overwritten coda to this reminiscence images of everyman should take over—with Bunyan's hero banishing Hardy's—Merrick's personal myth imposing itself upon Treves's fiction.

It is interesting to notice that Treves's reminiscence, like Merrick's autobiography, ends by polarizing the inner man and his outer image. Stressing the gap between surface and substance, beastly flesh and aspiring spirit, Treves romanticizes Merrick. In doing so, he demonstrates his own likeness to the Elephant Man, his sensing the Treves in Merrick and recognizing the Merrick in himself. Rhetoric aside, Merrick emerges from the details of Treves's account not as the exemplar of "human dignity" we later see in Montagu's study or the razor of intellect we see in Pomerance's play, but as something more surprising, an ordinary mortal. The details of Treves's narrative show a Merrick capable of courage, ambition, magnanimity, perseverance—but also of vanity, worldliness, sentimentality, and self-delusion. None of the negative qualities should be considered surprising or lamentable, especially in light of Merrick's age, background, education, and experience. The very fact that he could cherish the mundane interests and impulses of a normal social being—in spite of his potentially alienating deformity and in the face of the callous or brutal treatment it could provoke in his fellow humans—reveals both strength and charity. But within Treves's reminiscence there is virtually no evidence of the extraordinary talent and perceptiveness that are later accretions to the Elephant Man myth. Indeed, how could there be such evidence? The nuances of Merrick's ideas, such as they were, must have remained relatively obscure, for his disorder did make him a sort of Man in the Iron Mask, did deny him eloquence of tongue and expressiveness of feature alike. And anyway, with the notable exception of Treves himself, the kindly, generous people who enter Merrick's life as presented in the reminiscence come partly to *see* him (whether out of curiosity, fashion, or the desire to oblige Treves) and partly to confer favors on him—not really to engage in the equal interchange that is the forum in which we develop and articulate our own sensibilities and come to appreciate the sensibilities of others.

It all comes back to "A Question of Hats," really.[14] Among the hats that Treves literally or figuratively puts on his head (those of writer, surgeon, fellow practitioner, duke) is to be found that veiled "yachting cap" in which Merrick crossed over to the London Hospital. Treves is to some degree like the romance-loving protagonist of "The Elephant Man"—less in terms of what he reads than in terms of how he writes. As we have seen, Treves's choice of words and selective recollection of incidents often take refuge in, or attempt to gain luster from, allusions and quotations, literary situations and cultural commonplaces of his time. In one sense it cheapens Merrick's individual struggle to draw such parallels; in another sense the connections allow Treves and his readers to get beyond obsession with anomalous particulars. Likewise Treves shares Merrick's romantic and conventional view of women, though where Merrick's attitude (as depicted by Treves) stresses the idealizing side of stereotypic thinking, the condescending side is more prominently displayed in Treves's comments on and handling of the nurses, the widow, the actress, the princess. It would be most unjust to condemn either of the men depicted in the reminiscence for thinking about women in the conventional terms of their age—but it would be wrong to suggest that either transcended the age's values. And again like Merrick, with his partly absurd and partly incisive reading of his own needs in asking for the silver-fitted dressing bag, Treves fashions his own personal myth, this reminiscence, in a mixed and ultimately very human way. At times Treves seems blind to the fact that this story reveals his own insensitivities and ineptitudes, qualities exaggerated in some later treatments. Yet ultimately, we think, most of those short-comings emerge only because Treves is honest, insightful, and brave enough to acknowledge them.

Despite his biases and his errors of fact, the reminiscing Treves is probably more faithful to the essence of Merrick than any subsequent articulator could ever be. This is true in part because, unlike subsequent tellers of the story, he had been a denizen of the same culture, because once we exclude the considerable differences of education, class, health, and fortune, his and Merrick's biases were largely the same. Yet more important, Treves holds a unique advantage among the students of Merrick we are studying here. Some of the people whose accounts we have read saw Merrick. Others whose work we go on to examine have interpreted him. Gifted with opportunity and imagination, Treves alone both saw and interpreted. The two actions conjoined come as close as one can get to knowing Merrick.

4

Merrick as Exemplar
Ashley Montagu on Maternal Love

Frederick Treves's reminiscence of the Elephant Man seems to have fallen into comparative obscurity until it was returned to public notice by the prolific and multifaceted anthropologist Ashley Montagu, who published *The Elephant Man: A Study in Human Dignity* in 1971. Montagu encountered the reminiscence in his youth and found that it endured among the furnishings of his mind because it combined three of his keenest interests: human nature, bones, and the late Victorian London of Henry Mayhew. As its double title suggests, Montagu's book tries to connect a concrete and particular case—Merrick's—with a broad and abstract theme—what is necessary to make humanity humane. Montagu's ideas on the large topic had cohered years before he got around to writing on the small one, so his approach is essentially deductive. And though it is to Montagu, who rescued Treves's account from the cultural dustbin, that a whole generation owes its knowledge of Merrick, *The Elephant Man: A Study in Human Dignity* does not add much to what Treves's reminiscence tells us of Merrick the man. Montagu's book is more an appropriation of Merrick's story than an exploration of it—more a creative shaping of amorphous material than a descriptive account of extant configurations.

In the preface to the second edition of this book (1979), Montagu describes his own long-standing fascination with the story and the difficulties attendant on bringing it to light. When Montagu first read

Treves's book in 1923, he found the title story "the most dramatic and moving" of the twelve pieces.[1] Some years later, about 1940, he became interested in securing a copy of the book, which "had become a great rarity." Through a "happy chance," a friend in Cairo came upon a paperback copy, issued in 1941, and sent it to Montagu. "To this day," Montagu observes, "it is the only copy I have seen since 1923. None of the booksellers' catalogues in which I have hunted through the years has ever listed a copy." Montagu's persistent devotion to Merrick's story continued to be tested as he sought a publisher for the book he "wanted to write on 'The Elephant Man' and his rescuers." For some thirty years he tried in vain to find an editor interested in his idea, and it seemed "that [he] had a story to tell that no one wanted to publish" (xiii–xiv). Finally Montagu succeeded in persuading a beginning publisher, David Outerbridge, to take a chance on his project. The resulting book elicited a response that, as Montagu puts it, was "astonishing": not just a vigorous readership and transatlantic editions, but a number of artistic treatments of the Elephant Man's story, several of which we discuss in the following chapters.

At the close of his preface, Montagu explicitly aligns himself with the "rescuers" of the Elephant Man (and particularly his earlier memorialist): "My hope that my book would rescue John Merrick and his benefactor from the oblivion into which they had fallen has been satisfied beyond all expectation" (xiv). Indeed it is possible to read Montagu's whole preface as a reenactment of Treves's experience with Merrick. Montagu's difficulties in finding Treves's book, in recovering the story, parallel Treves's own avowed difficulties in arranging to see Merrick and bring him to the hospital. Montagu's discouraging series of encounters with uninterested publishers recalls the suppression of Merrick's exhibition as one of the things that could not be allowed. The "astonishing" reaction to Montagu's book finds its obvious analogue in the outpouring of benevolence to Merrick—both the public generosity that made possible his continued residence at the London and the particular favors of such prominent people as Princess Alexandra and Mrs. Kendal. All these parallels might have been intentional, but yet another similarity is clearly unintentional: the matter of gaps between when the two discoverers first encountered their exotic subject and when they came to write about him. As we have seen, Treves met Merrick in 1884, reencountered him in 1886, and wrote about him in 1923.

Montagu first heard of the Elephant Man in 1923, thought to reacquaint himself with Merrick in 1940, and finally wrote about him some thirty years later. Thus, in writing about Merrick, both Treves and Montagu returned to a matter that had opened for them years before. For Treves and Montagu alike, there is something about Merrick's story that recurs or remains. The Elephant Man is not just a curiosity to be exploited in a professional context (though both the surgeon and the anthropologist found him extraordinarily useful, if in different ways)—his story holds, for Montagu as for Treves, a powerful significance that must be confronted and expressed.

One of the paradoxes of Montagu's presentation of the Elephant Man story is that though its purposes are distinctive, and despite certain changes of emphasis that we explore in this essay, it closely—and often uncritically—follows Treves and thereby implicitly grants authority to his account. Directly after his prefaces and a brief introduction, Montagu gives a lengthy biographical sketch of Treves—not of Merrick, his title character—and then reprints Treves's reminiscence in full. The biography of Treves emphasizes his public career as a surgeon and his love of literature, an attachment evidenced by Lady Treves's remark "that her husband was never happier than when he had a pen in his hand" (8). Such love Montagu attributes in large measure to Treves's Dorset schoolmaster, the Reverend William Barnes (1801–66), author of *Poems of Rural Life in the Dorset Dialect*. In his early comments about Barnes's formative influence on Treves, Montagu points toward the heroic resolution in the face of tragedy that marks his later analysis of Merrick's character. For instance, Montagu quotes with approval Llewllyn Powys' judgment of Barnes's poetry: "These bucolic poems, so innocent and so sturdy, instruct us how to become accessible to the wonder latent in every mode of natural existence, teach us to be grateful for the privilege of life on its simplest terms, with firm purpose and serene minds, to face our inevitable lot of sorrow and death" (3). Here we recognize many of the terms in which Treves has described Merrick: the wonder, simplicity, and gratitude. To these qualities Montagu adds his own emphasis on Merrick's firmness in the face of sorrow and death. In short, Montagu sees Barnes's influence as a way of preparing Treves to experience Merrick.

In light of this careful introduction to Merrick's chief "rescuer," it is surprising to be given so sparse a biography of the Elephant Man himself. But Montagu adds very little indeed to the substance of Treves's reminiscence. He perpetuates Treves's habit of calling Merrick "John" rather than Joseph—and even adds an incorrect middle name, Thomas. In a note Montagu mentions "Joseph Merrick" as the name given by Carr Gomm and the *Times* report of the inquest on Merrick's death. But he dismisses these references out of hand with the assertion that "in all other references to him the name is given as John Merrick. Merrick's actual given name was John" (40). What this claim overlooks is that the "other references" derive in one way or another from Treves. As this detail suggests, Montagu does not go behind Treves to confirm his facts and thus offers a Merrick who is still very much Merrick as presented, and even rechristened, by Treves.

Montagu's own preconceptions may have led him to misidentify Merrick from Leicester birth records. In the preface to the second edition he mentions that "further research in England has enabled [him] to throw some new light on the early history of John Merrick," and he seems to be working from a birth certificate when he gives Merrick's Christian names as John Thomas and his birth date as April 21, 1864. He mentions using a birth certificate in the identification of Merrick's parents: "On his birth certificate his mother's name is entered as Jane Merrick. Under 'Name and surname of father' the space is left blank, indicating that the child was born without a legal father" (39). Howell and Ford, however, have identified Merrick (again from a birth certificate) as Joseph Carey Merrick, born August 5, 1862, to "Joseph Rockley Merrick, warehouseman," and "Mary Jane Merrick, née Potterton."[2] Because this identification accords with the name given in Merrick's pamphlet autobiography—and indeed with a whole pattern of additional detail Howell and Ford supply—it, not Montagu's, is more likely the proper one.

What might have led to the misidentification? Our answer is inevitably speculative, but we think the speculations reasonable ones. The first factor seems to be Montagu's respect for Treves's authority, which would lead to the not unreasonable assumption that Treves would have known and used Merrick's correct name, an assumption that would have guided Montagu to search for a John Merrick. Such respect also would make it less likely for Montagu to discover or attach significance to a document not known or valued by Treves (notably *The Autobiography of Joseph Carey Merrick*). A second factor involves the prevailing confusion about Merrick's actual age and birth date. Merrick's own inaccuracy about his age would permit or require a researcher to examine an abnormally wide span of time for pertinent information—and thereby would facilitate a mistake that would be far less likely in cases where a definite date, or at least year, of birth is known. Third, John Thomas Merrick's being "born without a legal father" may have effectively and prematurely confirmed the identification for Montagu, as this detail fits neatly into his larger developmental theory of Merrick's personality. That theory—the elaboration of which seems the real underlying purpose of Montagu's study—stresses the crucial role of maternal love, especially during the early childhood years, in the development of a well-adjusted adult. Indeed the importance of a mother's love is a recurrent emphasis in much of Montagu's wide-ranging writing, where such nurture sometimes becomes the key not only to healthy personal development but also to the growth of enlightened, truly human societies.

Montagu's analysis of Merrick's personality and the place of that analysis in the larger intellectual pattern constituted by his long and prolific career is examined later in this chapter. What matters at the moment is that Montagu's focus on maternal love might crucially contribute to the misidentification of John Thomas Merrick as the Elephant Man, for a fatherless Merrick who cherished a portrait of his mother would constitute a perfect example of Montagu's theory at work. Montagu's having responded to the fatherlessness of John Thomas emerges clearly in his comment about the blank space on the child's birth certificate: "This explains why Merrick knew nothing of him and never spoke of him" (39). To be sure, these inferences are based on Treves's recollection that Merrick "knew absolutely nothing" of his father; but because his own ideas run the same way, Montagu has been all too quick to accept Treves's claim uncritically. As Howell and Ford have shown, Merrick most certainly did know his father, with whom he lived until his early teens,[3] but fatherlessness fits the theoretical model more satisfactorily, as is evident when, for instance, Montagu argues that "the absence of the father may well have worked to the advantage of the child, for without the presence of a husband Merrick's mother may have been able to devote most of her available time to her pathetically misshapen child" (65).

Fitting facts into theory rather than deriving theory from facts does not promote the clearest view of things existent, and Montagu is occasionally vague about other details of Merrick's life. He refers first to Merrick's "maternal uncle Charles Merrick" being present at the inquest, but he later speaks of a "paternal uncle" being present at that hearing—and that "paternal uncle" in the source cited is Charles Merrick.[4] The unresolved contradiction here is obviously related to the misidentification of Merrick as one who derived his surname from his mother. Montagu also uncritically accepts, and even embellishes, Merrick's story of the fright his mother received from an elephant during her pregnancy. In Montagu's version of the incident, the unfortunate woman "was crippled in an accident by a circus elephant" during her pregnancy (41). Mary Jane Merrick does seem to have been crippled,[5] but there is no reason to connect this condition with Merrick's story of his mother's mishap—except insofar as such a connection heightens the association between the two afflicted sufferers, mother and child. Likewise, Montagu leaves vague the particulars of Merrick's institutionalization at the Leicester workhouse and hospital. He quite rightly sees that Merrick could not have gone to the workhouse as early as Treves implies (perhaps at no more than three or four years of age); but he mistakenly claims that Merrick was "placed in the workhouse by the local authorities" (42) rather than electing to go there himself after he could no longer work.[6] Montagu also creates the erroneous impression that Merrick spent much of his time from early youth until his seventeenth year at the Leicester hospital. This pattern of misreading creates a Merrick deprived of all agency, an endlessly suffering waif dominated by overpowering forces: "As his disorder progressed he was shuttled from workhouse to hospital to workhouse and back again to hospital. It could hardly have been a more miserable existence" (44). Stressing misery and constraint and minimizing autonomy, Montagu's account of the pre-exhibition years can be seen as a sort of counterpoint to Merrick's resolutely plucky sentences on this period in his *Autobiography*. Such a contrast highlights the fictive component of both texts by showing us that each man tells the story as he needs to tell it, or as his genre demands that it be told. We can be better readers of Montagu if we recognize that, despite its particular, generic, explicit, and implicit claims to authority, his study, like Merrick's autobiography and Treves's reminiscence, is a "monster"—part description, part interpretation, and part creation.

Throughout his study, Montagu deploys a rhetoric that furthers his interpretative and creative goals. A dramatically heightened language emphasizing Merrick's suffering is evident from the opening pages, where Montagu articulates the questions he finds posed by Merrick's story: "What is a human life? A pulse in the heartbeat of eternity? A cry that begins with birth and ends with death? A brief and tempestuous sojourn on an inhospitable shore, where there is really neither joy, nor love, nor light, nor certitude, nor peace, nor help for pain? Or is it, is it, something more?" (1). A leading question if ever there were one, were one. The echoes of Matthew Arnold's "Dover Beach" here work together with an epigraph from Shelley's elegy on Keats, "Adonais," to establish Montagu's romantic and existentialist framework for the story. The lines from Shelley, read in the context of Merrick's life, inevitably evoke the fateful elephant that trampled Merrick's mother and marked her boy:

> Life, like a dome of many-coloured glass,
> Stains the white radiance of Eternity,
> Until Death tramples it to fragments.

Merrick, in the work introduced by these opening gestures, becomes a kind of proto-Heideggerian hero, living out his being toward death with "supreme human integrity." With phrase after phrase, Montagu piles up the misery inflicted on Merrick in his "living purgatory":

> Hideously deformed, malodorous, for the most part maltreated, constantly in pain, lame, fed the merest scraps, exhibited as a grotesque monster at circuses, fairs, and wherever else a penny might be turned, the object of constant expressions of horror and disgust, it might have been expected that "the Elephant Man" would have grown into a creature detesting all human beings, bitter, awkward, difficult in his relations with others, ungentle, unfeeling, aggressive, and unlovable. (1–2)

The rhetoric of the above passage is characteristic of Montagu's tendency to exaggerate Merrick's ill-treatment. By giving Merrick circumstances of personal mortification and public abuse comparable to those inflicted on the monster in *Frankenstein*, Montagu makes Merrick's enduring benevolence more remarkable, the paradoxes of his story more extreme. Thus Montagu presses the shape of Merrick's life toward a question demanding an answer: How could the alien, tormented Elephant Man also be the humane, affable Merrick?

Answering this question takes up approximately one-third of *The Elephant Man: A Study in Human Dignity* and constitutes by far the greatest part of Montagu's original contribution to the volume. The nature of his answer is again signaled by an epigraph, this one from Laurens Van der Post on the heroism of love: "Of all man's inborn dispositions there is none more heroic than the love in him. Everything else accepts defeat and dies, but love will fight no-love every inch of the way" (39). [7] The love that counts most for Montagu is that which enables all subsequent love—the mother's love for her child. In a section entitled "Mothering and Personality," Montagu argues that Merrick "constitutes an intriguing case history" in the "light of present-day psychological theory" (48). Montagu does not address the questions of whether there is enough available material about Merrick for an adequate case history—or how one would reliably obtain such material from and about a person so innately inexpressive as Merrick. Rather, what he wants to do with Merrick's history is to test the already formulated generalization, for which "there exists a great body of evidence," that "maternal love or its equivalent is fundamentally important for the subsequent healthy development of the personality" (48). Before conducting this "test," however, Montagu defines two terms that are crucial to his argument. Because he believes, as the Van der Post epigraph suggests, that the disposition to love is deeply rooted in human nature, Montagu needs a definition of that difficult concept, and what he arrives at is "the expression of the interaction between our genetic potentials and the environmental challenges and pressures (we may consider consciousness part of the environment) to which those genetic potentials have been exposed and to which the individual has responded" (48). Equally necessary is a standard by which to judge Merrick—and for Montagu that standard is a triune one, combining Freud's pairing of the ability to love and the ability to work with a third attribute, the ability to play.

But before Montagu can argue the importance of maternal love to the development of Merrick's character, he must first establish that Merrick's mother did, in fact, love him. Doing so puts him at odds with Treves, who in his reminiscence characterized Merrick's mother as "worthless" and "inhuman" and claimed that she had "deserted him when he was very small."[8] The miniature painting that Merrick carried about, a possession mentioned by Carr Gomm in his letter to the *Times* of December 4, 1886, now becomes a major piece of evidence in Montagu's reading, contra Treves, of the relationship between Merrick and his mother. Treves does not mention the portrait of Mrs. Merrick, a fact that Montagu attributes either to his forgetting about it during the thirty years that intervened between his life with Merrick and his writing about it or to Treves's possible prejudgment of Merrick's mother, his falling into a "censorious view" consistent with the prevailing opinions of a century that "was not kind in its judgments of women." Montagu maintains that the portrait was Merrick's "most precious possession" (41), a claim that goes considerably beyond the language Carr Gomm had used in his letter to the *Times*. Montagu also implies, and correctly, as Howell and Ford have shown, that Merrick probably did have much more memory of his mother than Treves credits him with having because he was not abandoned to the workhouse at the early age insisted upon by Treves. Montagu thus thinks it quite possible that Merrick's mother was in fact beautiful, as he remembered her —a recollection dismissed as a happy fiction by Treves. Montagu himself begins to fictionalize in the language characterizing the importance Merrick attached to his mother. We have already suggested that the words Carr Gomm uses about the miniature do not fully warrant its being described as Merrick's "most precious possession"—but now that portrait is exalted to something akin to a religious icon "which he had always with him," a phrase that echoes Christ's promise to be with the faithful always (Matt. 28:20). Whether beautiful or not by public standards, Merrick's mother was, Montagu asserts, "sustaining and beautiful" to her son—"and that is what really mattered" (44). The word "sustaining" here carries especially marked religious overtones. It suggests the revered maternal presence continuing to feed Merrick day by day as he carries about the portrait.

Much of Montagu's argument for the crucial influence of maternal love on Merrick's personality depends on a contrast between the gentle, amiable Merrick and Alexander Pope, who, in this account, is seen as having responded to "the ineradicable and intolerable image of his bodily self" with "vanity, malevolence, lying, doubledealing, rage, and contempt for others" (51). Several flaws weaken this phase of the argument. First is the overly schematic approach to personality on which the contrast depends. The syllogisms set up by Montagu go something like this:

—Merrick, deformed, was gentle and kindly;
—Pope, also deformed, was nasty and vindictive;
—therefore Merrick was loved by his mother and Pope was not.

It would not be easy to accept such reductive causal reasoning about complex matters of temperament even if the two subjects were living and available for psychological interviewing. Sensing, perhaps, that such an approach is too limited, Montagu introduces several pages of comment on matters of heredity and environment, with special attention to possible genetic explanations of the differences between Merrick and Pope. Unfortunately he can arrive at no more specific conclusion than that genes have a "highly probable" likelihood of producing "some" of the differences between the men—but what these differences may be he cannot specify.

Quite apart from the fact that both Merrick and Pope are dead, the tasks of determining the one man's benevolence and the other's vindictiveness are equally problematic for opposite reasons. Merrick was insuperably inarticulate; Pope, extraordinarily articulate—which is not to say that his utterances are as transparent as they are eloquent. There simply is no information on which to base a scientific interpretation of Merrick, and though Pope's words survive in profusion, we think that Montagu fails to demonstrate his credentials as a sound interpreter. For instance, the following aphorism is cited as evidence of Pope's perceived need "to pillory his detractors": "The malice of my calumniators equals their stupidity. I forgive the first, pity the second, and despise both" (50). What rancor is there in forgiving malice, pitying stupidity, and despising both? Elsewhere, we find Pope's feelings being confused with those expressed by one of his personae, Eloisa, as she writes to Abelard of her impossible love for him:

Hearts so touch'd, so pierced, so lost as mine.
E're such a soul regain its peaceful state,
How often must it love, how often hate!
How often hope, despair, resent, regret,
Conceal, disdain—do all things but forget. (51)[9]

This literary naïveté is ultimately less damaging than is the inability to demonstrate that Pope's parents actually neglected him. In fact, Montagu's own language presents them in quite the opposite light: "Pope all through his childhood and youth received a good deal of attention from his parents and was greatly admired by his early teachers." If this assertion is to hold, then Pope's alleged vindictiveness cannot convincingly be attributed to lack of maternal or parental love, although later in the essay Montagu does make an unsubstantiated, and somewhat contradictory, attempt to explain away the problem: "While Pope's parents may have doted on him in his later childhood, it is quite probable that they did not give him all the attention he needed during his first three years" (62). The "quite probable" conclusion definitely begs the question: It is based not on evidence but simply on circular argument. Maternal love in the early years makes for sweetness of spirit in the adult—Pope was scheming, vindictive, and cruel—therefore his parents "quite probably" did not give him enough self-confirming love in his early years.

If the section devoted to Pope is finally an exercise in question begging, the larger case for the influence of maternal love on Merrick is also essentially circular. Montagu does not really prove that Merrick was sensitive and amiable because he had received his mother's love in his early years. In fact, how could one prove a hypothesis that explains the mystery of personality in terms of a single causal factor? What Montagu shows instead is that Merrick had the kind of character one would expect to belong to someone who had received strong maternal love in early childhood (though observation would show that some unloved children might also demonstrate such traits and some loved children might deviate from the profile). Next, deducing from his theory of maternal love's importance to personality development, Montagu concludes the likelihood of Merrick's being deeply loved by his mother. The argument is lengthy, but its basic structure is evident in the following passage:

> John Merrick's behavior strongly suggests that he had been much loved in his early years. Put another way, if mother-love in the early years of the child's development is as effective in securing the development of a healthy personality as theory and observation suggest, then it is very

likely that John Merrick received a considerable amount of love from his mother during the significant early years of his life. (62–63)

To complete the circular presentation, Montagu returns to the only piece of real evidence he has concerning Merrick's relation to his mother: the miniature portrait mentioned by Carr Gomm.

Perhaps the least satisfactory feature of *The Elephant Man* is Montagu's apparent refusal to let human behavior be sometimes mysterious, his need to account for everything. His elaboration of the maternal-love theory ultimately renders Merrick personally insignificant—and if, from reading Treves either in his own volume or in Montagu's, we have become interested in Merrick's story, we are offended by this flattening out of a complex and fascinating person into a "case" that does not even do much to validate the theory it is invoked to support. This diminution or exploitation of Merrick does not seem in any way deliberate—as we have seen, the opening signals of Montagu's preface show him reenacting Treves, and this gesture bespeaks a comparable empathy for the man whose stage name becomes the title of Montagu's (like Treves's) book. But, as we have seen above, to *The Elephant Man* Montagu appends a subtitle: *A Study in Human Dignity*— and these words accurately indicate the drift of the study. Montagu the writer and scholar is intrigued by Merrick but unable or disinclined to enrich, correct, diverge from, or amplify on Treves's account. Perhaps, then, his contribution can involve relating Merrick's particular life to some larger issue—such as the theory of maternal love.

Accordingly, to see why Montagu's treatment of Merrick develops as it does, we need to understand the crucial place that the theory it is made to serve occupies in Montagu's prolific career. It seems fair to say that maternal love is, for Montagu, the most important of all cultural values, a much-needed counter to the widespread dehumanization of a too exclusively technical civilization. In *The Meaning of Love* (1953), for example, Montagu grounds the need for love in the "very organization of living matter," in the "integrative, essentially cooperative relations of the particles constituting matter."[10] The "highest integration" of organisms occurs at the human level, in the complex interdependence of a culture based on signs, symbols, and meanings, on symbolic thought. Whatever variety of symbolic forms love may take in a given culture, Montagu believes "it will be found upon analysis [to be] . . . traceable to the need for the kind of love which is biologically determined, predetermined, to exist between mother and infant." "As our knowledge of man increases," Montagu continues, it becomes evident that "all human beings undeviatingly require . . . the pattern of love which exists beween mother and child" and that "in every human being something of the maternal and something of the child in relation to the mother remains, and in order to love and be loved this is necessary and highly desirable."[11] Or, as he puts it in *The Direction of Human Development* (1955, 1970), "the next best thing to being a mother is to behave like one."[12]

This last volume advocates a broad, school-based program of education in "the development of this maternally based capacity for love," a necessary corrective to what Montagu sees as the destructive tendencies of Western civilization, which in his view has largely emphasized the need for discipline and competitiveness rather than cooperation. To Montagu, fathers seem especially responsible for perpetuating unloving patterns of behavior, and Christianity represents an attempt to create a God of love "to compensate for our unloving actual fathers."[13] Montagu finds the problem of the "tyrannical father" less prevalent in the United States than in Europe but generalizes that even "if one's own father is satisfactory, it would seem that the fathers of a great many other men and women are not, to judge from the state in which the world is at the present time. Men are too hostile; wars threaten death and destruction."[14] Conceiving of human nature as good, loving, and cooperative, Montagu views hostility and conflict as unnatural. Accordingly, he has been particularly concerned to refute the theories of innate human aggressiveness put forth in such widely popular books of the 1960s as Robert Ardrey's *Territorial Imperative* and Konrad Lorenz's *On Aggression*. Montagu sees such views as transmutations of the discredited religious doctrines of original sin and innate depravity. He asserts quite bluntly that "the views of Ardrey and Lorenz and others like them concerning human nature have no scientific validity whatever."[15]

As Montagu sees it, the greatest danger of such "invalid" theories lies in their diverting "attention from the real sources of man's aggression and destructiveness, namely, the many false and contradictory values by which, in an overcrowded, highly competitive, dehumanized, threatening world, he so disoperatively attempts to live."[16] The problem is not human nature but our collective (Western) nurture, toward which Montagu has remained strongly critical in his more recent writings. *The Dehumanization of Man* (1983), written with Floyd Matson, concludes with a denunciation of Western nihilism and the call for an "evolutionary leap." Once again, failure of love seems at the very center of this "fatal disorder of the modern world, generated systematically out of the mainsprings of advanced industrial society and nurtured by a purely technical intelligence cut off from those balancing attributes of human nature invidiously categorized as sentimentality." What the evolutionary leap requires is the development of a "new and higher consciousness" that would marry (the metaphor is Montagu's) thought and feeling. Thus the species must be transformed from *Homo sapiens* to *Homo humanus*, a transformation that "rests upon our recovery of the lost world of fellow feeling, the source of all human connection."[17] And while Montagu does not explicitly say so in *The Dehumanization of Man*, that recovery of fellow feeling must be based— to put it in the context of all his writings— on the individual retention of the patterns of maternal love.

It now should be easier to see the place of John Merrick, part real man, part creation, in Montagu's systematics of love. Cherished by his mother, fortunate enough to have been reared without a tyrannical father, Merrick grew into an exemplary representative of *Homo humanus* despite his deformity and ill-treatment. In fact, Montagu's study reverses the ordinary meanings of normality and abnormality. Merrick becomes an example of healthy development in a dysfunctional society: "The truth seems to be that in most ways he achieved a kind of mental health that defies most human beings, the ability to love, to work, and to play" (74). Montagu's Merrick demonstrates the fallaciousness of Ardrey's or Lorenz's theories of human aggression based largely on analogies with animal behavior. When he first came to the London Hospital, Merrick seemed a beaten animal— "anxious, timid, frightened, haunted-looking and alarmed when his door was opened" (74)— but as he became convinced that his "future was secure" and, above all, that "he was a human being whom other human beings valued and treated with respect, he lost all his defensive reactions, and without in the least ever becoming froward, aggressive, or presumptuous, he became a changed man" (75).

One would like Montagu to comment further on the precise ways in which Merrick conforms to his definition of mental health—the ability to love, work, and play. Putting aside the matter of love (which cannot be adequately gauged through expression, least of all in Merrick's case), it is not immediately clear how Merrick could be said to work once he had taken up residence in the hospital, and the exact nature of his play also deserves discussion. If, for instance, Merrick's dressing up, playing the gentleman to his parade of callers, is a kind of play, it would be valuable to have Montagu's thoughts on the meaning of such activities. But still better than asserting Merrick's conformity to a definition of health that fits him poorly would be interrogating the definition itself in order to test its adequacy as a measure of health.

We suspect that one of Merrick's activities that Montagu considers a kind of work, though he never directly says as much, is the habit, mentioned in Carr Gomm's first letter to the *Times*, of making cardboard models to send to people who treated him with kindness. In fact, this occupation might be said to blend work with play and love (it is thus "healthy" in the fullest sense)—and the single surviving example of Merrick's models, a rendering of Saint Phillip's church in London, receives considerable attention from Montagu, who argues that "it speaks volumes for the acuity of his vision, his intelligence, his imagination, his manipulatory skill and his ability to make the most refined judgments as to distance and proportion" (66). For Montagu, Merrick's construction of the model church takes on something of the importance of a vocation, and the process is carefully described. Once Merrick has settled into his "new life" at the London and into the rooms from which he was able to see both the "Church of St. Phillip at the corner of Oxford and Turner Streets, and also St. Augustine's, the hospital church that was being built at the time," he "embark[s] upon the ambitious task of making a model of a great church or cathedral." The result is "really quite magnificent," an edifice in which "every stone, every tile, indeed, every detail the imaginative eye could possibly see in such a building is represented with singular fidelity" (66–67). Without employing the tired phrase "a labor of love," Montagu interprets the venture as just such a blend of industry and fervency—and in fact he apologizes for the inadequacy of the photographic representation of the model included in his book.

For Montagu, Merrick's church building constitutes the grand symbolic gesture in his career as hero of love. Despite all physical handicaps, from "bits of carefully chosen pieces of colored paper and cardboard" he erects an "impressive edifice" (66), an imagined place of fellow feeling and human connection. (If, as Howell and Ford assert, Merrick's nurses procured the materials and aided in their deployment, the venture was not the literally single-handed one Montagu envisions, and the community and cooperation—church building on the relational level—were real enough.)[18] Montagu's focus on Merrick's church building gains significance when seen in light of his other writings on the church. In *The Meaning of Love*, for instance, Montagu urges churchmen and scientists to learn from one another. Both groups are devoted to understanding human nature, and science needs to recognize what the church has long known: that the "most significant ingredient" in the "structure" of human nature is love. In *The Direction of Human Development*, Montagu insists that the church, along with the school and the home, must become the source of a new education in loving.[19] Furthermore, although Montagu tends to discount a supernatural reality, he does affirm an immortality of thought or works. The following passage, defining two kinds of immortality in the terms of J. T. Shotwell, has interesting relevance to Merrick and his model of Saint Phillip's:

> the immortality of monuments,—of things to look at and recall; and the immortality of use,—of things which surrender their identity but continue to live, things forgotten but treasured, and incorporated in the vital forces of society. Thought can achieve both kinds. It embodies itself in forms,—like epics, cathedrals and even engines,—where the endurance depends upon the nature of the stuff used, the perfection of the workmanship and the fortune of time. But it also embodies itself in use; that is, it can continue to work, enter into other thought and continue to emit its energy even when its original mold is broken up.[20]

Merrick's model of Saint Phillip's would seem to possess both kinds of immortality. It is something to be looked at but also something that continues to work by entering into the lives, thoughts, and hopes of human beings such as Montagu, Pomerance, and Lynch. The Shotwell quotation also provides insight into what Montagu is doing in his book, the reembodying of a story "forgotten but treasured" in order that it can continue to animate and enable other thought. Montagu's work enables

Merrick's immortality while at the same time adding another stone to the edifice that is Montagu's theory of love, built up through many volumes. Not coincidentally, the Shotwell extract in *Immortality, Religion, and Morals* follows directly upon Montagu's quoting the same lines from Arnold's "Dover Beach" that echo in the opening passage of *The Elephant Man: A Study in Human Dignity*. The antidote, then, to Arnold's fears about the futility of life on the "darkling plain" is to be found in the building of a community of fellow feeling, a community comprising both the living and, as George Eliot puts it, "those immortal dead who live again/ In minds made better by their presence."[21] The central place Montagu accords Merrick's church building suggests that in this act of courage, patience, and creativity is to be seen a shadowing forth of the immortal community of love.

In his discussion of Merrick's life at the hospital, Montagu follows Treves in emphasizing the role of women, though particularizing (as Treves does not) their role as bearers of love. Montagu credits Merrick's female visitors specifically with effecting the "transformation" in him. Surprisingly, despite his high esteem for the feminine nurturing instinct, Montagu, like Treves, seems unable to imagine women—the London Hospital nurses, for instance—freely offering even the smallest kindness. As Montagu presents it, Merrick's transformation begins with Treves as agent, woman as instrument. The pretty young widow who, at Treves's request, visits Merrick and shakes his hand renews the pattern of love established by his mother: "Apart from his mother the young widow was the first of her sex who had ever smiled at him" (75). Perhaps because her benevolence to Merrick involved some initiative, the actress Mrs. Kendal receives Montagu's special notice and praise. Indeed she is allowed to have something of the final word about Merrick in Montagu's book, for he includes material from her autobiography as the last of the many appendices to his study. There is considerable gallantry in the placement of these pages, where Mrs. Kendal mentions Merrick's sending her the church model, alludes to having given him her picture, and claims to have been the person who raised funds for Merrick's support in the hospital—but does not indicate that she ever visited him. By excluding this firsthand material from his text proper, Montagu is enabled there to praise Mrs. Kendal's generosity himself instead of relaying her self-congratulation. He is freed from the obligation to comment on the discrepancies between her claims about fund-

raising and the other documentary evidence or on her curious decision
to promote Merrick's welfare and accept his gratitude without taking
the opportunity to meet him in person, a chance seized on by so many
fashionable Londoners, from Princess Alexandra down. If both Pomerance's play and Lynch's film tend to exalt Mrs. Kendal's role in Merrick's life, Montagu's account is their precedent. [22]

Montagu largely follows Treves in his interpretation of Merrick's
death, one innovation being to heighten its pathos by stressing how it
cut short Merrick's long-denied but recently achieved happiness and
security: "His health was good. He was happy. It would seem that he
would now enjoy many happy years in comfort and security. But it was
not to be" (76). Because Montagu accepts at face value Merrick's remark to Treves that "I am happy every hour of the day" (75) and does
not quibble with Treves's characterizing Merrick's health as good ("as
good as could be expected" might be more accurate), he does not explore the possibility of suicide. Instead, without fully committing himself to the possibility, Montagu suggests that Merrick "may have" tried
the experiment of lying down to sleep "like other people," with "consequences that were fatal" (77). This subtle and quite plausible distinction between a death wish and a conformist urge so strong as to
overshadow the ordinary sense of cause and effect finds its way, though
in sharply distinct forms, into both Pomerance's play and Lynch's film.
In analyzing the actual physical causes of death, Montagu again follows
Treves rather than the doctors quoted in the inquest. Noting that the
coverlet of the bed was undisturbed and that there were no other signs
of a struggle for breath, he thinks it "unlikely" that the cause of death
was asphyxia. Instead, Montagu argues that Merrick was killed by his
head's falling backward, not forward, thereby dislocating the neck and
either rupturing or fatally compressing the spinal cord. The instan-
taneousness of such a death would explain the absence of signs of
struggle.

After his section on Merrick's final years and death, Montagu includes a chapter on Merrick's condition, which he judges to have been
neurofibromatosis, or von Recklinghausen's disease, as it was once
called, after Friedrich von Recklinghausen, the German physician who
described it in 1882. Actually such a condition would be not a disease
but a disorder, a distinction Montagu preserves with care. A disease,
he points out, "is an acquired morbid change in any tissue of an organ-

ism or in an organism as a whole; it has a specific micro-organismal source and has characteristic symptoms." A disorder, on the other hand, "may be either acquired or inborn" and is "a disturbance of structure or function or both due to a genetic defect or to a defect in the development of the embryo, or as the result of external causes such as chemical substances, injury, or disease" (80). As Montagu observes, many disorders have no relation to disease. Hemophilia, caused by a gene deficiency on the X chromosome, is an example, as is phocomelia, the condition that came to world attention during the 1950s, in the children of women who had used the drug thalidomide during pregnancy.

Montagu locates the cause of Merrick's disorder in a genetic mutation. He recognizes that neurofibromatosis "often has an hereditary basis," but in this case he discounts parental transmission on the ground that there was no known family history of deformity. (The quick and easy dismissal of heredity seems puzzling given that Montagu elsewhere has claimed that we know nothing of Merrick's father and does not make any rigorous attempt to prove that Mrs. Merrick's lameness was the product of accident or disease rather than a congenital condition.) Instead, Montagu argues, Merrick's disorder resulted from a mutation that expressed itself in "faulty control of the growth of the cellular elements of both the skeletal and cutaneous organs of the body." Perhaps inevitably, Montagu compares the disorder to that modern *bête noire* among diseases—cancer, which involves a similar "failure of cellular control," sometimes triggered by a "defective genetic system" (85). Perhaps without recognizing it, Montagu here has pointed to one reason behind the fascination the Elephant Man retains for readers and theatergoers: Merrick's disease does seem to mirror "the destructively anarchic multiplication of cells . . . run wild throughout the body" (85) that we fear in cancer, the metaphoric disease of our culture and time, as Susan Sontag has shown in *Illness as Metaphor* (1978).[23]

Neurofibromatosis refers simply to "the tendency to develop tumors of fibrous and nervous tissues," called neurofibromas. These masses may be firm or soft and may "range in size from a few millimeters to diffuse growths which hang in folds from the face, neck and shoulders, all the way down to the abdomen" (86–87). In the "vast majority of examples," however, the disorder "is so minor as to cause little in the

way of symptoms—perhaps a small, soft swelling that can be felt beneath the skin, or a few warty pimples hidden from sight beneath normal clothes, or a patch of lightly pigmented skin."[24] Café au lait spots
on the skin are present in more than 99 percent of patients with neurofibromatosis.[25] That Merrick was never described as having these
nearly definitive café au lait spots figures centrally in a recent argument by Drs. J. A. R. Tibbles and M. M. Cohen, Jr., contesting the
diagnosis of neurofibromatosis for Merrick. They point, too, to the fact
that Merrick's "manifestations were much more bizarre than those commonly seen in neurofibromatosis."[26] For Tibbles and Cohen, Merrick
suffered not from neurofibromatosis but from the Proteus syndrome—a
diagnosis discussed at greater length in chapter 7.

For Montagu, what seems especially significant about Merrick's
condition is the correlation between skin involvement and disorder of
the bones. As he explains, "sheathed (myelinated) and unsheathed
(unmyelinated) nerves enter a bone along with the blood vessels that
supply it. The nerve fibers can often be traced as far as the bone-
forming cells" (89). From the correlation between disordered bone and
"disordered overlying integument," Montagu theorizes "that the disorder spread along the course of the connective tissue cells of the nerve
sheaths and those between and around the nerve fibers originating from
the same main nerve trunks or branches" (91). Montagu notes that in
most cases of neurofibromatosis the bones are not affected and comments further that Merrick seemed unaffected in areas free of bone:
"The external genitalia, penis, scrotum, and testes, appear to have
been entirely normal and free of any form of disorder." For Montagu
these facts of physiology "independently tend to confirm" Treves's
statement that Merrick would have liked "to have been a lover" and add
to the tragedy of Merrick's life, for being a lover "was, alas, an experience Merrick was never to know" (90).

The generous selection of illustrations Montagu provides in his
monograph warrant some comment, for they offer a concrete and particular counterweight to the theoretical abstraction that is his chief intellectual contribution to Treves's basic account. The apparently simple act of including pictures proves crucial to Montagu's success in
reviving the story of Merrick—for Merrick's disorder was so extraordinary that even the most precise words do not suffice to characterize it.
Indeed, even visual representation can only begin to convey Merrick's

somatic difference from the human norm. The illustrations Montagu includes are a diverse array: pictures of the Mile End Road and of the model church so important to his interpretation of Merrick's character; sketches, casts, and photographs of Merrick, and, most moving of all, photographs of his skeleton. Merrick's face and voice were hampered by his disorder from displaying emotion or nuance, the signals that perhaps even more than features and colorations distinguish human beings from one another. His appearance was unique but not expressive. How curious, then, that whereas the "skull beneath the skin" is a mortal leveling, much the same for the beautiful and the plain alike, Merrick's skull is individual—that where most human skeletons are, except to the forensic eye, anonymity lying beneath superficial diversity, Merrick's bones are uniquely true to the surface that once sheathed them. Perhaps the point is that we can inure ourselves to surface deformities, even extreme ones, but our sensibilities must respond to bone-deep evidence of the bodily alienation a fellow human can be—and has been—called upon to bear.

In this chapter we have been describing an account of Merrick that essentially follows, but occasionally refutes, Treves, one that presses Merrick's story into the service of a larger cause, that of the theory of maternal love. When this account has seemed unsatisfying to us, the essential problem has not been the disproportion and discrepancies between substantiated facts and Montagu's speculations. Creative interpretations of a compelling story such as Merrick's have their own place. The speculative nature of Montagu's monograph becomes a problem only because that work has been seen as a source of facts— partly by his intention, partly because for years no alternative was readily accessible. When used that way, Montagu's study has in some ways misled readers. Of course, readers, viewers, and audiences might also rely upon a yet more radically fictionalized and interpretative account (such as Pomerance's play) to constitute their sense of the "whole truth" about Merrick and Treves. But the generic conventions of drama should alert them that such reliance would be ill-founded, just as it would be to assume that Shakespeare's representation of Richard III is a true and sufficient account, as well as a rich and memorable one.

But Montagu's *Elephant Man* is not just a reenactment of Treves's reminiscence, a sometimes flawed report of factual detail, and a deductive exercise in connecting one human being's life to an overarching theory of humanity. It is also a reembodiment of Merrick, whose story stayed alive within Montagu. The success of this achievement is to be observed in its effect, its having brought the story of Merrick and Treves back to the world's attention—and also, oddly enough, in its very shape. Montagu's book adopts Merrick's disorder as its own order. Its distinctive formal characteristic is the presence of appended and extrusive masses (Treves's reprinted narrative, unassimilated source materials, the Pope digression, theoretical arguments, numerous illustrations) that complicate, enrich, deform the simple human facts of Merrick's story. Through its own structure, then, *The Elephant Man: A Study in Human Dignity* pays tribute to the man whose eloquent bones it exhibits.

5

Merrick at Center Stage
Bernard Pomerance's
Elephant Man

The Elephant Man: A Study in Human Dignity gave rise, during the late 1970s, to a number of dramatic treatments of Merrick and Treves's story. By far the best known of these was the Tony Award–winning Broadway play *The Elephant Man* by Bernard Pomerance. The March 7, 1979, edition of *Variety*, however, mentioned at least three other plays specifically: one by Thomas Gibbons that played in Philadelphia; another by William Turner presented in Pittsburgh; and a third by Roy Faudree, performed first at Holyoke Community College, then at several theaters in Northampton, Massachusetts, and eventually at the Performing Garage Center at Canal Street Station in New York. *Variety* also mentioned three other productions, which, "according to unconfirmed reports," had taken place in Milwaukee, Chicago, and Denver.[1] We have been able to confirm at least one of these reports— of the Milwaukee play, created by Jed Harris and Ric Gruczynski— and have learned as well that there was at least one opera planned for production, though it is unclear whether this piece was ever performed.[2] This chapter focuses on the Pomerance play—on the way it presents Merrick and Treves, on the medical issues it raises, on the reasons for its success. Chapter 6 addresses the ways in which Gibbons, Turner, and Faudree have chosen to tell the story.

The Pomerance play first appeared in London on November 7, 1977, a co-production of the Foco Novo Company and the Hampstead

Theatre, for which Pomerance had done an adaptation of Brecht's *Man's Man* in 1975. After revisions, it reopened in London in early 1978 and then began "a sellout run" at the Theatre at St. Peter's in New York on January 14, 1979. Later it successfully moved to Broadway, where it was produced at the Booth Theatre on April 22, 1979, with Kevin Conway as Treves and Philip Anglim as Merrick, a part later assumed by rock-music star David Bowie.[3] In the introductory note to the play, Pomerance explains the way the story came to him through the books of both Treves and Montagu: "My own knowledge of it came via my brother Michael, who told me the story, provided me with xeroxes of Treves' memoirs until I came on my own copy, and sent me the Montagu book." In commenting on Montagu's book, Pomerance mentions specifically the photographs of Merrick and of his model of Saint Phillip's church, the building of which Pomerance places at the center of his play : "I believe the building of the church model constitutes some kind of central metaphor, and the groping toward conditions where it can be built and the building of it are the action of the play."[4]

People who know something of Merrick's story but nothing of Pomerance's play are in for at least one major surprise in the play: The face and body of the Elephant Man are not naturalistically deformed. Pomerance's introductory note explains that "any attempt to reproduce his [Merrick's] appearance and his speech naturalistically—*if* it were possible—would seem to me not only counterproductive, but, the more remarkably successful, the more distracting from the play" (v–vi). Later, on the page preliminary to the cast lists, Pomerance warns actors against the perils of the play's title role in an interestingly double way: "*No one with any history of back trouble should attempt the part of* MERRICK *as contorted. Anyone playing the part of* MERRICK *should be advised to consult a physician about the problems of sustaining any unnatural or twisted position.—B.P.*" (ix). On one level, perhaps, these words are a considerate or practical *caveat actor*, words that will keep people from being hurt and productions from being sued. At the same time, however, such warnings exalt the lead role by setting its unusual athletic demands apart from and above other parts. And most intriguingly, the final phrases point in two different directions—toward the literal and obvious "get a doctor's advice before embarking on this rigorous course" but also toward the subversive message "if you want to know all about existence over time in an abnormal and bent (moral) posture, talk to someone who lives in that shape by profession." Thus Pomerance first suggests the deformity of normality that he develops throughout the play in his characterization of Treves.

Both of the passages mentioned above are theatrical gestures preceding the rise of the curtain—verbal ways of setting a stage (or conditioning an audience) not unlike the "crudely painted" sideshow advertisement for Merrick's exhibition. A central assumption of our discussion treating Pomerance's play and various other dramas on the same subject is that the playwrights' choices depend on both how they understand Merrick's story and what the dramatic form demands or makes possible. This last implication, as we later see, is one of the recurring themes of Pomerance's *Elephant Man*, where Treves is distorted, abstracted, and flattened out for ideological purposes at least as much as Merrick is remade for the sake of argument in Montagu's book.

Reviewers generally approved of Pomerance's decision to have Merrick's deformity suggested through his actor's physical contortion rather than through naturalistic makeup. Writing in *The New Republic*, Stanley Kauffmann, lauding the play as the best by an American since Sam Shepard's *Tooth of Crime* (1972), observes that any such makeup would be more appropriate to a horror film and that it "would make Quasimodo look like Puck."[5] Pomerance enables us to know what the real Merrick looked like by having Treves point to slides of him in a scene suggesting Treves's exhibition of Merrick before the Pathological Society. While Treves is doing this, the actor portraying Merrick first comes on stage, clad only in a breech cloth; soon his "right arm appears to elongate, becoming heavy and useless, his body twists, his legs grow clumpish, difficult to manage." The result is, in the words of Gerald Weales of *Commonweal*, "a marvelous extension of the conventional collusion of actor and audience which allows a performer to become a character." Anglim "turns into the horribly deformed Merrick. Yet his face, unlike Merrick's, remains unchanged, so that the audience can at once perceive the man and the freak."[6] Or, as Steve Lawson of *Horizon* puts it, Pomerance "insists that we make a mental leap with him and realize the 'normality' of the Elephant Man under the ghastliness of his 'true' physical appearance."[7]

Serious reservation about Pomerance's manner of representing Merrick is expressed, however, by Martha Bayles of *Harper's*, in one of the best considered of the negative commentaries on the play. Bayles compares the play unfavorably to David Lynch's film of the same name, which does use makeup to represent the physical deformity of Merrick. For Bayles, Pomerance's "imaginary-invalid routine" is a bit of "avant-garde old hat," a by now completely expectable Brechtian strategy for breaking the illusion of the theater and setting up a live interaction between the actors and the audience. But here that interaction works "in a direction just the opposite of Brecht's. Instead of rattling us, it soothes us, lulls us into a sense of moral superiority." We are saved from being gawkers, elevated above the characters onstage, and thus prepared for some of the play's sleight of hand, which Bayles finds ultimately dishonest. The play's indignation at the repressiveness of societal views of the normal is made possible only by the removal of Merrick's physical deformity from the stage. "By giving us a physical fact instead of a mental construct," the film, on the other hand, "renders moot the majority of the play's preoccupations. Denunciations of society, for example, don't seem very important when it is obvious society didn't cause his [Merrick's] main problem."[8] Deeply troubling to Bayles, too, is the play's implication that the hospital is no better than the freak show, Treves no better than the freak-show hawker. Such simplistic judgments are possible only because the play has placed its audience in a false position of moral superiority by preventing them from becoming gawkers. What the play appeals to is a posh radicalism as stale as some of the theatrical techniques themselves.

Most of the reviewers of *The Elephant Man*, however, did not share Bayles's reservations. Several reviewers complained that the second half of the play did not fulfill the promise of the first; that the "emotional high point" of the play, Merrick's meeting Mrs. Kendal, occurred too early in the play; or that the play was occasionally too obviously didactic in its insistence on the tyranny of the normal.[9] But for the most part, the reviews were highly laudatory. Dean Valentine of *The New Leader* found it "one of the most moving, original plays in a decade"; Walter Kerr of *The New York Times* placed it at the top of his list of plays for 1979; and even John Simon, though not without his reservations, judged it "the liveliest new play in some time."[10] Steve Lawson noted how the story seemed to be one of those that have the effect of telling us more than we knew, not only about its subject, but "about ourselves as observers." He placed Pomerance's work among a "small torrent" of recent plays that used "disease or debilitation or mental waywardness" as a locus. Such plays as Peter Shaffer's *Equus*, Michael Cristofer's *Shadow Box*, and Arthur Kopit's *Wings* were, in Lawson's view, the expression of a decade marked by a "general turning inward from the world at large to the crises of the self." Lawson preferred *The Elephant Man* to all of these, for Pomerance had been able to "link private anguish" to larger concerns, to "the question of humanity itself."[11] Several other reviewers compared the play—greatly to Pomerance's advantage—to Brian Clark's rather formulaic dramatization of the questions of autonomy and paternalism in medical decision making, *Whose Life Is It, Anyway?*[12] Finally, at least one commentator found the play to have serious religious implications. Writing in *The Christian Century*, Janet Karsten Larson argued that the center of the play was the "story of the overwhelming need for faith in the face of malignant nature and one-dimensional culture." Most surprising of all to Larson was Pomerance's laying "Pascal's wager on the bare possibility of salvation."[13]

Nearly all the reviewers mentioned the concern with normality that lies at the heart of the play. In a scene entitled "The English Public Will Pay for Him to Be Like Us," Carr Gomm and Treves discuss what to do with the funds that have come in for Merrick's care. When Carr Gomm, who is fresh from a conversation with Bishop How on the white man's burden, asks Treves cynically, "Well, Jesus my boy, now we have the money, what do you plan for Merrick?" Treves answers, "Normality as far as is possible" (21). As they were for Treves in his own reminiscence, women here are "the key to retrieving [Merrick] from his exclusion" (29). Pomerance collapses all of the women who came to see Merrick into the one figure of Mrs. Kendal, whose relationship with Merrick climaxes in a scene in which she undresses for him, perhaps as a way of helping him to be like other men. Treves interdicts that scene, lecturing Merrick later in a rather unpleasantly stuffy way about propriety. The immediate context is a discussion about the link between religious faith and moral judgment. Asked by Merrick why he sent Mrs. Kendal away even though he does not believe, Treves responds, "Don't forget. It saved you once. My interference. You know well enough—it was not proper." Merrick, who exhibits a kind of razor wit throughout much of the play, returns a pair of questions—"How can you tell? If you do not believe?"—and then parrots ironically Treves's answer about "standards" in the language he has learned from his doctor and caretaker: "They make us happy because they are for our own good" (55). That the rules make us happy because they are for our own good is the burden of much of the moral education the paternalistic Treves offers Merrick in the play. For the most part Merrick is willing enough to play his part; as Treves says of him near the end of the play, "he is very excited to do what others do if he thinks it is what others do" (64). Yet as he watches Merrick internalize the standards of normality and become a cause célèbre to a brilliant array of visitors, Treves comes to question his society's and his own assumptions.

What especially distresses Treves late in the play is the essentially narcissistic way in which all the characters look upon Merrick. Instead of being a continual reminder of difference, Merrick "makes all of us think he is deeply like ourselves." Yet because Treves has, through his life with Merrick, become more deeply aware of difference, he knows that "we're not like each other" and thus concludes that Merrick's seeming like others is only the result of our "polish[ing] him like a mirror" so that we "shout hallelujah when he reflects us to the inch." Treves, who has set out to bring Merrick to normality as far as is possible, "grow[s] sorry" for his success (64). Pomerance stresses the narcissism of Merrick's visitors particularly in scene 12, titled "Who Does He Remind You Of?" Just before this scene, Merrick has received a number of exquisite personal items as gifts for Christmas. Because these are not things he has asked for—as they are in Treves's reminiscence—the effect of the gift giving in the play is to emphasize the insensitive and egocentric nature of the givers rather than Merrick's desire to outfit himself like the gentlemen who have come to call. Among his gifts are some "silver-backed brushes" and a comb from the Countess, pheasants and woodcock from the Prince of Wales, ivory-handled razors and toothbrush from Mrs. Kendal, and a cigarette case full of cigarettes from Treves. Treves opens scene 12, then, with a question about the propriety of some of these gifts, "Why all those toilet articles, tell me? He is much too deformed to use any of them." Mrs. Kendal answers him, saying that they are "props" with which Merrick can make himself, as she makes herself. Her response thus initiates a motif that is carried through the scene. Bishop How, Carr Gomm, the Duchess, and finally Treves himself join Mrs. Kendal in testifying to the way Merrick reminds them of themselves. He is religious and devout like the Bishop, though with some of the "same doubts" that How has had in seminary; he is practical like Carr Gomm and aware enough of "daily evil to be thankful for small goods." The Duchess finds in him a familiar discretion, while Mrs. Kendal sees him as odd, and hurt, "and helpless not to show the struggling," as she also sees herself. Finally Treves closes the scene by reflecting ironically on his own relation to his patient. Aware, as the others are not, of the way each has poured his or her own content into the expressionless Merrick, Treves muses at once on his own success as well as Merrick's failing health and growing popularity: "Merrick visibly worse than 86–87. That, as he rises higher in the consolations of society, he gets visibly more grotesque is proof definitive he is like me. Like his condition, which I make no sense of, I make no sense of mine" (39–41).

Earlier in the play, Merrick has seemed free of the narcissism that afflicts all of the other characters. His suffering and his lack of a firm sense of self cause him to live beyond himself, in religious dependence, in what theologian Arthur McGill calls an ecstatic identity.[14] He is thus truly able to attend to the needs of the other. In Belgium, for instance, he reveals his empathy for a group of Pinheads who are mistreated by their manager. They are being rehearsed for a performance at the Brussels Fair in honor of "Leopold's fifth year as King of the Congo." During their rehearsal, they sing a parody of the song they are supposed to be learning, one that exposes the coercion and violence that underlie imperialism: "We are the Queens of the Congo / The Beautiful Belgian Empire / Our niggers are bigger / Our miners are finer / Empire, Empire, Congo and power / Civilizuzu's finest hour / Admire, perspire, desire, acquire / Or we'll set you on fire!" (10). The song contributes on one level to the play's critique of imperialism, which, despite platitudes by Bishop How on the white man's burden, is treated as a forceful eradication of difference parallel to the normalizing of Merrick. In its more immediate context, however, the song evokes the anger of the Pinheads' manager, who threatens them: "Get those words right, girls! Or you know what." Merrick, who is being exhibited at the same fair, sympathizes with the Pins: "Don't cry. You sang nicely. Don't cry. There there." When a Belgian policeman appears on the scene to ban Merrick's exhibition as a "public indecency," the Pins turn ironically on their comforter. The policeman cuffs Merrick viciously, denouncing him as an "indecent bastard" who would be "better off dead." As this is going on, Merrick's concern is that the Pinheads not be disturbed by his being beaten: "Don't cry girls.

Doesn't hurt." But they share none of his other-directedness, turning on him with a violent echoing of the official guardians of their culture: "Indecent, indecent, indecent, indecent!!" (10–11).

Merrick displays similar compassion in scene 8, "Mercy and Justice Elude Our Minds and Actions," which takes place after his move to the hospital. The scene begins with Treves telling Merrick that the funds have now been received that will make possible his staying for life at the hospital. After Carr Gomm assures Merrick that "no one will bother [him at the hospital]," two workmen, Porter and Snork, come to gape at him. Carr Gomm sacks Porter on the spot for doing so, despite Porter's plea that his wife "ain't well" and his "sister has got to take care of" their children. After Carr Gomm exits, Merrick and Treves engage in a dialogue about home, a word quite unknown to Merrick. Treves also gives Merrick his first lesson in the value of the "rules," which "make us happy because they are for our own good." Merrick echoes Treves's teaching, but as the scene closes, Merrick's remembering his years in the workhouse leads to an ironic undercutting of Treves's ideas of mercy and discipline: "The workhouse where they put me. They beat you there like a drum. Boom boom: scrape the floor white. Shine the pan, boom boom. It never ends. The floor is always dirty. The pan is always tarnished. There is nothing you can do about it. You are always attacked anyway. Boom boom. Boom boom. Boom boom. Will the children go to the workhouse?" (22–27).

The contrast between Merrick and the ordinarily self-centered Treves is made apparent by Treves's response: "What children?" The children are nothing to him, protected as he is by the ordinary social logic of individual rights and freedoms: "Of necessity Will will find other employment. You don't want crowds staring at you, do you?" For Treves, Carr Gomm was "merciful" in his sacking of Porter, a point he wants to impress upon Merrick: "You yourself are proof. Is it not so? Well? Is it not so?" Because Merrick as an exhibition freak has been a man for others, and is thus far completely untutored in notions of private right, he can ask a radical question of Treves: "If your mercy is so cruel, what do you have for justice?" That this is one of the first moments in which Merrick's questions begin to shake Treves's sure sense of himself is indicated by his first response, "I'm sorry," but he goes on to offer a tired defense as well: "It's just the way things are" (27). Later in the play, when Merrick has come to have a surer sense of his own identity and private worth, he repeats Treves's line to Ross, his ex-manager, when the latter comes, impoverished and ill, to implore him to return to exhibition as the Elephant Man. Our reaction at that point is curiously double. We of course cannot expect or hope that he will go back to working for Ross, but, on the other hand, we feel the loss involved in the diminishment of his regard for others. He has become a man like others, not a god, one for others, as the last lines of the scene suggest:

> *Merrick:* I'm sorry, Ross. It's just the way things are.
> *Ross:* By god. Then I am lost. (53)

Merrick voices his concern for the other as other in the pivotal scene 10, "When the Illusion Ends He Must Kill Himself." The scene, which brings Mrs. Kendal and Merrick together for the first time, adumbrates the play's later preoccupations with love, art, and the church. The scene opens with the play's first mention of Merrick's model of Saint Phillip's. As Treves and Mrs. Kendal enter Merrick's room, the home where he is now established, Merrick is making sketches for his model. The scene's first turn on the relationship of nature and art emerges from Merrick's greeting of Mrs. Kendal: "I planned so many things to say. I forget them. You are so beautiful." Soon he reveals this apparently spontaneous, natural compliment to have been, in fact, an artifice; he has "planned" to say "that I forgot what I planned to say." When Mrs. Kendal follows this lead by asking him if he agrees that "real charm is always planned," Merrick makes an enigmatic reply, one that asserts the power of the unplanned, of nature, of what Treves's beloved Hardy called "Hap": "Well, I do not know why I look like this, Mrs. Kendal. My mother was so beautiful. She was knocked down by an elephant in a circus while she was pregnant. Something must have happened, don't you think?" After Mrs. Kendal returns an inconclusive answer to his question—"It may well have"—Merrick suggests an alternative explanation for his head's being so large, one that is quite important to the later allusions in the scene and to the role of dreams in the play as a whole: "It may well have. But sometimes I think my head is so big because it is so full of dreams. Because it is. Do you know what happens when dreams cannot get out?" (31–32).

The next turn of the conversation works toward associating Merrick with Mrs. Kendal as creators of illusion, as players on exhibit for others. Merrick makes the connection himself, commenting that Mrs. Kendal, as a "famous actress," must "display" herself, just as he has, for a living. Mrs. Kendal seems at this point to want to distinguish between her role and herself, responding to Merrick: "That is not myself, Mr. Merrick. That is an illusion. This is myself" (32). Her lines are doubly ironic, for she is, throughout her meeting with Merrick, playing a part that Treves has urged upon her, the part of making women "real" to Merrick in order to retrieve him "from his exclusion." Moreover, as she has made clear to Treves in the previous scene when accepting her part, she is, as a woman, always playing a role in response to the imaginative projections of men. Treves has said to her naively, in arguing her suitability to help Merrick "become a man like other men," that as an actress she is, "unlike most women," trained to hide her "feelings and assume others." Mrs. Kendal's rejoinder stresses the essential theatricality of all women's performance: "You mean unlike most women I am famous for it, that is really all" (29).

Mrs. Kendal's distinction between herself and her "illusion" elicits an echo from Merrick, one itself replete with ironies: "This is myself too." The echo of Mrs. Kendal underscores the strong association of Merrick with women at work both in the play and in other accounts of Merrick's story as well. Like Mrs. Kendal, Merrick has played his part for others, and under the gaze of others, and that part has been one traditionally allotted to females: the role of passive sufferer, one acted upon rather than initiating action, one viewed rather than viewing, other rather than self. But it is possible to hear in Merrick's simple "this is myself" the desire, too, to break through the layers of illusion that prevent his truly meeting Mrs. Kendal. She, however, seems unwilling or unable to meet him truly, preferring instead to discuss their new relationship through another medium of illusion: "Frederick says you like to read. So: books." The essential insincerity of Mrs. Kendal emerges in her overstated reaction to Merrick's revelation that he is reading *Romeo and Juliet*. Mrs. Kendal "adores" love stories, whereas Merrick more simply and genuinely "like[s]" them "best" (32).

In his understanding of *Romeo and Juliet*, Merrick naively reads himself into the part of Romeo. Here Pomerance may be following fairly closely Treves's reminiscence, with its suggestion that Merrick in his reading seemed to make little distinction between his own world and the fictional worlds of literature. "If I had been Romeo," Merrick tells Mrs. Kendal, "I would not have held the mirror to her breath." Mrs. Kendal provides an essential gloss on Merrick's allusion: "You mean the scene where Juliet appears to be dead and he holds a mirror to her breath and sees ——— ." The suspension of Mrs. Kendal's line heightens the importance of the familiar Shakespearean word Merrick supplies to fill the gap: "Nothing. How does it feel when he kills himself because he just sees nothing?" (32–33).

Later in the scene Merrick reintroduces the image of the mirror, using it again to comment on Romeo's failure to love but also seeming to imply a more generalized point about the process of mirror gazing: "Looking in a mirror and seeing nothing. That is not love" (33). Merrick's line functions in several ways as a comment on his own experience. First, he has largely been denied the experience of looking into a mirror, for Treves has specifically prohibited his having one in his room. Second, if a mirror serves to reconfirm one's sense of one's own ego, the boundaries of the self, then Merrick's experience of looking into the mirror would reconfirm only the fluidity of his self, the instability of his ego, for his condition itself involves the continual alteration of his image and boundaries. What would make this experience of seeing himself change especially dramatic to Merrick is his inability to defend against it by theatrical self-expression. His face is inexpressive; when he gazes on it, he sees its nakedness. He cannot prepare a face to meet the faces that he meets. Thus Merrick looks into a mirror and sees nothing, a vacancy over which he has no control.

Yet Merrick would not kill himself at seeing nothing. Merrick interprets Romeo's suicide as evidence that he "does not care for" Juliet but rather only for himself. If he had been Romeo, he would have taken Juliet's pulse or gone for a doctor; "If I had been Romeo," he tells Mrs. Kendal, "we would have got away." Mrs. Kendal's response adumbrates a theme developed more fully later in the play in scene 14, a scene with many specific parallels to scene 10. If Romeo and Juliet had gotten away, she tells Merrick, "there would be no play" (33). Art depends on the destruction of life, the frustration of love; it presents an illusion of life to a spectator who knows him- or herself as an onlooker, an observer, separate from the action or the text, no matter how fully he or she suspends disbelief. But Merrick is naive in this regard; he reads himself into the role of Juliet's lover and refuses Mrs. Kendal's distinction between art and life: "If he did not love her, why should there be a play?" (33). Pomerance suggests that Merrick's ability to enter the play is evidence of his extraordinary ability to love, his orientation to the other. This ability is suggested, too, by the speech that closes Merrick's one-on-one encounter with Mrs. Kendal. After she has called his comments on *Romeo and Juliet* "extraordinary," Merrick says of his newly found capacity to be understood: "Before I spoke with people, I did not think of all these things because there was no one to bother to think them for. Now things just come out of my mouth which are true" (34). Here Pomerance attributes to Merrick a language of pure love, one that speaks what is true because it is not driven by the demands of the ego but oriented to the needs of the other. Such would be a loving, giving, faithful speech, an offering.

Merrick's comments on his speech represent the closest he is able to come to overcoming the separation between Mrs. Kendal and himself. Treves enters, intervening between the two and announcing a course for his patient that is quite different from the sublime other-directedness of Merrick's loving speech: "You are famous, John. We are in the papers. Look. They have written up my report to the Pathological Society. Look—it is a kind of apotheosis for you." Treves's enjoining Merrick to "look" encourages the development of his patient's self-consciousness: To look at himself in the papers is to learn to look at himself as others see him—thus the acute irony of Treves's speaking of Merrick's "apotheosis." For Treves, Merrick is apotheosized by becoming the object of the public's fascinated gaze, a gaze in which he is now invited to participate. Earlier in the scene Pomerance has suggested a quite different kind of "apotheosis" for Merrick as one who utters a godlike speech of truth in love. The rest of the scene, then, intimates the way Treves's notion of his patient's apotheosis will dominate Merrick's future. Mrs. Kendal offers to make it her "task" to make him "acquainted with the best, and they with him"—a purpose Treves enthusiastically endorses. After she pronounces the line Treves has formerly scripted for her, "it has been a very great pleasure to make your acquaintance," Mrs. Kendal and Treves exit, the latter declaring this meeting "a wonderful success." Merrick, however, is left sobbing *"soundlessly, uncontrollably"* (34–35), perhaps in gratitude for what has truly been given him, perhaps in gratitude even for the somewhat mistaken efforts of others to help him, perhaps already in mourning for the loss that his development of self-consciousness will entail.

Scene 10 acquires additional resonances of meaning through its intertextual play with *Romeo and Juliet* and its engagement with that word so paradoxically rich for Shakespeare: "nothing." Romeo succumbs to his vision of nothing, going down into the tomb to join his beloved and reunite with the earth. As David Willbern has pointed out, act 5 of *Romeo and Juliet* is "a set of variations on the theme of womb and tomb."[15] As such it implies the creative possibilities of nothing even as Romeo is acting out his murderous and suicidal intentions. Just before killing Paris, he curses the tomb in language rich with suggestions of nothing:

> Thou detestable maw, thou womb of death,
> Gorged with the dearest morsel of the earth,
> Thus I enforce thy rotten jaws to open,
> And in despite I'll cram thee with more food.[16]

While the primary sense of nothing here is destructive, negative—the tomb as devouring maw—the passage itself depends on an inversion of the positive sense of nothing as potential for creation, nothing as womb. The inversion itself is extraordinary and perhaps suggests a deep parallel between Romeo's story and Merrick's that would account for Pomerance's allusions to Shakespeare's play. The oral nature of Romeo's fantasy—as well as of his later suicide—indicates the degree to which he feels reduced to a condition of infantile dependency. What he seeks is to undo the creative, nurturing feeding of the mother by forcing himself as food down her devouring jaws. In this sense of dependence, of fatedness, lies Romeo's similarity to Merrick. Romeo repeatedly expresses the sense that his life's course is beyond his control, determined by "inauspicious stars" whose "yoke" he seeks to shake in death. His response to dependence is anger, and in this, too, his experience points intertextually to issues raised in Pomerance's play, specifically to scene 16, in which Treves and Merrick consider the appropriateness of anger as a response to Merrick's own dependence.

Romeo's rage leads to his focusing only on the negativity of nothing, his going down into the devouring maw in the churchyard. Merrick, however, is building the church model even while Pomerance is causing him to speak intertextually on Shakespearean nothing. His response to seeing nothing is to love, to take Juliet's pulse or get her a doctor, to seek reconnection. The scene thus comments reflexively both on Pomerance's drama itself and on Merrick's building of the church. The scene suggests that for Pomerance, as for Shakespeare, the creative nothing, the generative space of symbolic connection and reconnection, is the theater itself. Here in this creative play space, orality becomes potent, the word working with and against the surrounding silence to generate meaning. Merrick's pointing to the creative possibilities of nothing helps us to understand specifically why Pomerance has chosen not to represent his central character's deformity naturalistically. The play space conceived as a creative nothingness depends on its audience's participation in relationship with what is being represented on the stage. Depending on the actor's gestures alone to represent Merrick's deformity emphasizes this role of the audience, which is given an absence from which to create a presence, a nothing from which to imagine something. Scene 10 suggests finally, too, an analogy between the theater and the church. Like the theater, the church is a rich potential space for symbolic relationships, one in which the word is spoken out of silence. Thus it seems felicitous that the New York run of *The Elephant Man* began at the Theatre at St. Peter's. Such a context must surely have enhanced Pomerance's suggestive analogy of theatre and church.

Scenes 11, 12, and 13 focus on the process of Merrick's becoming "acquainted with the best, and they with him" (34), while also keeping his work on the church model squarely before the audience's eyes. He works on the model throughout scene 11, for instance, as the Duchess, Countess, Lord John, Princess Alexandra, and eventually Mrs. Kendal and Treves come bearing Christmas gifts. At the end of the scene, Mrs. Kendal calls attention to the model, in a moment that develops the idea of Merrick as artist adumbrated in the previous scene. After Treves pronounces Merrick's work "remarkable," Merrick responds wittily, with a line that suggests his ironic sense of the social condescension he enjoys or perhaps endures: "And I do it with just one hand, they all say." Mrs. Kendal follows by proclaiming Merrick an artist, a comment that prompts his most sustained reflection of the play on what he is doing in building the church: "I did not begin to build at first. Not till I saw what St. Phillip's really was. It is not stone and steel and glass; it is an imitation of grace flying up and up from the mud. So I make my imitation of an imitation. But even in that is heaven to me, Mrs.

Kendal." Treves hears in Merrick's comments the echo of Plato, and the scene closes with a brief dialogue on the relationship between idea and creation:

> *Treves:* That thought's got a good line, John. Plato believed this was all a world of illusion and that artists made illusions of illusions of heaven.
> *Merrick:* You mean we are all just copies? Of originals?
> *Treves:* That's it.
> *Merrick:* Who made the copies?
> *Treves:* God. The Demi-urge.
> *Merrick (goes back to work):* He should have used both hands shouldn't he? (38)

The first allusion here is specifically to book 10 of *The Republic*, where Socrates argues that artists should be excluded from the ideal city because they make imitations of things that are themselves imitations of the ideal forms. Thus imitative art for Plato is at best "an inferior uniting with an inferior and breeding inferior offspring."[17] Treves's later reference to the Demi-urge would seem to have in mind the *Timaeus*, in whose creation myth the Demi-urge fashions this world of becoming, much as a craftsman would, after the ideal order of being.

Despite Treves's linking Merrick's artistry here with Plato, Merrick's comic closing question—his casting the Demi-urge as an *imago hominis elephanti*—suggests the difference between his own sense of his work and Platonic imitation. In building his model of Saint Phillip's, Merrick does not seek to bring it into conformity with a preexistent ideal form of church. His sense of Saint Phillip's reality is more dynamic than the Platonic model of imitation allows: The church is "an imitation of grace flying up and up from the mud." That the church is not simply the shadowing forth of an idea is indicated, too, by Merrick's curious opening statement: "I did not begin to build at first." It is difficult to understand quite what Merrick means here, for if he was not beginning "at first," then what was he doing? Perhaps what Merrick means to suggest is that it was not simply himself, his "I," who began to build. Additionally, his language perhaps points to the inadequacy of building—imaged as in the *Timaeus* as the act of a craftsman standing outside and shaping his material—as a description for what he was doing at first. To understand Merrick's comment requires attending with some precision to his reference to grace. He has a sense of givenness, of giftedness, prior to his coming to himself, his becoming an "I." That Merrick should have such a strong apprehension of grace is perhaps attributable to his experience of his body. Not only does Merrick's body represent his fundamental givenness—as the body does for each of us—but in his case it also suggests how fully that givenness is beyond his full control, his conscious building or construction.

Merrick does not, then, "build at first"; instead he responds to, participates in, a building already begun. If the dialogue cited above plays ironically against Plato, it perhaps also alludes to Paul's comments in the First Letter to the Corinthians on building the church, the well-known master builder passage. Paul tells the Corinthians, "Ye are God's building," and then goes on to insist that the wise master builder builds only on God's grace in Christ:

> According to the grace of God which is given unto me, as a wise master-builder, I have laid the foundation, and another buildeth thereon. But let every man take heed how he buildeth thereupon.
>
> For other foundation can no man lay than that is laid, which is Jesus Christ.[18]

Thinking about Merrick's church building in the Pauline context enriches the significance of his act and helps explain why Pomerance emphasizes its centrality so strongly in his introductory note to the play. For Paul, and for much of the Christian tradition, the church is a body, the body of Christ, a point made especially by the master builder verses with their insistence that the Corinthians are "God's building" and later God's "temple" (3:16). In building his model, then, Merrick is building a body—one that can contain his body, one that reflects his own bodily experience, and one in which he would be understood truly as an *imago Dei.*

Scene 12 underscores the need for the church as a place where Merrick can be understood as an image of the God who is never fully graspable, knowable, possessible. For in this scene, as we have noted previously, Pomerance shows how all of Merrick's associates—from Mrs. Kendal to the Duchess to Treves—see in him an image of themselves. After each has said how Merrick is so clearly "like me," the final spot falls on Merrick *"placing another piece on St. Phillip's,"* building a context in which his identity can never be fully known, his self never reduced to a mirror of others, his freedom never exhausted because he stands in relation to a God who is ultimately mystery. The final moment of the scene also introduces a note that will come increasingly to dominate the latter part of the play: Treves's own growing puzzlement, professional anxiety, and self-doubt. As he notes that Merrick is "visibly worse than 86–87," Treves reflects on his own condition, perhaps with some ironic awareness of the inadequacy of simply reading his patient in terms of himself: "That, as he rises higher in the consolations of society, he gets visibly more grotesque is proof definitive he is like me. Like his condition, which I make no sense of, I make no sense of mine" (41). Once again it is possible to hear the echo of Shakespeare's "nothing" here. Through its defiance of Treves's diagnostic abilities, his surgeon's faith in aggressive intervention, and his social pretension, Merrick's "condition," both physical and social, calls into question all of Treves's ways of ordering his world. He can make nothing of Merrick's or his own nothing. But perhaps this very inability to make sense can become in Treves the ground for his own symbolic reconstitution of relationships, as is suggested by the dreams he has in scenes 17 and 18. Perhaps Treves's making no sense of himself can even provide an opening for God to do something in him, for the doctor's confused reflection, his new sense of his own grotesqueness, is framed in the scene by Merrick's last gesture, his putting a piece on Saint Phillip's.

The parallel between Merrick and Treves is stressed in another fashion in scene 13, one that introduces plot complications that seem in ways quite unjustified. The scene opens with a conversation between Treves and Lord John that reveals the latter to have broken certain unspecified "contracts" involving other people's money—including Treves's. Lord John is in the midst of a further appeal to Treves for funds when their conversation is interrupted by Carr Gomm, who rescues his prized surgeon from further bad investment. Thus, as Treves has "risen fast and easily"—the phrase is Carr Gomm's—he has become open to exploitation in the same way as the quickly rising Merrick. What is more interesting for the play's deeper motifs is Carr Gomm's imagery in describing Lord John, with its emphasis on a devouring orality:

> He has succeeded in destroying himself so rabidly, you ought not doubt
> an instant it was his real aim all along. He broke the contracts, gambled
> the money away, lied, and like an infant in his mess, gurgles and wants to

do it again. Never mind details, don't want to know. Break and be glad. Don't hesitate. Today. One-man moral swamp. Don't be sucked in. (43)

Carr Gomm's language defines an orality that is antithetical to the creative orality of the stage. For the rabid Lord John, in Carr Gomm's version, others are objects to be consumed, food to be eaten; he is all, and everything else functions merely to sustain him. In its infantile quality, such a response is equivalent to Romeo's spiteful desire to force himself as food down death's devouring jaws. Romeo would be devoured; Sir John would devour all. Both represent ways of rejecting life, or rejecting mortality both for oneself and for others. Both attitudes seek omnipotence (Romeo would undo death by suicide) rather than limited mortal existence together with others truly understood as other and not simply as narcissistic reflections of oneself.

Overhearing Treves and Carr Gomm's conversation about Lord John's dishonorable behavior, Merrick begins to fear that Treves may not be able to keep their own agreements. His fear emerges in a brief interchange with Mrs. Kendal which also includes the play's one direct reference to Merrick's mother's picture. Responding to Mrs. Kendal's assurance that Frederick is his "protector," Merrick asks "if he is in trouble," at the same time picking up a "small photograph," about which Mrs. Kendal asks in turn: "Who is that? Ah, is it not your mother? She is pretty, isn't she?" (45). Merrick's action underscores the link between his seeking the lost mother and his constitution of symbolic relationships with others. For at the same moment Merrick introduces the language of contract for his relationships with Treves and Mrs. Kendal himself:

> *Merrick:* Will Frederick keep his word with me, his contract, Mrs. Kendal? If he is in trouble.
> *Mrs. Kendal:* What? Contract? Did you say?
> *Merrick:* And will you?
> *Mrs. Kendal:* I? What? Will I? (45)

Clearly Merrick's language mystifies Mrs. Kendal. She has not considered herself to have entered into any relationship of obligation to Merrick. Merrick, on the other hand—perhaps because of his less sure sense of ego boundaries—understands himself in relation to both Treves and Mrs. Kendal. But Merrick's contractual language also suggests that he is coming to have a clearer sense of his own separateness than he has previously. Once again the scene closes by suggesting a relationship capable of including Merrick's lost yet sought-after connection to his mother and his contractual involvement with others: He puts another piece on Saint Phillip's.

The structure of scene 14 closely parallels that of scene 10, the Romeo and Juliet scene, to which it also repeatedly alludes. The scene focuses on Mrs. Kendal and Merrick, who is described as "working," presumably on his church model, and is ultimately interrupted, like the earlier scene, by Treves. The opening lines, however, mark the change in Merrick's sense of self from scene 10. Whereas earlier he has chastised Romeo for caring only for himself, not for Juliet, now he has discovered personal desire, as well as the double entendre of speech directed toward its fulfillment: "The Prince has a mistress. (*Silence.*) The Irishman had one. Everyone seems to. Or a wife. Some have both. I have concluded I need a mistress. It is bad enough not to sleep like others" (46). Mrs. Kendal first pretends to misunderstand this, restricting the significance of Merrick's comment about not sleeping like others to his need to sleep sitting up in order to support the weight of his head. But when Merrick makes clear that sleeping alone is "worst of all" (46), what results is a witty engagement between the two that leads ultimately to Mrs. Kendal's undressing for Merrick. It would be tempting to read the scene, then, as a representation of Merrick's achievement of (or perhaps fall into) male selfhood, defined by his assuming the role of spectator, of subject looking on Mrs. Kendal as object. Such a reading would treat the scene as presenting a simple reversal of Merrick's own earlier condition. Whereas he had been the object of the gaze of others and had, as he tells Mrs. Kendal, "never even seen a naked woman," now Merrick becomes the viewer. Moreover, Mrs. Kendal seems to understand her own beauty as absence or lack, as women have been figured under patriarchy. She tells Merrick "it has no really good use" and "does not signify very much" (48). Signification—the argument would run—is of course the privilege of the male, of the phallus, and here Merrick—possessor of that curiously normal penis—comes into his full masculine inheritance by looking on the naked Mrs. Kendal, who in herself signifies nothing.

While the scene almost invites the kind of reading detailed above, such an interpretation would be overly schematic, insufficiently at-

tuned to the context of Mrs. Kendal's undressing. She prefaces her act
with a very important comment on the nature of her relationship to Merrick: "Trust is very important you know. I trust you" (48). Her emphasis
on trust suggests the inappropriateness of reading her relation to Merrick within any paradigm of master-servant relations, of domination
and oppression. She does not strip for a man who would reduce her to
an object to be subjugated; she undresses—not only for Merrick but
also for herself—before one whom she trusts to regard her with a loving
gaze. The structural parallel between this scene and the earlier scene
10 reminds us that the basis of her trust lies in Merrick's love for Juliet,
his difference from Romeo. Moreover, Mrs. Kendal's undressing takes
place within the framing action of Merrick's building of the church, a
place of trust where all master-slave, subject-object relations are to be
overcome. Within these contexts Mrs. Kendal's insistence on the justice of her act becomes clear. She reveals to Merrick that she has seen
photographs of him, and he asks whether she means "the ones from the
first time, in '84?"—those of Merrick naked. Mrs. Kendal's answer to
Merrick's question is implicit in her response: "I felt it was—unjust. I
don't know why. I cannot say my sense of justice is my most highly
developed characteristic. You may turn around again. Well. A little
funny, isn't it?" (49). Mrs. Kendal undresses for herself as well as for
Merrick, for in doing so she relinquishes her privileged role as viewer,
as pornographic voyeur, and, in trust, opens herself to another. Indeed
she seems self-consciously aware of relinquishing the performance of
her gender. As she undoes her hair, she notes ironically the inadequacy of the line she has earlier developed, under Treves's coaching,
for her first meeting with Merrick: "There. No illusions. Now. Well?
What is there to say? 'I am extremely pleased to have made your acquaintance?'" (49). What the hollowness of her line suggests is that
perhaps there is nothing to say. As she and Merrick enjoy a privileged
moment of mutual recognition, they escape momentarily the realm of
the symbolic, the fallenness of language. Mrs. Kendal calls this state
"Paradise," with some precision, when Treves suddenly interrupts:

> *Treves:* For God's sakes. What is going on here? What is going on?
> *Mrs. Kendal:* For a moment, Paradise, Freddie. (She begins dressing.)
> *Treves:* But have you no sense of decency? Woman, dress yourself
> quickly.

(*Silence.* MERRICK *goes to put another piece on St. Phillip's.*)
Are you not ashamed? Do you know what you are? Don't you know
what is forbidden? (49–50)

Treves serves as a figure of the law, reenacting the announcement
of the Fall and defining the relationship between Merrick and Mrs.
Kendal as one of desire and transgression. He breaks Merrick's, and
perhaps our own, wordless moment of loving gaze on Mrs. Kendal, and
she becomes again a forbidden object to be viewed and desired from a
distance. Treves effectively insists on the ego boundaries, the separateness, of both Merrick and Mrs. Kendal. The scene follows the biblical pattern closely and obviously in its treatment of shame. Mrs. Kendal begins to cover herself, and Treves asks Merrick explicitly if he is
ashamed, that is, aware of himself as a separate person and as an object in the view of others. An additional biblical allusion rings in
Treves's last address to Mrs. Kendal. In this context one is inevitably
reminded of Jesus' admonition to the woman taken in adultery in the
eighth chapter of John: "Woman, go and sin no more." The parallel
between the woman of John and Mrs. Kendal is quite instructive. Mrs.
Kendal's crime is a kind of adultery, a confusion of boundaries, of limitations (significantly, Jesus marks with his finger in the sand before he
speaks, though his intent, it must be remembered, is not to define the
adulteress as sinner but to diminish the distinction between the Phar-
isees and her, between the patriarchal order and the woman). It is
entirely appropriate, then, that Treves addresses Mrs. Kendal as
"Woman," for here she is playing the role of woman under patriarchy as
that which resists containment, demarcation—as Other. What is most
intriguing, however, is Merrick's gesture—accomplished in silence
and inserted between Treves's insistences on separation and shame—
of putting another piece on the church. As Pomerance has earlier established the analogy of church and theater as creative spaces in which
the word can be spoken, Merrick's action here suggests his comple-
mentary creation of the church as a place of preverbal, presymbolic
silence. The whole pattern of Merrick's building begins to point toward
the church as the space where silence and word enrich and complete
each other in their mutual dependence.

The allusion to John resonates throughout the following scene 15,
which reintroduces Ross, the entrepreneur who has earlier exhibited

Merrick and robbed him of his funds. For Ross, all human relations are matters of prostitution. Merrick is, in his view, still selling his aristocratic visitors "the same service as always," making them "feel good about themselves by comparison." When Merrick objects that this makes him sound like a whore, Ross responds, "You are. I am. They are. Most are. No disgrace, John. Disgrace is to be a stupid whore. Give it for free." When Merrick refuses Ross's plea that they strike a deal again, Ross asks him, with implied promise, whether he's "had a woman yet." For Ross, this is what would make Merrick "a man like others." Life is a business of having and being had, with looking on and sexual intercourse conflated as processes of objectification, especially of male objectification of women. Ross's world thus stands in the starkest contrast to the play's image of the church as context for the overcoming of such objectification. What heightens this contrast is Ross's own wickedly parodic implicit comparison of his own service to that of the church. He comes to Merrick as to a god, asking "forgiveness," and he repeatedly says during their conversation that he would be happy with "ten percent" (51–53). Moreover, his own role as manager has been at least quasi-priestly in its mediation between the crowd and a sacred mystery—sacred in the precise sense of both attractive and repellent.

Indeed the scene strongly suggests the scapegoat function Merrick has played earlier during his exhibition by Ross. Ross wants Merrick to resume his role as either a god or an animal, as one for others, and it is a measure of Merrick's development of a self that he rejects returning to this role of other-directedness: "I'd lose everything. For you. Ross, you lived your life. You robbed me of forty-eight pounds, nine shillings, tuppence. You left me to die. Be satisfied Ross. You've had enough. You kept me like an animal in darkness. You come back and want to rob me again. Will you not be satisfied? Now I am a man like others, you want me to return?" (53). What is somewhat disconcerting here is the weakness of the defense Pomerance gives to Merrick. Being "a man like others" is a phrase thoroughly undercut by much of the play (quite apart from Ross's own reduction of the phrase to mean one who has "had" a woman). Throughout most of the play, the phrase does not mean that one possesses a sure sense of one's ego boundaries or of personal and moral self-worth. It means rather that one has learned to live under the tyranny of the normal and to look on others only as reflections of oneself. Merrick seems even more callous in his next, and final, rejection of Ross, who is given a very affecting plea by Pomerance: "Then I'm condemned. I got no energy to try nothing new. I may as well go to the dosshouse straight. Die there anyway. Between filthy doss-house rags. Nothing in the belly but acid. I don't like pain, John. The future gives pain sense. Without a future—*(Pauses.)* Five percent? John?" To this Merrick can respond only with the tired justification he has learned from Treves: "I'm sorry, Ross. It's just the way things are" (53). Treves has used precisely these words earlier in the play to justify Carr Gomm's sacking of Porter for staring at Merrick. What is trou-bling, then, is that the repetition of the phrase tends to suggest that there is little moral distinction between that sacking and Merrick's re-fusal of Ross. Pomerance comes perilously close to suggesting that there is somehow a loss in Merrick's new defense of his own integrity, his refusal to become again one for others, one at the disposal of others. The logic of the scene comes perilously close to lamenting Merrick's break from the role of scapegoat.

Scene 16 returns the play's focus to the relationship of Merrick and Treves. It presents their last interchanges in the play, although Merrick does appear later in a scene representing Treves's dreams. Mrs. Kendal is also present in her absence here—she has apparently been ban-ished from Merrick's presence by Treves—and many of the scene's motifs parallel those of the powerful earlier scenes 10 and 14, in which the three characters have appeared together. In the foreground of scene 16 are issues of medical and moral paternalism as exercised by Treves in his care of Merrick. Merrick, working on his church, begins by ask-ing Treves about his religious convictions:

> *Merrick:* Frederick—do you believe in heaven? Hell? What about Christ? What about God? I believe in heaven. The Bible promises in heaven the crooked shall be made straight. (54)

Merrick's comments here make explicit what he has earlier said of love to Mrs. Kendal in their dialogue on Romeo and Juliet. As Merrick would seek to restore the apparently lost Juliet, so too his belief in heaven is a way of seeking reconnection and the fulfillment of love in the face of possible nothingness. Merrick here even reads his own con-dition in a kind of negatively dialectical way: His "crookedness," while seen as a lack, nevertheless points to a promise, a fulfillment that breaks the ordinary logic of this world. That ordinary logic is Treves's.

He avoids Merrick's direct questions about his faith, answering first that the rack also made people straight and that, for the time being, he would "settle for a reliable general anesthetic" as an alternative to heaven. But he then goes on to tell, with a certain mock-seriousness, the story of a patient's near-death experience. The patient was a woman, on whom Treves operated for "a woman's thing," using "ether to anesthetize." For five minutes she seemed without vital signs, "a big white dead mackerel," but then "fretted back to existence, like a lost explorer with a great scoop of the undiscovered" (54). Treves continues:

> Well. I quote her: it was neither heavenly nor hellish. Rather like perambulating in a London fog. People drifted by, but no one spoke. London, mind you. Hell's probably the provinces. She was shocked it wasn't more exotic. But allowed as how had she stayed, and got used to the familiar, so to speak, it did have hints of becoming a kind of bliss. She fled. (55)

Despite Treves's attempt to exercise some control over the woman's story here—as in the witty remark about hell and the provinces—what emerges again is the motif of a woman's breaking of boundaries, here even those presumably absolute ones of life and death.

Treves's paternalistic attitude toward Merrick appears in its baldest form as their conversation continues. In a question reminiscent of Dostoevski's argument that without God everything is permitted, Merrick asks Treves: "If you do not believe—why did you send Mrs. Kendal away?" When Treves rather feebly alludes to "standards" we still must live by, Merrick presses him on the question of whose standards these are. Treves can only respond: "Everyone's. Well. Mine. Everyone's" (55). One can well imagine the laugh this rather broad irony would elicit from an audience inclined to resent the traditional authority of physicians. Indeed, the scene opts for an easy irony rather than for a serious engagement with the issues of medical paternalism or the complex living reality of the relationship between the historical Merrick and Treves. Here Treves's socializing Merrick is reduced to caricature, as patient ironically parrots the line on standards he has learned from his mentor: "They make us happy because they are for our own good" (55).

What prevents the treatment of the medical relationship from being intolerably simplistic at this point in the play is the image of the church that Merrick has been fashioning. Pomerance's giving centrality to that image suggests that the play is working at a more nuanced understanding of the relation between patient and care giver than the dialogue by itself communicates. Christian ethicist Stanley Hauerwas has written of the vital relationship between medicine and the church, and we think it quite possible to read what is happening in Pomerance's play in terms of some of the themes Hauerwas explicates. For Hauerwas, medicine is fundamentally a moral art characterized by "the willingness of patient and physician alike to be present to one another in times of suffering."[19] Because the church is a community of people called out by God to be present to one another in sin, suffering, and pain, it can serve medicine as a "resource of the habits and practices necessary to sustain the care of those in pain over the long haul." Moreover, because the church is a community commanded and pledged to welcoming the stranger, it can be of particular service to those involved in care of the ill, for "illness always makes us a stranger to ourselves and others,"[20] and the world of the ill and of those who care for them is always in danger of becoming separate from the rest of us. The church offers, in other words, a more embracing community, nourished by God's presence among us, capable of binding together the ill and the whole in our common journey with finitude. Such a community could provide a context, too, in which physicians could exercise legitimate authority without that exercise becoming an arbitrary paternalism, for both physician and patient would understand themselves to be mutually dependent, supported in their roles by a story and wisdom carried by the church, and sustained by God's presence.

To return these ideas to the play, we might say that Merrick's endeavor in building the church is to create a context in which he and Treves could have a relationship that would transcend the paternalistic model depicted in scene 16. We might see Merrick, too, engaged in creating a context that would break down the alienation between us and him. Having been taken as a stranger into an institution whose roots are religious (Hauerwas reminds us of the connection between hospital and hospitality), Pomerance's Merrick takes up the motif, building a church within the hospital as a welcoming sign to us, that we need not fear being with one so obviously marked by finitude. It is no accident that the historical Merrick's mere building of a church model from a kit has come to be so central in the story as told by both Montagu and Pomerance. For it has been a deeply religious story from the first: one about receiving the stranger in our midst and one about a suffering that medicine could not simply relieve or render meaningless, a suffering that had to be given meaning within a larger story.[21]

Issues of paternalism and the doctor-patient relationship continue to dominate scene 16 as Merrick presses Treves on the banishment of Mrs. Kendal. He begins by asking Treves whether the standards they abide by include "that woman's, that Juliet"—referring here to the woman whom Treves has described as dying and then coming back. Merrick's line performs an important function in the working of the scene, for it tightens the link between 16 and the earlier Romeo and Juliet scene, establishing the former as a kind of subtext for all that follows. Recalling his own experience with Mrs. Kendal, Merrick then asks Treves whether he has seen the woman "naked," to which Treves replies: "When I was operating. Of course." Merrick then shrewdly traps Treves, asking with seeming innocence what differentiates Treves's looking on his patient from his own looking on Mrs. Kendal:

> *Merrick:* Is it okay to see them naked if you cut them up afterwards?
> *Treves:* Good Lord. I'm a surgeon. That is science. (56)

When Treves insists on a distinction between science and love, Merrick asks him if that is why he's "looking for an anesthetic," suggesting that such a division in the surgeon's own psyche can be accomplished only through an emotional deadening. When Treves maintains again that "love's got nothing to do with surgery," Merrick asks simply, "Do you lose many patients?" For the Merrick whose response to seeing nothing is to love, losing patients would seem a spur to love, to seeking reconnection. Treves admits that he does lose "some," and Merrick responds simply, "Oh," a primitive word reminiscent of Shakespeare's pregnant "O," signifying a deep sense of loss but an equally deep longing for the reestablishment of relationship (56–57).

Treves seems angered by Merrick's "Oh," as if perhaps he is unwilling to simply acknowledge and wonder dumbly at loss, as if he needs to fill the wound quickly with meaning, words:

> *Treves:* Oh what? What does it matter? Don't you see? If I love, if any surgeon loves her or any patient or not, what does it matter? And what conceivable difference to you?
> *Merrick:* Because it is your standards we abide by.

> *Treves:* For God's sakes. If you are angry, just say it. I won't turn you
> out. Say it: I am angry. I am angry! I am angry!
> *Merrick:* I believe in heaven.
> *Treves:* And it is not okay. If they undress if you cut them up. As you
> put it. Make me sound like Jack the, Jack the Ripper. (57)

Clearly Treves is the angry one here, and his anger seems the cost of
his need to maintain the separation within himself between his understanding of surgery as science, as technique exercised upon an object,
and his care for his patients. Pomerance makes use here of the historical coincidence of Merrick's residence at the London and the Jack the
Ripper murders in Whitechapel, murders whose location and nature
cast suspicion on the London's doctors. Treves knows he is not like Jack
the Ripper, but he is not very clear here about what differentiates
them. Merrick's questions, his very presence, erode Treves's distinctions. If love is irrelevant to his surgery, if his work is truly science,
technique exercised upon objects, then what distinguishes him from
Jack the Ripper? Of course Treves would answer, quite rightly, that
what he does is for the patient's own good. But Merrick has also cast
doubt on his sure sense that he knows the patient's own good. What,
then, prevents the merely arbitrary imposition on the patient of the
physician's idea of his or her welfare? Once again the issues raised by
the dialogue suggest the richness of the image of the church toward
which Merrick and the play are, to use Pomerance's word, "groping."
    Within the church, the complete split of love from science would
never be forced on surgeons or physicians, for they would always understand themselves as co-participants with patients in a reality transcending them both. Surgeons could even afford to love patients—in
the sense of intending, hoping for, even praying for, their good—and
would indeed find that love underwritten within a body of people com-
mitted to intending the good for all persons. Physicians' love would be
empowered, paradoxically, by their being freed from total responsibility for their patients' fates. What Hauerwas has called a "fallible
medicine" would be made possible.[22] Physicians would be free to offer
patients the very best exercise of their skills, at the same time knowing
that everything does not depend upon medical efforts. For the church
knows that tragedy is not always avoidable, but that life can be lived
nevertheless because it is sustained by God's presence. Physicians,

too, could come to understand their skill not as a Promethean accomplishment, but as a gift made possible by the sacrifices of generations of both patients and practitioners. Not the least of what the church could offer physicians is the knowledge that patients have resources with which to suffer and even to die. Physicians would be freed from the demonizing need to relieve all suffering and to defeat death at all costs. This is not to say that physicians should forsake their traditional obligations to relieve suffering and combat death. But it is to insist that medicine has a certain tragic dimension: Not all suffering is avoidable and death cannot ultimately be kept at bay. Physicians need to know that patients have resources with which to confront these facts of suffering and death; otherwise they will be tempted to treat their patients as mere wards, incompetents, to be protected "for their own good."

This last point returns to the curious way in which scene 16 closes, with Treves apparently protecting either Merrick or Mrs. Kendal, or both, from the knowledge of Merrick's impending death. Merrick has asked Treves if Mrs. Kendal will return to visit him. Treves answers vaguely that he does not think she will, because "there are other things involved. Very. That is. Other things." Merrick picks up Treves's phrase, "other things," repeating it twice as he exits, again with the question: "Why won't she?" The scene closes then with Treves's single line: "Because I don't want her here when you die" (58). It is difficult to know just how to read this last line, to understand why Treves would want to prevent Mrs. Kendal from seeing Merrick die. It does suggest his physician's need and self-imposed burden, however, to bear alone the tragic secret of Merrick's death, and of his own inability to do anything about it. The wisdom of the church as context for medicine is implicit by contrast, for the church is a place where the scandal of all our deaths—and medicine's ultimate failure to do anything about them—can be acknowledged, confronted, and overcome.

As the play moves to a conclusion, Pomerance represents Merrick's unsettling effect on Treves through two scenes representing Treves's dreams, dreams in which physician and Elephant Man reverse their roles from the play's early scenes. In the first of these, Mr. Merrick, "of the mutations cross the road," comes to Carr Gomm—who plays a Ross-like role as Treves's exhibitor—requesting the opportunity to examine Treves. In the second dream, Merrick stands at the lectern describing Treves in great detail in a parody of Treves's exhibition of

Merrick before the Pathological Society of London. Merrick's language in the dream of course suggests Treves's doubts about his own profession and his project of helping Merrick to become, as much as possible, "like us." For the Merrick of the dream, the normal represents a kind of insensitive, egocentric individualism:

> *Merrick:* The most striking feature about him, note, is the terrifyingly normal head. This allowed him to lie down normally, and therefore to dream in the exclusive personal manner, without the weight of others' dreams accumulating to break his neck. From the brow projected a normal vision of benevolent enlightenment, what we believe to be a kind of self-mesmerized state. (61)

The language of the rest of the dream associates the physician with both the brutal exhibitor of freaks and the imperialist: "Due also to the normal head, the right arm was of enormous power; but, so incapable of the distinction between the assertion of authority and the charitable act of giving, that it was often to be found disgustingly beating others—for their own good." The speech also develops the idea of Treves's repression of sexuality, as suggested earlier by his embarrassment over Mrs. Kendal's questions about Merrick's genitals and his disruption of her disrobing for Merrick in scene 14. Pomerance here extends the metaphor of imperialism to Treves's treatment of the body: "The left arm was slighter and fairer, and may be seen in typical position, hand covering the genitals which were treated as a sullen colony in constant need of restriction, governance, punishment. For their own good" (62). In short, Treves subconsciously indicts himself for a variety of sins against the creed of postmodernism: a Cartesian commitment to mind over body, a repressed sexuality, an insistence on the control and manipulation of nature, a belief in the necessity of authority, and an obsessive focusing on the self to the exclusion of empathy with others. The tour de force is brought to a close by the entrance of the Pinheads, who now appropriate the Voice that has spoken earlier during Treves's exhibition of Merrick to the Pathological Society. In their judgment, returning Treves to his "prior life" is now something that ought not "to be permitted," a "pity and a disgrace," a "danger in ways we do not know."

Scene 18 is superb theater, if judged by its ability to elicit a particular reaction from the audience. Nevertheless it remains troubling for several reasons. The first is a matter of fidelity to history, and we say that with all regard for the playwright's freedom to revise history. The scene's implicit denunciation of Treves's shaping Merrick toward the normal insufficiently values Treves's simple and prior willingness to be present to Merrick in suffering. Second, to present the historical Treves's care purely in terms of a paternalistic shaping of Merrick toward some model of the normal radically oversimplifies the dynamic of authority and agency, protection and empowerment, that Treves's account of their relationship reveals. Third, to present normalization merely as repression and restriction is to undervalue the historical Merrick's own simple personal ambition for a life of some basic fellowship: It is to keep Merrick in the role of freak or scapegoat, as one supplying vicarious experience to an audience that would like to consider itself sophisticatedly alienated from oppressive "normality" while of course, for the most part, being quite comfortably and recognizably within middle-class norms. Recognition of this bad faith may be what motivates Martha Bayles' objection to the play's sleight of hand in not using naturalistic makeup for Merrick. As we have seen, Bayles argues that making Merrick up would make it perfectly obvious that his primary problem is not, as the play would have it, society. We think it not accidental that this objection to the play is raised by a woman, for what she is taking exception to is the play's romantic figuring of Merrick as liberating nature over against an oppressive culture—and being figured as nature over against culture is an old story for women.

The transformation of Treves into an Elephant Man is the motif of scene 19, which presents Treves first with Carr Gomm and then with Bishop How. As Merrick was inexpressive in his earliest encounters with Treves, now Treves finds it impossible to make himself understood to his associates. In response to Carr Gomm's asking what "has gone sour" for him, Treves offers the play's most concise reflection on the irony of normality:

> *Treves:* It is just—it is the overarc of things, quite inescapable that as he's achieved greater and greater normality, his condition's edged him closer to the grave. So—a parable of growing up? To become more normal is to die? More accepted to worsen? He—it is just a mockery of everything we live by.
>
> *Carr Gomm:* Sorry, Freddie. Didn't catch that one. (64)

Here the play's sleight of hand is fairly evident, for it is Merrick's physical condition, not his social one, that has edged him closer to death. Treves's reading of the "parable" can be glossed in various ways. One could say, with Ernest Becker, for instance, that to develop a character is to live a vital lie, to repress some possibilities in favor of others, and therefore, in a way, to die.[23] Or to put this in a somewhat less desperate, and more affirmative, light, one could say that becoming a self means growing into a particular community, with a particular understanding of what constitutes a good life. This involves a death of sorts, the repression of possibilities. But not to do this is to be nothing. One cannot be everything; one must be something. The play's equivocality about the very process of becoming a self among others emerges in Treves's speech. Treves (Pomerance) would seem to prefer the play's earlier apotheosized Merrick as one wholly oriented to the other. But to bear the weight of others' dreams is to be a god, a scapegoat, a freak, not a person. Once again the play intuits something on the level of the image that it does not make clear on the level of discourse. For in fashioning his church model, Merrick creates a place, or space, in which the person can participate in the gathered hopes and dreams of others without losing his or her own identity.

Bishop How finds himself no better able to understand Treves than Carr Gomm has. He and Merrick have been visible in the background of the scene during Treves and Carr Gomm's conversation. Now he engages Treves, telling the doctor that Merrick has "leaped" at the suggestion that he might be confirmed. Treves responds first that Merrick "is very excited to do what others do if he thinks it is what others do" and then amplifies his sense of Merrick's function as a reflector of others' narcissism when the Bishop asks, "Do you cast doubt, sir, on his faith?":

> *Treves:* No sir, I do not. Yet he makes all of us think he is deeply like ourselves. And yet we're not like each other. I conclude that we have polished him like a mirror, and shout hallelujah when he reflects us to the inch. I have grown sorry for it.
> *Bishop:* I cannot make out what you're saying. Is something troubling you, Mr. Treves? (64–65)

A difficulty with Treves's comment is that it does not follow very well from the portrayal of Merrick in his last major scene, the discussion with Treves over the banishment of Mrs. Kendal and the relationship between love and surgery. There Merrick seemed anything but a reflector of Treves as he wittily debunked several articles of the surgeon's personal and professional self-understanding. The inconsistency in Merrick's characterization springs from the unresolved problems in Pomerance's views of self-development. He wants Merrick to stand for a kind of sublime other-directedness, over against Treves's bourgeois individualism, but this other-directedness seems difficult to distinguish at times from mere slavish absorption of others' values. On the other hand, Pomerance needs to use Merrick as an acutely critical intelligence to undermine Treves's self-satisfaction. Yet given his views of normalization as oppression and repression, Pomerance cannot really account for the source of this intelligence in Merrick.

As the scene continues, Bishop How repeats his incomprehension of Treves several times, confirming the physician's new status as freak, outsider, Elephant Man. The burden of Treves's new knowledge is to see deformity everywhere. What's troubling him is "corsets," Treves tells How, as Pomerance takes his cue from a pamphlet, *The Influence of Clothing on Health,* written by the historical Treves on the ailments caused by these concessions to fashion. Treves finds his own work co-opted by a system that destroys nature and health at all levels. He spends his Sundays in the poor wards, treating "twenty-year-old women who look an abused fifty with worn-outedness" and "young men with appalling industrial conditions." These last he "turn[s] out as soon as possible to return to their labors." His middle-class patients "overeat and drink so grossly" as to destroy nature in themselves, while those above them in the social scale, "bulged out by unlimited resources and the ruthlessness of privilege," exhibit "the most scandalous dissipation yoked to the grossest ignorance and constraint." Treves sees in this monstrous destruction of nature the sign of a pervasive will to death. His own response is despair: "Science, observation, practice, deduction, having led me to these conclusions, can no longer serve as consolation. I apparently see things others don't" (65).

"Consolation" has been an important word in the play from the opening scene, where Carr Gomm predicts for Treves "an FRS and 100 guinea fees before you're forty," adding that these will be an "excellent consolation prize." Treves fails to understand what he will need consolation for, but the scene suggests this quite clearly through Carr Gomm:

"Ignore the squalor of Whitechapel, the general dinginess, neglect and poverty without, and you will find a continual medical richesse in the London Hospital" (1–2). "Richesse," riches, then are what one gets for deadening one's sensibility to others' pain, for abandoning the thirst for justice. Such consolation sounds very much like that Jesus referred to in the first malediction of the Sermon on the Plain: "But woe unto you that are rich! for ye have received your consolation."[24] The biblical ring of the word is reinforced in scene 2 by its association with other biblical language—Isaiah's description of the suffering servant, applied originally to Merrick by Treves in his reminiscence—in Ross's definition of Merrick as "a despised creature without consolation."[25] Merrick resists this definition in his simple commitment to justice and hope for fulfillment, spoken to Treves, also in the language of Isaiah, at the beginning of scene 16: "I believe in heaven. The Bible promises in heaven the crooked shall be made straight."[26] Merrick speaks always of heaven, of fulfillment, rather than of consolation, with its sense of something given in exchange for something lacking and yet incommensurate with the loss. Thus it is a sign of the difference between Bishop How's conception of the church and Merrick's when the Bishop says to Treves, after the latter's admission that there is no longer consolation in science for him. "I do wish I understood you better, sir. But as for consolation, there is in Christ's church consolation." Treves is closer to Merrick's religious spirit, and it is a measure of his patient's influence on him, when he replies to the Bishop: "I am sure we were not born for mere consolation." But Treves cannot sustain the sense of hope and hunger for fulfillment implicit in his phrase. After an angry denunciation of the Bishop for patronizing Merrick, he asks, weeping, for his help. The stage direction then notes, "BISHOP *consoles him,*" as Merrick, rising, puts the "*last piece on St. Phillip's*" and declares, "It is done" (65–66). Merrick's *consummatum est* works in at least two ways here. His "work" in Treves is finished when the physician, deprived of his former idol, science, acknowledges his dependence, his need for help. His work is accomplished, too, insofar as his experience points to the disjunction between Bishop How's church, with its emphasis on solace and comfort, and his own vision of the church as a bearer of hope and a sign of the promised fulfillment.

His work accomplished, all that is left Merrick, in Pomerance's telling of the story, is to die. Scene 20, "The Weight of Dreams," opens with Merrick, alone, looking at his model. After a brief conversation about the "chance-y" nature of death with Snork, who brings him lunch, Merrick "*breathes*" on his model (as if to impart to it his spirit?), polishes it, and then, to quote the stage directions, "*goes to bed, arms on knees, head on arms, the position in which he must sleep*" (67). The importance of these directions lies in their signaling Pomerance's departure from Treves's account of Merrick's death, with its suggestion that his asphyxiation resulted from Merrick's experiment in lying down in the normal manner. Pomerance thus insists that Merrick does not accede, at least consciously, to the desire to be normal; he continues to sleep in the position that suggests his role as scapegoat or god, bearing, as the scene title suggests, the weight of others' dreams. He has not learned to dream "in the exclusive personal manner," associated earlier in the Treves dream sequences with a normal and uncaring bourgeois individualism. Yet because Pomerance also wants to have Merrick killed by the normal, he conjures a dream for him, sung by the Pinheads, whose major emphasis is on the oppression, the death, involved in coming to be like others:

> We are the Queens of the Cosmos
> Beautiful darkness' empire
> Darkness darkness, light's true flower,
> Here is eternity's finest hour
> Sleep like others you learn to admire
> Be like your mother, be like your sire. (67–68)

As they sing, the Pins "*straighten* MERRICK *out to normal sleep position. His head tilts over too far. His arms fly up clawing the air. He dies*" (68). Thus Merrick remains a heroic figure resisting victimization by the normal; like the Pins, he has been colonized, his very dreams possessed by those who would shape him for his own good. Pomerance's treatment of the death avoids asking to what extent Merrick actively sought normality, and it clouds rather than clarifies his relationship to others. Pomerance wants Merrick to bear the dreams of others, yet it is others' dreams that kill him. The scene does not tell us how one remains related to others without their dreams destroying one, and in a way that avoids the prevailing mode of atomistic individualism. Still the whole play has groped toward an image of that kind of possibility in the church.

Pomerance's final scene deals explicitly with the question of authority over Merrick's story. Carr Gomm reads to Treves as he composes his letter to the *Times* of April 16, 1890, giving an account of the death of the Elephant Man. The account stresses the kindly philanthropy of those who gave their money to make Merrick's refuge possible, the good offices of all those at the hospital who sought "to alleviate his misery," and the patient's own unassuming and grateful manner. When Carr Gomm asks Treves if there is anything he would like to add, the surgeon first mentions Merrick's intelligence, "acute sensibility," and "romantic imagination" but then withdraws, as he is now "really not certain of any of it." Carr Gomm then concludes his history of Merrick as willing object of Victorian charity, giving an account of his disposition of the remaining funds and thanking the *Times* for its insertion of his letter of 1886, which "procured for this afflicted man a comfortable protection during the last years of a previously wretched existence." The play then concludes with an exchange between the two men, Treves wanting to add to the official story, Carr Gomm willing it closed:

> *Treves:* I did think of one small thing.
> *Gomm:* It's too late, I'm afraid. It is done. (*Smiles.*) (71)

Pomerance's Treves has of course come to understand the inadequacy of telling Merrick's story simply as the account of a wretched existence made less miserable through public and institutional good will. The play's conclusion calls our attention to the issues of control and authority in authorship, to the way we tell our own and other people's lives. Even in his desire to close Merrick's story, Carr Gomm unintentionally points to its openness, its ability to be told and read in various ways. For his *consummatum est* ironically echoes Merrick's words on finishing the church, where the story can never be pronounced "done" by any human voice.

6

Merrick on the Fringe

Plays by Thomas Gibbons, William Turner, and Roy Faudree

In the previous discussion of Pomerance's *Elephant Man* we have stressed the intellectually provocative nature of the play—the ideas it offers and the comparisons or connections it encourages an audience to make. Something of the play's power and effectiveness is innate to its subject, the story of Merrick, but Pomerance's distinctive imaginative use of that subject is yet more crucial. It is his remaking of the story that brings about its dramatic efficacy; and remaking, whether through selection, emphasis, or invention, unavoidably involves parting company with fact. Pomerance alters Merrick's story so that it may better illustrate a particular theme—the tyranny of the "normal"—and it is no small irony that Pomerance's play has overshadowed the various other dramatic adaptations of the Elephant Man story through precisely the sort of tyranny it describes. Pomerance's *Elephant Man* attracted the widespread popular and critical notice that eluded other plays on the subject because Pomerance's remaking, far more than those of the other dramatists, offered that mass tyrant the ticket-buying audience just what it wanted to see in 1979. Pomerance's departures from fact (and from Treves's and Montagu's narratives) are not just intellectually provocative, they are also shrewdly pragmatic, deftly calculated to enhance the story's stage potential and to give its contemporary audience the blend of comfort and challenge that makes for healthy box offices.

In most ages, audiences have favored a romantic interest in even the grimmest story: hence the creation of highly charged relationships between Treves and Mrs. Kendal, and yet more important between Merrick and Mrs. Kendal. Late twentieth-century theatergoers tend to prefer antiheroics to heroics and would rather see a triumph of the underdog (individual or collective) than an endorsement of an established power group; and in the 1970s and 1980s a popular formula for providing such gratification involved the juxtaposition of an apparently empowered but actually insecure doctor (or other sort of therapist) and a severely handicapped yet somehow triumphant patient (or other sort of help receiver). This formula proved doubly effective. Not only did it minister to the tastes of the age, but it also offered a wide range of potential challenges for the actors playing the "handicapped" roles. A few of the best-known plays falling into this group are *Equus* (1974), with a deranged seventeen-year-old blinder of horses; *Whose Life Is It, Anyway?* (1979), with a sculptor paralyzed from the neck down, *Children of a Lesser God* (1980), with its brilliant, angry deaf woman, and *Duet for One* (1981), with a violinist suffering from multiple sclerosis— the last play based, like Pomerance's, on a true story, that of former cellist Jacqueline Du Pre. With the exception of *Children of a Lesser God*, which highlighted the acting talents of a deaf actress, each of these plays has enabled a "normal" man or woman to demonstrate his or her talent by plausibly impersonating debility and rendering the debilitated character not only interesting but also downright charismatic. Exploiting this particular dramatic situation is at once humane and exceedingly canny—it widens the sympathies of the audience (people made uncomfortable by actual handicaps allow themselves to contemplate the disturbing when it is stage illusion), and it maximizes the chance for favorable audience response (who could be so unfeeling as to dismiss a handicapped protagonist or to deprecate the acting of someone who has taken on the task of portraying a handicap?). Thus there is something formulaic in the "originality" of Pomerance's play, which flattens out a real surgeon, Frederick Treves, into an archetype of scientific, patriarchal, imperialistic authority, and then punctures his authoritarian certainties by the words of his own self-doubting aspect, by the yet more powerful arguments of a woman, Mrs. Kendal, and by the supremely logical, intellectually honest, eloquently expressed insights of a severely disabled member of the underclass, "John" Merrick.

But because the triumph of Pomerance's handicapped hero depends on ideas and ideas depend on words, the dramatist must diverge from convention in an important way, one that distinguishes Pomerance's Merrick from all the other imaginative renditions of disability mentioned above and from the dramatic versions of Merrick discussed in this chapter. As we have already seen, the title character does not look anything like the real Merrick (the audience must sympathetically imagine the physical particulars of his disorder), and he articulates insights that the real Merrick could never, given his disability, have put into spoken words. In using a more or less normal-looking, highly verbal being to suggest a highly abnormal-looking, more or less nonverbal one, Pomerance stands in radical opposition to Thomas Gibbons, William Turner, and Roy Faudree. The difference between Pomerance's approach and those taken by the other dramatists resembles that existing between Mary Shelley's evocation of the monster-hero in *Franken-stein* and the subsequent theatrical treatments that popularized her tale. Like Shelley's novel, Pomerance's play works through articulated ideas to create a sensitive, philosophical being whose engaging and superior mind constitutes his primary reality for us. Like the Frankenstein melodramas, the plays of Gibbons, Turner, and Faudree rely heavily (though in different ways) on the spectacle of Merrick, each making him a chiefly visual presence for us.[1]

Thomas Gibbons' *Exhibition: Scenes from the Life of John Merrick*, drafted when the author was a senior at Villanova, given a staged reading by the Philadelphia Company in February 1977, and presented in fifth draft by that troupe in March 1979, is a one-act play with four scenes and only two characters, Merrick and Treves.[2] Throughout, Merrick is presented in the "crossing the Mile End Road" costume described by Treves (cloak, yachting cap, veil) with the further addition of a glove hiding his deformed hand. The play is set up to be a retrospective that jumps about in terms of time and place. An aged Treves, in the last year of his life, conjures up memories of the relationship that continues to fascinate and torment him; Merrick, in like manner at the end of his (much shorter) existence, thinks back over his days at the London and the sad years of exhibition that went before. The play is curiously noninteractive—much of the time Merrick and Treves speak in sequential monologues rather than in dialogue. The words themselves are frequently quoted rather than original—words straight out of the title piece from *The Elephant Man and Other Reminiscences* and *The Autobiography of Joseph Carey Merrick*. Interestingly, despite his awareness of this latter source, Gibbons follows Treves's published account naming Merrick "John," not only in Treves's speeches but even in the play's subtitle and in Merrick's reference to himself.

In the first scene, Merrick and Treves deliver alternating expository accounts of the Elephant Man's life. Treves sometimes reads from a "leatherbound journal" containing words from his reminiscence or speaks extemporaneously, these remarks (with the exception of a brief professional autobiography) also deriving from the reminiscence. Merrick's first three speeches come from his *Autobiography;* his subsequent remarks are imaginary monologues created by Gibbons, one a night piece combining present thoughts of walking in the hospital garden with earlier experiences of darkness, the next a recollection of how, as a thirteen-year-old in the workhouse, Merrick first encountered a mirror and thus lost his "peculiar virginity"—ignorance of the fact that his face was fully as alien as his body. The brief second scene, set in the hospital garden in 1887, shows Merrick first refusing the social companionship Treves, in hopes of "humanizing" his patient, wants to bring to him at the London but finally agreeing to see (or be seen by) others—to resume his exhibition, as it were. Scene 3 takes place in November 1889, at which time Treves has arranged a country holiday for Merrick. Here, in a series of conversations and retrospective soliloquies, we are led to the crucial moment in Treves's relationship with Merrick, which hinges on the possibility of transformation through touch, as if the two men were acting out some myth of metamorphosis. In the final scene, it is 1923, the final year of Treves's life, and the surgeon is alone with his journal and Merrick's mask and walking stick. His soliloquy blends extracts from the journal (which now contains bits from his travel writing as well as words from "The Elephant Man") and recollections of a long and eminent life, amid whose many encounters the relation with Merrick seems central, even obsessive.

As we have already seen, the real Merrick and Treves and the documentary evidence of their relationship serve Pomerance as a springboard: What he offers is effective theater that has rather little to do with historical fact or plausibility. Gibbons, in contrast, works so closely with the sources that he gives up much of the dramatic potential inherent to the story. When it is possible to allow Treves and Merrick their own published words, he does so—and when he creates thoughts, aspirations, regrets for the two men, he takes far fewer liberties in presenting them than Pomerance does. His Merrick is no 1970s wit but rather a wistful Victorian, no intellectual and social construct but a believably corporeal being. In Gibbons, Merrick looks to his fellow human beings not for the intellectual exercise of conversation or for the social status brought by courtesy visits, but for basic emotional and physical acknowledgment—for the touch of a caring equal.

The forms that such acknowledgment might take are various; but clearly Treves's medical touch, presented in scene 2, where he examines Merrick's "flawless" left arm, is not enough. Speaking of his nocturnal perambulations with a nurse (though never the same one), Merrick muses, "Sometimes, walking in the garden with the nurse at my side, it almost seems. . . . If I forget certain facts: that this is a hospital, that she is a trained nurse, that I wear this. . . . *(Touches mask.)* In the end there are too many things to be forgotten" (9). Unlike the Pomerance Treves, who indignantly terminates that brief moment of "paradise" between Merrick and Mrs. Kendal, this Treves recognizes Merrick's creaturely needs, though his understanding is as partial as his solution is unacceptable: "Perhaps the kindest thing would have been to find some . . . woman, from Whitechapel, and bring her to his room one night; give her enough drink, and when she was insensible, unaware, bring him in from some dark corner and . . . let him" (15). Finally, however, the emotional and physical contact for which Merrick asks is parental. He senses in the act of touch a potential, if temporary, liberation from his role as exhibited object, a possibility of metamorphosis: "If someone would *touch* me, I'd be human . . . for a moment. Please. The way a father does touch his son." Treves can offer kind words—"John. I am . . . your friend"—but he cannot confer what Merrick needs. With his failure, Treves in turn is metamorphosed from friend or doctor to exhibitor, as Merrick, with killing kindness, implies: "My last showman stole everything I owned. But I give these to you" (21). What Merrick refers to here are the costly but valueless "rings and walking-sticks, diamond stickpins and pretty photographs" that the so-called friends who have called at his so-called home have offered as unconvincing evidence that he could be one of them. Merrick cannot, as Treves just has proved; and a few moments later Merrick retreats from "I-you" personal relationships and takes up his old

role in his last speech of the play, which, like his first one, is characterized in the stage directions as *"a recitation"* and drawn from the
Autobiography sold in the places of exhibition.

Gibbons ends his play with Treves facing a world without Merrick.
The sense of bereavement is more obsessive than in Pomerance (an
effect heightened by setting the last scene in 1923 instead of 1889),
though in both plays the surviving Treves becomes something of an
Elephant Man. For Gibbons, this involves Treves's recognizing an emotional deformity in his "deepest self" analogous to Merrick's physical
disfigurement; for Pomerance, Treves takes on the mantle (or mask) of
Merrick in becoming able to see things that others do not. The differences here are consistent with the differing methods and preoccupations of the two dramatists. Similarly, the methods of presenting a reversal or metamorphosis in Treves demonstrate the differences in the
two works. In Gibbons, Treves picks up Merrick's mask and dons it *"in
silence, in a gesture oddly formal, ceremonious,"* his objective being an
attempt "to see what he saw"—and later, in the college museum where
Merrick's bones are exhibited, Treves recalls that "I stood there, in the
darkness, in the silence . . . and looked at the skull. . . . I looked
into the sockets that his eyes peered from, thirty-three years ago . . .
and tried to remember the intelligence imprisoned there" (23). These
responses are modest and immediate—attempts rather than successes, practical, physical gestures rather than theoretical, cerebral
observations. Here Treves remains a physician confronting his specific
limitations as physician: "But for Merrick's pain, what mere operation
was there?" Rather than punishing himself for what he has done in
socializing Merrick, he instead laments that he could not "do anything
more than stand guard over him in his solitude" (23). Gibbons' Treves,
then, is only himself, in contrast to the sinister synecdoche of the intel-
lectualized dream sequence where Pomerance's Treves, embodying the
whole power class in which he participates, punishes himself and his
class by putting himself in Merrick's position, and Merrick in the role
of medical exhibitor. Thus, as he has been from the beginning, Gibbons remains more interested than Pomerance in Merrick's (and
Treves's) corporeal reality. Even in death, Merrick's experience is not
really available to Treves. Bodily beings remain themselves; they are
not interchangeable ciphers.

If one impediment to the theatrical success of Gibbons' play lies in its staying closer to the sources than is usual for a dramatic venture, William Turner's play takes many more liberties with its historical characters than is customary in mainstream theater—even in speculative drama of the Pomerance sort. Turner's *Elephant Man*, staged by Pittsburgh's Theater Express, ran from December 14, 1978, until January 7, 1979. The director was Jed Harris, who, having played in a previous Milwaukee production based on the Elephant Man's story, encouraged Turner to write on the subject for Theater Express. Because Turner is dead and his play has not been published, our comments are based on typed pages from the original workshop production graciously provided by Harris, who has identified this version as his favorite.[3] The curious angle of the Turner play is the prominence it gives to Princess Alexandra, who, rather than Treves, is set up to be Merrick's analogue. Female, lame, deaf, Danish, married to a fat philanderer who infected her with syphilis, the Princess, though she seems to be at the top of English society, is in her own way and in her own eyes the marginalized Merrick's counterpart. Princess Alexandra makes this point clear during "the new revised elephant dance" she performs for, or with, Merrick, who earlier in the play has spoken of his days at the London as "learning to do a new dance"—a dream regimen that "always sent . . . [him] into the arms of George Eliot."

Turner's Treves, far from being sympathetic to or parallel with Merrick, is insensitive and repressed. Responding to the question "did you begin to have a personal relationship with the patient," Treves replies with a brutality absent in Pomerance's or Gibbons' plays (or in the narratives of Treves and Montagu, for that matter): "in a sense but no relation ship could be complete because of the defect in his speech and the complete expressionlessness of his features in this sense it was much like trying to communicate with a pet animal although i was not able to feel the unashamed affection which one usually associates with pet/ owner relationships." A little further on, he accounts for the "unnamed hence i presume unnameable barrier between you" in the words, "i never was able to tell how john would understand what i said he sometimes i thought he would misunderstand me i was always afraid he might suddenly unexpectedly touch me touch me before i was ready." Treves's medical profession and surgical specialty become particularly voyeuristic and invasive in Turner's play: "i have always loved bursting into the heart of a situation," confesses Treves, who goes on to speak of his enduring childhood delight in eavesdropping and how he continues "to this day to relish the thrill of willfully invading people's privacy as a doctor is so eagerly urged to do."

Turner's Merrick, like Pomerance's, is not presented through makeup or costume. Turner observed in an interview that "since the disease gets worse and worse as the play goes on, the make-up job would be on too large a scale. So we decided not to use a representational costume. Instead, we decided to portray the disease through imagery."[4] But if the disease is portrayed through imagery, the man suffering that affliction does not emerge clearly—for extreme, perhaps even complete, alienation is Merrick's ruling attribute here. Neither through the eyes of others nor from his own remarks do we discover much about him, though to be sure part of the unknowability lies in readers having to rely on words alone to intuit what stagecraft, with its additional resources, might have made clear to the audiences of this experimental piece. What emerges most vividly is how difficult it is for someone with Merrick's various afflictions to make human connections—whether with other characters in the play or with the audience. As Turner observed, his play "shows that it's not possible for such desperate people like Merrick to have a relationship."[5]

The impossibility of relationship mentioned by Turner proves central to Roy Faudree's *Elephant Man,* though in Faudree's play rigid class prejudices, repressive gender roles, and constrictive fashions (such as corsets and stiff collars) deform the women and men surrounding Merrick in such a way that *all* are freaks, emotional or physical analogues to the title character. This play, first written for a large cast, premiered at Holyoke Community College in October 1975. In August and September of 1976, a revised version using seven actors for twenty parts was presented at the Globe of Northampton. Two years later, *The Elephant Man* was revived by Faudree's own theatrical company, the No Theater, which staged the play in Northampton during May and June before taking it to New York's Performing Garage, where it ran from July 27 until August 13, 1978. In May 1987 the No Theater brought back the play for three performances as part of a thirteen-year retrospective of its work.[6]

Although Faudree's play is a far more sophisticated piece of theater than either Gibbons' or Turner's, it is not calculated to engage the sensibilities of a wide audience as is Pomerance's play, which it predates by four years. Far from adhering to familiar Broadway conventions, Faudree's *Elephant Man* is experimental theater with a form as difficult to characterize as was Merrick's own body. The program from the Performing Garage run describes Faudree's play as a "melodrama," but in fact it is more closely allied to pantomime (the popular, highly spectacular subgenre that was playing at Drury Lane the night of Merrick's attendance) or extravaganza. Like English pantos, Faudree's play takes its title story as a point of departure rather than as a focus. Like pantomime, it offers topical, satirical social criticism interlaced with plenty of slapstick comedy, intricately staged pursuits and evasions, farcical cross dressing, and the crucial device of transformation (a recurrent strategy in Faudree, but a possibility sadly denied, despite the unrealistic format, to the title character himself). For all its freedoms, though, pantomime follows a more conventionalized form than is encountered in *The Elephant Man* and has a more purely comic tone and resolution. The amorphous nature of Faudree's play and its complex blend of humor and pathos make it yet more closely resemble the extravaganza, a fantastic, irregular form defined by its creator, J. R. Planché, as "whimsical treatment of a poetical subject as distinguished from the broad caricature of a tragedy or serious opera, which was correctly described as burlesque."[7]

It is interesting to see that while Pomerance's decisions about remaking Merrick's story ironically serve to put the supposedly marginalized Elephant Man at center stage (both within the play itself and in the contemporary consciousness), Faudree's avant-garde strategies enact what they assert about Merrick. Faudree's play, like its protagonist, remains on the fringe, and within the play Merrick himself is far from prominent. Although his presence is always felt and often noticed, the bulk of attention goes to the other characters, who are more articulate, more attractive, better suited to interest an audience with their highly verbalized bustlings than is the mostly silent and never entirely intelligible cloaked and hooded presence of Merrick. In Faudree's play, the Elephant Man is a character so uncharacterized that he can be, and is, played by many different actors in the course of the play.

The particular conventions of such forms as pantomime and extravaganza being much more familiar to British audiences than they are to American ones, it is no surprise that from 1975 on reviewers have found themselves puzzled by the play; but perhaps the most compelling quandary for anyone familiar with the facts of Merrick's life is how his story can be construed as the stuff of comedy. Faudree commented on this matter in an interview: "Usually people with a disease or deformities are treated with a sort of reverence, a solemn sort of respect. But the play is a comedy. It's very different from the treatment you'd expect. We're not trying to say 'how noble this person must be, to have this horrible handicap and still be able to remain a sensitive, caring individual, after all he's been through.' "[8] Faudree's *Elephant Man* can be comic precisely because it is not narrowly focused on the Elephant Man. If Victorian society is the villain in Pomerance's play, here it serves as the foolish collective protagonist, its individual members either self-deformed or misshapen by constraints placed on them by others. We are not meant to care about these comically warped characters as individuals but are to see them always in connection, as component parts of their intricate and absurd society.

This situation is perfectly presented through Faudree's stage set consisting of "five doors, all facing out towards the audience; two large staircases on opposite side[s] of the stage and an elevated playing area that connects the two sets of stairs and with them form[s] a proscenium that frames the upstage five doors."[9] One stair is elaborate, used for all the society scenes, and the playing area atop it is elegantly Victorian. The other stair leads to the isolation ward of the London Hospital and is correspondingly Spartan. Suspended above the whole playing area is "a large striped canvas tarp that is rigged so that, depending on the way it is flown, it can function as a circus tent, show curtain, canopy." With Faudree's set, parallels suggested thematically in Gibbons', Turner's, and Pomerance's plays can have spatial reality. For example, as Merrick is being brought a lonely meal in his ward, the Gomms and Treveses are having a convivial, but equally repressed, dinner on the "society" side; and Treves's highly unorthodox after-dinner description of Merrick's symptoms (information teased out of him by Mrs. Gomm, here presented as a Victorian feminist chafing under the conventions governing ladylike behavior) seamlessly transforms into Treves's presentation to the Pathological Society. Besides keeping the audience aware of analogous situations and of parallels straightforward and ironic, the set announces its own theatricality—the proscenium *within* the stage setting and the versatile, overarching tent or curtain keep the audience aware that the play is only a play. The Faudree troupe's highly mannered, even parodic, acting style commented on by various reviewers would further this sense of artificiality, as would the blatant juxtaposition of incongruous, unassimilated elements—for from the first scenes, where a cacophony of carnival cries gives way to fashionable medicine (Dr. Treves examining, and seducing, Mrs. Kendal), the play is a verbal and histrionic equivalent to the jumble sale or three-ring circus suggested by the striped fabric enclosing its set.

The hotchpotch constituting Faudree's play includes direct quotation from Treves's clinical description of Merrick (interestingly, this part of the reminiscence is cited verbatim by every reteller of the tale mentioned thus far) and other bits from his essay, along with recurrent reference to his anticorseting tract *The Influence of Clothing on Health.* The play also includes borrowings from two plays of the period, Henrik Ibsen's *Doll's House* (1879) and W. S. Gilbert's *Pygmalion and Galatea* (1871); from H. G. Hibbert's *Playgoer's Memories;* from George Du Maurier's 1880s *Punch* cartoons; from the Parker Brothers game Clue; and from the conventions of Japanese Kabuki theater. The borrowings are obvious, their differences from one another and from Faudree's original lines stressed rather than smoothed over. Absurdities (such as the presence of Clue suspects among the real and fictional names dropped) abound. So do anachronisms. The snobbish Lady Midas, asking the identity of Mrs. Kendal, is told that she is "the Duchess of Bayswater. She was a Lady Jacqueline Bouvier, you know." And the confusion over Merrick's Christian name is given a decidedly 1970s twist. Here, it is Mrs. Kendal who is uncertain—"Is it John or Joseph?"—and Treves's answer amplifies the confusion: "David. John! No, it's John." The play's incongruities are deliberate, as Faudree acknowledges: "I like the sort of naive, ill-formed quality of the play. It keeps it from being precise and historically documented."[10]

The fact that these mix-ups are deliberate has not kept some of the play's reviewers from deprecating their effect, but there are a number of ways in which they prove highly appropriate. First, the inaccuracies and blatant theatricality keep an audience fully aware that the production is Faudree's fiction. There is no confusing this Treves, who in fact is not much further removed from the historical Treves than is Pomerance's, with the real-life surgeon. Second, the outrageous juxtapositions enact Merrick's disorder. If the Elephant Man is not one of the leading characters in Faudree's play, his body is the model along whose lines the extravaganza is constructed. Third, the absurdities encourage the audience to think associatively—to intuit truths instead of chopping logic—to supplement, even subvert, the rational, scientific, linear way of proceeding that does not much help Treves, or anyone else, to understand Merrick.

For instance, the very basic "John-Joseph-David" confusion takes us back to that old inaccuracy of Treves's and reminds us how ultimately unknowable Merrick was—but simultaneously undercuts its serious import with the trivial anachronism, conjuring up as it does the well-known name of a contemporary Broadway producer and thereby indirectly reminding us that we are not Victorians and that what we are experiencing is theater, nothing else. The mental agility cultivated by this moment helps us to make mental leaps—as does the "Lady Jacqueline Bouvier" allusion, which, if we untangle it, is a clever hybrid: a real American lady's marriage into an imaginary British dynasty here being doubly apt, partially applicable to two actual unions, Jacqueline Bouvier's with future president John Kennedy, and Kathleen Kennedy's with the marquess of Hartington, who, had he lived to succeed to his family's primary title, would have made her duchess of Devonshire. Assembling what coherence can be gained from fragmentary evidence and penetrating theatrical surfaces for such glimpses of reality as are available in a world where all is theater—these skills are necessary if we are all, as Faudree sees it, Elephant Men and Women.

The allied processes of dramatist juxtaposing and audience associating operate at larger levels throughout the play. Merrick's story begins at the time of his arrival back in London with Treves's card. Along with occasional flashbacks to supply earlier information, there are scenes representing his permanent installation at the London, Treves's growing interest in Merrick's mind and introduction of Mrs. Kendal to him (Mrs. Kendal here playing to an Elephant Man who is offstage except for his left hand), Merrick's presence at a pantomime (here presented as a Kabuki version of the Western tale *Beauty and the Beast*), and finally Merrick's death (here seen as coming just prior to the country holiday arranged by Lady Knightley, with the cause of death straight out of Treves's reminiscence, the attempt to sleep "like other people"). Interspersed with these scenes from the traditional, Trevesian Elephant Man story are other scenes of Faudree's invention. We glimpse the tyrannies of fashion over the female form in Treves's examination of Mrs. Kendal, the conventionalized relations of men and women at the Treves-Gomm dinner party, the snobbish social discrimination against actresses (even Mrs. Kendal) at a tennis match where Mrs. Treves, Mrs. Gomm, and the transparently fictive Lady Midas are spectators.

As the "normal" Londoners, especially Treves and Mrs. Kendal, become increasingly aware of the normal person beneath Merrick's bizarre exterior, they (and we) have a growing sense that their own circumstances are freakish and deforming. For Mrs. Gomm, this awareness takes the form of demanding extraordinary prerogatives after dinner: Offered tea and frivolous conversation with Mrs. Treves, she demands coffee, a cigar, and substantive discussion with the men. For the mature actress Mrs. Kendal, first seen tightly corseted and bound by the belief that "the function of clothing is [to] conceal not reveal the nude form of the female body," liberation takes the form of appearing opposite her husband in *Pygmalion and Galatea* without the foundation garment she has thought crucial to her continued existence as an "ornament of the stage." The curtain rises on the "uncorseted and scantily draped nude body" of the actress—and it seems delightfully ironic that despite this lapse from convention she is, as Victorian statues and ladies were both supposed to be, on a pedestal. Treves, who in this play is never the smug Victorian professional or the anguished transcendental overreacher we see in other versions, remains cheerfully bohemian throughout the play; but Faudree perceptively picks up his progressive sense of engagement with Merrick from the reminiscence. Treves begins by sheltering a freak but ends up cherishing a friend: "He's the kindest, most gentle man I have ever known. I feel more like myself when I'm alone with him than anyone else . . . than with any other man I mean." And Mrs. Treves, on whose account Treves has appended the insincere qualification to the assertion quoted above, undergoes the most radical transformation of all. Primly repressed in the early scenes (at one point we see her "facing the audience with a cloth harness strapped about her chin and head looking at herself in a mirror"—a striking image of what vanity will undergo in the service of beauty), she ends by reading her own life through Nora's in *A Doll's House*. The penultimate scene of the play, done in slow motion, presents her as Nora, going out the door with her suitcase in hand, looking back at Treves, who is moving toward her—though unlike Ibsen's play, Faudree's ends before the closing door ratifies the feminist deed.

All the changes mentioned above can shelter under the umbrella term "transformation"—a word that has been important to the understanding of Merrick since Treves's reminiscence, where the transformation of man into beast or beast into man is what proved so horrifying about the crude sideshow advertisement for the Elephant Man. Transformation is likewise crucial to English pantomime. An obligatory part of the pantomime structure, the transformation scene is effected through the agency of a benevolent being (usually a fairy godmother), who causes Harlequin, Pantaloon, Columbine, and Clown to emerge from whatever superficial forms (for instance, the characters of *Puss in Boots*) have cloaked them in the opening story: In effect, then, the trivial and particular roles fall away to reveal the essential and eternal attributes underneath. As Faudree's *Elephant Man* proceeds, this stock pantomime device comes to be both subject and vehicle. Costumes are stripped off or added on with lightning speed. Period underwear combines with a grandly elaborate article or two to suggest, and simultaneously subvert, Victorian propriety. Characters are in dishabille when they should be (shaving, being examined by the doctor, playing Galatea) and when they should not (at lawn parties or balls). Toward the end of the play, the cross dressing that is a perennial feature of English panto crops up. The actress playing Mrs. Gomm (in Victorian bloomers) puts on Mr. Gomm's coat and hat to become "Gentleman" at a ball, while the actors who also play, among other parts, Jack the Orderly and Charles the Butler appear in evening gowns as "Lady Knightley" and "Lady." Perhaps the most surprising such reversal, though, comes with the *hikinuki* or "quick change" that ends the Kabuki-pantomime-within-a-play of *Beauty and the Beast*, as the wig and kimono of Beauty fall away. The transformation here is exceedingly complex. There are reversed expectations on the metalevel—we encounter a Western tale and theatrical form in Eastern drag. Within the story, the reversals are multiple: Beast is supposed to transform, not Beauty, and when a lady's kimono unexpectedly drops in Faudree's play we have been conditioned to expect Mrs. Kendal underneath— not Treves. If we adjust our expectations to accommodate the fact that Beauty somehow turns to Treves, then Beast should not turn to "a young [male] lover"—as in fact he does—and because the scene has started out in the province of theater, with Merrick watching from the same box seat that served as Mrs. Treves's vantage point on *Pygmalion and Galatea*, it certainly should not end as it does with Treves thrashing about among the discarded costumes as if awakening from a bad dream and Mrs. Treves entering with the line "Frederick, I was beginning to think you were going to sleep the entire day."

Corsets and kimonos falling off, lab coats and bowler hats going on—men becoming ladies, a lady becoming a gentleman, a statue becoming a beautiful woman, Beast becoming Prince, Beauty becoming Treves, panto becoming Kabuki, a public performance becoming a private nightmare, Nora-as-Torvald's-wife becoming Nora-her-own-woman with both Mrs. Kendal and Mrs. Treves becoming Nora—all this transformation occurring thick, fast, and reflexive suggests by contrast the one transformation that never happens in the play. Of all the costumes, only Merrick's never changes. He is always draped in black when onstage and is always offstage when his cloak and mask are seen to be off him (for instance, they are in Nurse Ireland's hands while Mrs. Kendal makes his acquaintance, and only his normal left hand is in view of the audience). In a play where clothes, loose and constricting alike, come off with such frequency, Merrick's continued concealment is sure to prove horridly suspenseful—as potent a device for manipulating the audience as is the occasional nudity of the other characters—but it is more than a mere *coup de théâtre*. In the Victorian England of Faudree's play, as in the last reminiscence of Treves's *Elephant Man*, identity may ultimately come down to "A Question of Hats"—but Merrick must be alone in not taking his off. Nevertheless, if he is not like the others (and us), they (and we) are like him. Merrick may die from his sleeping experiment, from "the pathetic but hopeless desire to be 'like other people.' " Yet, as the end of Faudree's play suggests, the Elephant Man survives in all his survivors: The last thing the audience sees is the entire cast assembled in a dance of death, or curtain call, of Elephant Men. *"There is complete silence for a few seconds and then a whirling sounds [sic] starts to gradually build and the lid to the coffin flies off and an individual in the Elephant Man garb emerges as the otherwise empty set becomes dimly lit. Another Elephant Man appears in the doorway to Merrick's room. Another Elephant Man is seen descending one set of stairs and then another Elephant Man is seen descending the other set of stairs. Three more Elephant Men appear through different doors and all seven gradually make their way towards the audience softly laughing or humming as they affectionately bump against one another. The stage fades to a blackout before they make it to the downstage edge of the stage."*

Because he mediates his account of Merrick's death, reporting on it after the fact through the words of Treves's reminiscence, Faudree is not obliged to speculate on whether the fatal event was accidental or intentional. Similarly, Gibbons' and Pomerance's dramatic choices are such that they need not take positions on the matter. In Gibbons' play, Merrick's death takes place between the third and fourth scenes. In Pomerance's, Merrick's agency is also beside the point. His last moments take place in a dream sequence as the Pinheads, a bizarre pair of Fates, chant their "Queens of the Cosmos" lullaby and lay him out, to "sleep like others" and so to die. What interests all three dramatists is not how Merrick died but how he stayed alive in others. As we have seen, Merrick's visitors in Pomerance's play all saw him as a mirror, reflecting their identities rather than projecting his own; and yet as the play concludes, Treves has subsumed the essential feature of that identity, Merrick's rare gift of insight. Gibbons' Treves, still haunted and pained by the loss of Merrick nearly a quarter of a century after his death, comes at the matter another way, though his thoughts, too, turn on what was or was not there to be seen: "Why did people turn away when they saw him? Could it have been, truly, that he was so hideous? Or did they see in him, without realizing it, a blinding beauty? A beauty so rare and radical that it must walk cloaked and masked?"[11] In Faudree's play that "beauty so rare and radical" may have remained cloaked and masked for the audience, but it will not stay in the coffin. The danse macabre that ends the play signifies the Elephant Man's endurance, not his death, and leaves members of the audience thinking not of his absolute otherness but of their likeness (in otherness) to him.

7

"If Only I Could Find Her"
David Lynch and Merrick's
Search for the Lost Mother

If a great many people first learned about Merrick (and Treves) from Pomerance's play, even more first encountered them in Lynch's film, which came out in 1979, during the play's Broadway run. The great popularity and near simultaneity of these two treatments make the act of comparing them almost irresistible, as does the film's explicit disclaimer of influence—and several interesting comparisons of the two works (among them, Bayles in *Harper's*, Kawin in *Film Quarterly*, and Holladay and Watt in *PMLA*) do exist.[1] We spend some time in this chapter discussing similarities and differences of these two works, but what seems a more important part of our task here is seeing how the film employs, and departs from, the two works on which it claims to be based, Treves's account and Montagu's study. Besides examining these matters of influence, we want to consider in what ways the conventions of cinema and the distinctive features of the director's own artistic vision have reshaped materials found in Treves and Montagu.

Through a prologuelike screen that announces indebtedness to Treves and Montagu, the film suggests that these works are matters of fact rather than interpretations, or even fictions in certain respects, as we have shown.[2] Nonetheless, the film diverges frequently and radically from the view of Merrick's life offered by Treves. The sequence of events is altered, as is the nature of each principal character's relationship with Merrick. What the film does take from Treves is its conception of Merrick, who is closer to the being depicted in the reminiscence than are any of the stage Merricks at whom we have been looking. Whether the film follows the Treves account or departs from it, though, should not be seen as a matter of good or bad faith with regard to sources. Instead, the particular choices involve fidelity to an imaginative vision of what Merrick's story signifies—a vision deriving in part from the idiosyncratic view of the director Lynch but also in part, as we show, from the theories of Montagu.

The most important alteration in the sequence of events involves the placing of Merrick's period of exhibition on the Continent. While in fact Merrick's time abroad preceded his coming to live at the hospital, in the film it follows his permanent establishment in the Bedstead Square rooms. The London has become his "home" in a physical sense (as evidenced by the set design stressing the comfortable, even luxurious, furnishings of the room, with such signs of human connection as expensively framed photographs on the mantel), an emotional one (besides having welcomed London's fashionables, he has become "friends" with Treves, with a Carr Gomm much more personally interested than the facts suggest, and with a head nurse, the not-so-subtly-named Mrs. Mothershead, who has been invented as the third in this caring trinity), and even a vocational one (here he has found, and proceeded a long way toward fulfilling, his life's work, the construction of a model of Saint Phillip's yet more elaborate and engrossing than any account has suggested). Any removal from such a settled home would be a wrenching one, but here the Continental exhibition is more degraded and brutal than anything suggested by any other account; and rather than going off with a manager, he here is reduced to a piece of property, a "treasure" stolen by Bytes, the same vicious, self-styled "owner" from whom Treves and Carr Gomm have previously rescued him.

The film's altered sequence of events suggests the difficulty of Merrick's escaping his role as Elephant Man. Even welcomed by the hospital and surrounded by the care of his adoptive family, he remains vulnerable to the brutal intrusions of exhibitors: first the night watchman who brings paying customers to gape at him, then the sadistic kidnapper Bytes. The altered timing, combined with the presence of Bytes as obvious external agent of Merrick's degradation, also simplifies or even erases the complex questions of how active Merrick was in arranging his own exhibition and whether Treves, having brought Merrick to the

London and presented him to the Pathological Society, should bear any responsibility for returning him to his former life of exhibition. The reordering of events both makes the return to exhibition more horrible and allows Merrick time to develop the personal strength to withstand the indignities and brutalities of his resumed status as Elephant Man. His arrival in London at Liverpool Station is thus very different from that of the reminiscence. Here he is no "shapeless bundle" connected to humanity only through Treves's card. Instead he is able to assert his identity to a crowd of pursuers, who have cornered him in the station urinals: "I am not an elephant! I am not an animal! I am a human being!"[3] Weak and frightened though he may be, the film's Merrick does not wait, objectlike, to be reclaimed by Treves; supported by a policeman, he walks back into the hospital, reentering his home on his own agency.

How Merrick is first established in that home involves other major revisions of the events as presented in Treves's reminiscence. Although in successive scenes Mrs. Kendal and the night watchman are seen reading from Carr Gomm's letter to the *Times*, the film detaches the issue of Merrick's permanent residence at the hospital from the administrator's public financial appeal. The trustees vote to keep Merrick not because a generous flow of public donations has made it possible but because Princess Alexandra, speaking for no less a figure than Victoria herself, personally encourages them in this charitable act. Merrick's acceptance also depends, as it does not in the reminiscence, on personal welcome from the people working at the hospital: Treves of course, but also Carr Gomm, Mothershead, and her nurses. His official installation accordingly gains a symbolic weight it lacks in the reminiscence. No mere medical exigency, it signifies his acceptance into a human community, an event made tangible by the presentation of the dressing case (here, the staff's generous idea rather than Merrick's whimsical request).

We have seen how the theater productions of Merrick's story circumvent, in their different ways, the problem of representing his physical deformity. In contrast, the film offers views of an uncloaked, unmasked, heavily made-up Elephant Man whose grotesquely misshapen face and body do not precisely conform to photographs of the actual Merrick but are remarkable approximations that, augmented by the acting skills of John Hurt, create an illusion of reality. The acting task is different from, but no less difficult than, that required by the title role of Pomerance's play. Encumbered with layers of makeup in the film, Merrick's face must *seem* expressionless, but in fact it must (particularly through the eyes) convey enough expression to lead the audience in the right emotional direction. Combining the talents of make-up artist and actor to create a physically credible, potentially expressive monster is a stock device of classic horror films, but from the first the originators of the Elephant Man film stressed its difference from that popular subgenre. Director David Lynch, speaking about Merrick's realistic representation, said, "He did look like this. People did go past that, and learn to love him. We think it can happen again"; and executive producer Stuart Cornfeld characterized the project as "a classic treatment[,] a question of fascination rather than horror."[4]

Cornfeld's protestations gloss over the potent connection between fascination and horror, a connection exploited by any successful horror film and brilliantly illustrated by the suspense leading up to our first view of the Elephant Man. After a short, dreamlike passage juxtaposing the photograph of a woman, various images of elephants, and assorted sinister noises of industrial and animal brutality (this footage presents an impressionistic rendition of Merrick's genesis as he understood it), we find ourselves in a sinister sideshow. Here, with Treves, we enter a door marked "No Entry" and proceed down into a netherworld peopled by freaks: bearded ladies, Siamese twins. Finally we encounter a bottled embryo labeled "Fruit of the Original Sin" and next to it a painted curtain with a crude depiction of the Elephant Man. But we get no closer to the actual Elephant Man: Police, who are in the process of closing the show as one that "degrades all who see it as well as the poor creature himself," turn Treves away. Our suspense increases with the frustrations of his quest.

Later, at the private view paid for by Treves, the film presents a shadowy back glimpse of Merrick as first described in Treves's reminiscence—the "hunched-up figure" embodying loneliness, the "captive in a cavern." But although the screenplay indicates that a head-on view of Merrick and a close-up of his face were originally to follow this partial revelation, the film instead cuts to a close-up of Treves's face, which sensitively registers the horror or compassion of seeing a sight we are denied.[5] Before being offered any further direct view of the Elephant Man's body, we see him cloaked and masked in several scenes and view his grossly twisted silhouette from behind an illuminated screen at the Pathological Society. Again denied the view direct, we instead scrutinize the bewildered and concerned faces of the medical men who are given it. Finally, when Carr Gomm's interception of Treves makes it necessary for an insufficiently prepared young nurse to go into Merrick's room, we briefly see his face from her point of view. Classic cinematic devices prepare for, yet delay, the encounter: Foreshadowing (the association of elephants and harm to women established in the film's opening mind screen), a manipulative soundtrack (ominous music on double basses and thumps like heartbeats), physical obstacles (a long flight of stairs leading to the isolation ward, just as steps earlier led down to the netherworld of freaks, and a closed door), and crosscutting (between the nurse's ascent and Treves and Carr Gomm's conversation) all tantalize the viewer. When the much-deferred moment of revelation arrives, it offers the surprise of mutual revulsion. As we expect, the nurse is horrified at the sight we are prepared to see but she is not; and, after cutting to her response, the camera offers its first sustained shot of Merrick, who is cowering on his bed, afraid of the nurse or ashamed of being seen. Her scream elicits from Carr Gomm, several flights below, an exclamation of "the Elephant Man!" In the portions of conversation that Lynch shares with his audience, Carr Gomm has not been directly informed that Merrick is Treves's mysterious patient, but according to horror convention, he has a sure sense of the monster's presence. Viewers familiar with the details of Merrick's story may be reminded of a phrase from the historical Carr Gomm's letter to the *Times*—"women and nervous persons fly from him in terror"—but for anyone, Carr Gomm's exclamation makes explicit an association of female scream and violent, monstrous presence insisted on in the opening montage of Merrick's mother and the violating elephant.

This association is, however, ironically inappropriate. The Merrick intruded upon by the young nurse, and by us, shrinks from view; and once our suspense about seeing Merrick is dispelled, there is nothing horrifying about his appearance. Having faced Merrick as he is, we accept him as a pathetic alien, not a frightening one. If anything, the film domesticates him too quickly. Within minutes he is transformed from semihuman freak to outlandish-looking but otherwise conventional specimen of Victorian gentility, from inarticulate, uncomprehending "imbecile" or "complete idiot" (words used by Treves in the film) to a respectable being whose speech, though impaired, marks him as a member of the class to which Treves and Carr Gomm belong. What is lost in this facile transformation that quickly moves Merrick further toward normality than his brave struggles ever took him is the powerful strangeness that caused D. G. Halsted, who as Treves's house surgeon attended Merrick every day, to confess, "I could never quite overcome a feeling of uneasiness in his presence." In spite of his medical training, Halsted did not find it so easy to "go past" Merrick's difference as Lynch would have his audience do. Learning to "love" Merrick is made much easier on film.

Why should this be so? It is partly because of the way love is understood here, a matter to which we later return. It is also partly because a black-and-white film containing graphic visual representation of Merrick's disorder may remind us, as Martha Bayles suggested, that his immediate problem was always somatic rather than social, but sight and sound on celluloid do not give us the experience of being there with Merrick. We do not smell him, or worry about how or whether to touch him; he is not always present, for the camera does not linger uncomfortably long but cuts away, and very often to images of squalor and cruelty that are far uglier than Merrick in his clean white shirt. Another partial reason may be that, as members of a late twentieth-century audience, we do not perceive the film's Merrick as an aberration among us; instead, he is a strange being in a strange milieu. Accurately represented historical details combine with Lynch's highly disconcerting personal vision to make his Victorian London as alien to us as is the weird urban world of his preceding film, *Eraserhead*, or the intergalactic setting of his subsequent one, *Dune*. And finally, offering compassion or companionship to the real Merrick, however gentrified his accent and clean his tailored clothes, would involve facing a severely disabled being struggling insofar as possible to be normal, whereas anyone watching the film encounters John Hurt as Merrick, an extraordinarily talented normal person whose struggle is to seem severely disabled.

In cultivating love rather than voyeuristic detachment, *The Elephant Man* is unlike other Lynch films. The successfully sympathetic nature of the film depends in great part on its connection not to other Lynch works but to a familiar Victorian genre; for as Lynch presents it, Merrick's story is not just his own, it is also a variant on the tale of the deserving orphan (or outcast) making his or her way in a hostile London milieu. Perhaps the most widely known of these stories is Charles Dickens' *Oliver Twist*, and the resemblances between this novel (one Merrick most certainly would have enjoyed) and the film's rendition of Merrick's life are remarkable. Dickens' protagonist, one recalls, is an orphan arbitrarily assigned his name in the workhouse where he was born. The film does not stress Merrick's years in the workhouse, but his identity as "Elephant Man" is just as casually conferred. Each protagonist finds himself in unsavory East End company, but each remains a "good boy" despite the devilish surrogate father who has taken him in. Oliver Twist's fiend is the sadistic, implicitly pederastic Fagin (a cartoon devil in his appearance, and appropriately associated with greasy cooking fires and a toasting fork). Merrick's analogous fiend is Bytes, even crueler to his "treasure" than is Fagin to his "dear" and fully alive, as his overacted facial expressions and intonations obviously reveal, to the fundamental connection between eroticism and freakishness so well explained by Leslie Fiedler.[6] (Like Fagin, Bytes is frequently posed beside a fire, but the implement he brandishes is always a stick, first his own and later the elegant walking stick given Merrick by society visitors.)

Both protagonists suffer at the hands of other brutal men, younger and less intelligent than the devil fathers (Sikes and the Night Porter, respectively); due in part to the agency of these secondary villains, Oliver and Merrick alike are recaptured by their exploiters before finally returning to their respective "homes." Acting as buffer between Fagin and Oliver, sometimes serving the former and sometimes standing up for the latter, is that engaging rogue the Artful Dodger. Similarly, Bytes' constant companion is a boy who imitates the exhibitor at the "private showing" for Treves but later, during the Belgian interlude, pleads for Merrick, only to share in the physical abuse. Throughout his ordeals and despite his workhouse origins, Oliver Twist speaks like a perfect gentleman, his superior speech being one way Dickens indicates both his spiritual status and his rightful social position. In the same unbelievable manner, once Merrick overcomes his fear of speaking to Treves and Carr Gomm, he employs genteel inflection, pronunciation, and diction rather than the less-refined accents and words of Bytes, his boy, and the East Enders. At Mr. Brownlow's house, Oliver is fascinated with a picture of a beautiful woman, who turns out to have been the mother who died at his birth. Lynch's camera consistently plays up Merrick's attachment to the pocket-sized likeness of his mother that he draws out and comments upon at tea with the Treveses and later brings to the attention of Mrs. Kendal. Both virtuous, mother-loving boys are saved by middle-class rescuers (Brownlow and Treves) and established in bourgeois comfort (at Pentonville and Bedstead Square). In both Oliver's case and Merrick's, the virtue ultimately rewarded is extraordinarily passive. Neither character is capable of wrongdoing, and neither is capable of self-sufficiency. In a world where resourcefulness is shown to be most often selfish, brutal, or both, Oliver and Merrick demonstrate their goodness by not acting. What J. Hillis Miller and George Orwell before him have observed of the Dickens world is equally true in the film *The Elephant Man*: A curse hangs over all positive action, and only the passive can be sure, as Lynch's Treves is not, that they are good.[7]

Playing opposite this sympathetic Elephant Man created from Lynch's filmic choices and the generic echoes is not the historical Treves but Anthony Hopkins as Treves—and he is yet more of a revision than the film's Merrick is. The film's Treves—small (scarcely taller than Merrick), self-doubting, emotional enough to be moved to tears by his first sight of the Elephant Man—is very different from the hearty, athletic, extroverted man of action remembered by Halsted, Grenfell, Bland-Sutton, and others and presented in the recent Trombley biography. The film's interpretation of Treves takes as its point of departure the 1960s television formula of the idealistic young hospital medico, more ambitious and earnest than his jocular peers, eager to please the fatherly hospital administrator. What results is a Dr. Kildare with two sorts of period modifications—a figure designed to represent certain features of 1880s medical practice as understood by the late 1970s. At the heart of the film's self-conscious, soul-searching characterization of Treves is a conflict between his self-serving scientific use of Merrick to further his career and his compassionate personal involvement with Merrick. The disgusting Bytes first highlights the exploitative side of Treves when the two men strike the deal that allows for Merrick's examination and exhibition at the hospital. "We understand each other. . . . We understand each other completely," Bytes says as, in a conspiratorial gesture that begins as a handshake but ends as a repulsive embrace, he draws Treves close to him with an intimacy most inappropriate to the difference in their social stations. The opportunistic quality of Treves's interest in Merrick emerges clearly during the examination preceding the Pathological Society meeting. When he has gotten Merrick up to his rooms, Treves begins tentatively, attempting to take a personal history but bewildered by the inexpressive Merrick. Just after Treves asks Merrick about his father and mother, questions that elicit a disturbed moan, Treves's colleague Fox interrupts by rapping on the door and poking his head in.[8] The subsequent brief interchange with Fox focuses on Merrick as a medical freak-hunter's "find"; and when Treves goes back to the interview, his scruples about approaching the balky patient have disappeared. "I think I'll examine you now," Treves says. "I'll leave the questions till later." The scene ends with the lifting of Merrick's hood, and the prominently stitched aperture through which Merrick has viewed this encounter serves as a visual transition to the eyelike spotlight focused on Merrick in the next scene as he stands before the Pathological Society.

Treves as clinical presenter is Treves at his most unsympathetic. By now accustomed to the Elephant Man's bizarre disorder but not yet conscious of Merrick's intelligence and gentleness, Treves here seems the callous professional who distances himself through the heavily moral language too often used to distinguish the sick from the healthy, as in, for instance, "at no time have I met with such a perverted or degraded version of a human being as this man." The staging of the medical presentation further emphasizes Treves's distance. He brings the meeting to order by rapping a pointer in a gesture reminiscent of Bytes and executes his intentions through assistants, who, at appropriate moments, help Merrick to turn round and later untie the loose knot securing his loincloth. We see this last action in silhouette as Treves comments on the "interesting side-note" of genitals that "remain entirely intact and unaffected." Here and elsewhere, Lynch has stressed the correspondence of diverse sorts of privileged viewing: sideshow gawking, surgical operation (which takes place in a "theater"), medical exhibition, and, in a reflexive way, filmmaking and -watching. The emphasized presence of the single-eyed light, with its suggestion of the movie camera (in fact, it is called a camera in the screenplay), implicates both Lynch and his audience, lest we smugly distinguish ourselves from Treves or from Merrick's other viewers.

We never again see Treves behave in this detached, exploitative

manner, but his use of Merrick becomes a matter of self-reproach later
in the film. Bytes, who has come into the hospital to reclaim his "treasure," asserts an essential likeness between himself and Treves: "You
think you're better than me? YOU wanted the freak to show to those
doctor friends of yours to make a name for yourself." Later Mothershead takes Treves to task for encouraging the stream of fashionable
visitors who, as she sees it, are no different from those who paid to see
Merrick in earlier days: "If you ask my opinion, he's only being stared
at all over again." In thus challenging Treves's authority, she steps out
of her place in the social and medical hierarchy and at the same time
seems "rather harsh" to Treves, who reminds her that she "hardly
showed him much loving kindness when he first arrived." Mothershead
defends herself, implicitly asserting an earned authority of her own, by
reminding Treves of her daily attention to Merrick's bodily needs: "I
bathed him, I fed him and I cleaned up after him, didn't I, and I made
sure my nurses did the same! If loving kindness can be called care and
practical concern, then I did show him loving kindness, and I'm not
ashamed to admit it." Her comments carry a particular weight because
the issue in Merrick's case is indeed one of care, not cure—the nurse's
province, not the surgeon's. This theme is clearly stated in the scene
directly following Treves and Mothershead's encounter. "Can you cure
me?" asks Merrick; and Treves must reply, "No, no. We can care for
you, but we can't cure you." Precisely because Mothershead has provided so much of Merrick's practical care, her implied rebuke disturbs
Treves. Like Bytes' less completely just assertion, it increases Treves's
self-doubt, the inner uncertainty that comes to the surface in a scene
culminating with his asking his wife, "Am I a good man or am I a bad
man?" Mrs. Treves, blessed with the sort of sensible certainty that
makes practical life possible, does what she can to allay his fears.

We like Anne Treves the better for her commonsensical kindness
(she has demonstrated it earlier in welcoming Merrick to her house—
spontaneously taking him by the hand, a gesture the historical Treves
scripted for the "young and pretty widow" in his reminiscence and the
Pomerance Treves planned for Mrs. Kendal). And if we have become
sympathetically engaged by the film, we like Treves the better for needing her comfort. The conventionally masculine, action-directed certainty likely to characterize any successful Victorian surgeon and especially notable in the historical Treves is a quality not meant to be

admired in this film, whose images persistently conflate power with force, violence, and oppression. Thus, from the first we see a Treves with dual potential—ambitious, competitive, able to get along in the Victorian world of men and yet questioning his actions, empathizing, staying in touch with his own feminine side, to put it in 1979 terms. As the film proceeds, we see increasingly less of Treves's professional side and more of his personal side. Thanks to the instrumentality, if not agency, of Merrick, Treves progressively becomes less the opportunist and more the altruist, less the manly surgeon and more the mother.

Indeed the film might be seen as a demonstration of Montagu's proposition that the next best thing to being a mother is to act like one. Treves is but one of the film's metaphorical mothers. Despite her name, Mrs. Mothershead does not seem particularly maternal in the early segments of the film; instead, in a way parallel to Treves's conversion, her care and responsibility for Merrick make her worthy of her name. We first see her, primly and rigidly self-contained, presiding over the turmoil of the receiving room on the day of Merrick's first visit to the London. She pays little attention to the distress around her and regards the cloaked Merrick rather as a threat to good order than a mysteriously suffering human being in need. Here, and in her other early appearances with Merrick, she plays clearly the role of adjunct to the physician, impatiently seconding Treves's request to Merrick—"Will you come with me, please"—with her echo of his authority: "You heard what the doctor said. . . . Go on." Later, in Merrick's room, she tells Treves that all such patients understand is a "good smack" and asks, "Honestly, sir, what can you do for him?"—thus implying that Treves should give his time to those he can benefit. In short, she combines a certain desensitized quality—perhaps forced on her by the exigencies of her position—with an acceptance of the institution's distinctions between those who are worthy of treatment and those who are not.

The care of Merrick, however, brings significant change in Mothershead. As we have seen, she earns the right, and perhaps gains the confidence, to speak in her own voice, challenging Treves's decision to encourage the flow of upper-class visitors to Merrick's room. She thus defends her patient against the fascinated, yet secretly (sometimes even not so secretly) disgusted gaze of the detached, those who have no personal engagement with Merrick. She plays this role to the end, glowering disapprovingly as the patrons of Drury Lane rise at Mrs.

Kendal's request to salute Merrick with applause at the close of his visit
to the theater. The change in Mrs. Mothershead's relationship to Merrick is signaled by her participation, with Carr Gomm and Treves, in
welcoming Merrick officially into his home and, with Treves, in discovering his absence after the kidnapping by Bytes. Our sense of her
deeply felt connection to Merrick lies behind the satisfaction we feel at
seeing her "sack" the Night Porter, announcing his dismissal with a
blow to the head that renders him unconscious. Finally, it is Mothershead who rushes through the hospital corridors announcing the return of the wandering son when Merrick reenters the London after his
escape from the Continent and difficult journey back to England. All
these images confirm Mothershead's achievement of the status pre-
dicted for her by her name: Through the care of Merrick she has moved
from being the somewhat disinterested guardian of the hospital's official order to a passionately concerned defender and comforter of her
"lad. "

The hospital's official order receives its most passionate defense
from Mr. Broadneck of the governing committee, who finds himself opposed by yet another of the film's mothers, Queen Victoria, mother to
the empire. The issue is Merrick's fitness to be a patient at the London,
a general hospital not intended for the care of incurables. At a meeting
of the committee, Broadneck opposes Carr Gomm's request for autho-
rization to keep Merrick at the London with two powerful objections:
first, that it is inappropriate for the hospital to subvene "competitive
freak-hunting" by ambitious doctors concerned with building personal
reputations; and second, that the hospital's resources are better spent
on treating curable patients than on caring for Merrick, who should be
placed in one of the established institutions for incurables. The film
fails to give adequate attention to these potentially serious arguments,
opting instead to gratify its audience through the humiliation of Broadneck. Princess Alexandra makes a royal entrance into the governors'
meeting, is seated, and reads a letter from Victoria commending the
committee "for the charitable face" it has shown in providing "one of
England's most unfortunate sons with a safe and tranquil harbor, a
home." The Princess concludes by masterfully circumscribing the
committee's alternatives: "I am sure I can count on you gentlemen to do
the Christian thing. " As the scene has earlier been punctuated by a cut
to Merrick's room, where we see him working on his cathedral, Alex-

andra's word "Christian" receives a particular emphasis. The effect, made visible elsewhere by a rather elephantine portrait of Victoria displayed in one of the wards, is to conflate church and hospital with the benevolent action of the nation's matriarch concerned about the last and least of her sons, Merrick.

Of course the film's most prominent mother is Merrick's own. The abstract dream that opens the film begins with a lingering close-up of her miniature portrait, with special attention to her mouth, followed by a dissolve to a brutal rendering of Merrick's "conception": a close-up of his mother, her face shadowed; images of elephant ears, trunks, and faces accompanied by trumpeting and the pounding of dark, heavy feet; the mother receiving a powerful hit, falling, and screaming. Explicit enough even in the film, the odious sexual overtones of the scene are even more apparent in the screenplay, where the directions call for the elephant's trunk to "slide over Mother's face and breasts and stomach, leaving a moist trail." This introductory sequence establishes an important association repeated and varied throughout the film, where male violence blends into the powerful energies of the industrialized city-jungle, suggested through images and sounds of steam as well as shots of the surreal tangle of pipe and duct work needed to sustain the city's life. The screenplay interestingly implies that even the carnival music itself poses a threat to women. Although they are not present in the film's opening tour through the carnival, Anne Treves and her two daughters do accompany Frederick in the screenplay version. As Anne and the girls come into view, the directions suggest the calliope music's dangerous power: "The shrill, over-whelming music seems to engulf her. She looks discomfited, vulnerable, and protective of her daughters."[9]

Scenes such as the one described above richly evoke a sinister milieu surrounding its protagonist, a foul urban soup of smells, sounds, sights, and people from which the gentle, childlike Merrick clearly deserves to be rescued by some foster mother or another. The film portrays this world through details closely corresponding to images from Treves's other reminiscences collected with "The Elephant Man," most notably "The Old Receiving Room." For instance, just after the off-duty Treves has been turned away from the Elephant Man exhibit, the camera offers a scene of Treves on the job, attending the hideously maimed victim of an industrial accident. Here, besides showing a grisly spectacle just after Treves and the audience have been denied one, the camera graphically evokes the state of medicine in the late nineteenth century. We are given a view of a coal fire heating cauterizing irons (a visual transition from the sideshow scene, and a striking parallel with the flame that began that earlier scene), then the grim furnishings of the operating room: a black leather table, like the one in "The Old Receiving Room," also "a large sink, a cupboard containing dressings, gags, manacles, emetics, and other unattractive things."[10] Amid these surroundings, Treves, assisted by his colleague Fox, is operating on a chloroformed patient whose legs are restrained by ropes held tight by medical students, while antiseptics are sprayed as if from miniature fire hoses. "Abominable things these machines. You can't reason with them," remarks Treves. True enough—though shortly afterward, in another scene with Fox, he will similarly (and wrongly) dismiss that organic abomination the Elephant Man as similarly devoid of rational potential. In the operating scene as in others less directly connected with the principal characters of the stories (clips of violently brawling prostitutes, half-naked industrial workers monotonously ministering to the needs of their untiring machines, sufferers and spectators crowding the receiving room), the film evokes, in images closely allied to those of Treves's writing, a cruel and irrational environment whose workings are sometimes echoed and sometimes contradicted in the smaller world of Merrick and the people surrounding him.

The urban menace so clearly discernible throughout the film comes as much from sounds as from sights. The discomfiting use of engulfing music and sound is a hallmark of *The Elephant Man*, as well as of other films by David Lynch. The opening minutes of the film establish a powerful sequence of sounds: waltz music, to be heard again during the cruel scenes of Merrick's taunting by the Night Porter and those he brings to Bedstead Square; the throbbing of a heartbeat, used as accompaniment to the shots of Merrick's mother's picture; a chaotic blend of elephant trumpeting, foot pounding, and the rhythmic pulsing of industrialized noise; the explosion of steam from the calliope and the raucous music of the carnival. Later in the film Lynch returns to some of these sounds to create his most sinister effects. The pressure of mindless industrial humming, for instance, accompanies the Night Porter's first approach to Merrick as we see him walking down a long, darkened hall lit only by gas lamps. That constant pressing background roar is sharply and distinctly broken by the metallic sound of

his boots as they strike the hall floor, a crisp striking that blends with
the earlier rapping of Bytes' cane as he calls his audience to attention
and with Treves's tapping of the pointer in his own exhibition of Merrick. The screenplay is even more explicit than the film about the association of the menacing maleness of the Night Porter with that of the
original violating elephant and the equally monstrous industrial city.
In the play, the Night Porter rapes a woman in traction (her image recalling the victim of industrial accident, gagged and restrained by
ropes, on whom Treves operates in an earlier scene) immediately before
proceeding to Merrick's room. The language of the directions stresses
the shadowing and engulfment associated earlier with the violation of
Merrick's mother and the music's threat to Anne Treves: "The Night
Porter moves to her, his shadow engulfing her." To conclude the effect,
the screenplay calls for a cut from the Night Porter's moving in on his
victim to the opening of a door in another hallway, accompanied by a
squeaking sound "vaguely like the trumpeting of an elephant." This
was to be followed again by the metallic footfalls of the Night Porter,
moving this time toward Merrick.[11]

Lynch uses many of the same obsessive images and sounds to signal the change in Treves from the detached, exploitative self-promoter
to the compassionate, self-critical care giver. He does this by means of
a double dream sequence, perhaps suggestive of a larger collective
dream, involving Merrick and Treves. After Mrs. Mothershead has
taken Treves to task for exposing Merrick to his visitors, there is a brief
shot of Merrick's apparently seeing his own reflection in the window.
Following Merrick's view of himself as he is seen by others, we are
privileged to enter his inner world, which we do by going through the
single eye of his traveling mask. The sequence that follows begins with
a tour through an underworld of seemingly endless pipes, a journey
accompanied by the sound of bells and trumpeting. Next, images from
the dream of Merrick's mother's violation merge into shots of mindless-
looking men pushing heavy machines in a rhythmic repetitive motion.
Then, after the slow-motion approach of a sinister man carrying a mirror, sequential images of an elephant, of Merrick's face, and finally of
clouds lead us to a shot of Anne going downstairs to find Treves, sleep-
less in his dressing gown, as if himself struggling with a nightmare. At
this moment, Treves breaks into agonized self-reflection on his motives
for rescuing Merrick, reflection culminating in the question about his

essential moral worth discussed above, "Am I a good man or am I a bad man?" The cumulative effect of Lynch's imagery and sound has been to establish the male quality of the violent world that threatens and victimizes Merrick. Treves's awakened questioning indicates his movement away from the collective fantasy of power and domination in which he has participated.

The gendering of the world in *The Elephant Man* strikingly parallels the broad patterns of Montagu's thought. The film's male world of power and violence is rooted in the separation of intelligence from fellow feeling, a separation that results in the dehumanizing products of technical intelligence, on the one hand, and the fury of repressed passion on the other. The violating elephant is simply the dark side of the dream of a thoroughly rationalized industrial civilization. In the film, as for Montagu, maternal love provides the basis for healthy personality development within this otherwise nightmarish world and perhaps also the principle of a better social order. We see such love evinced by Mrs. Mothershead; by Princess Alexandra and through her, by Queen Victoria; and by Treves as he comes to question his distancing, intellectual approach to Merrick and relies more fully on their fellow feeling. Merrick himself cherishes the picture of his mother—which figures so importantly in Montagu's account of his personality—and defines his own search for happiness in terms of "finding" her. In a scene at Treves's home, he shares, for the first time, his mother's likeness, after being shown family pictures from the Treves's mantel. Prompted by trust in Anne Treves, Merrick asks, "Would you . . . would you care to see my mother?"—a question that brings amazed unbelief from Treves, for Merrick has revealed to Anne on their first meeting what he has hitherto concealed from his physician. After Anne remarks on Mrs. Merrick's beauty, Merrick offers his understanding of the curiosity of his own misshapenness: "I must have been a great disappointment to her." Anne, acting as a maternal substitute, speaks for Mrs. Merrick, reassuring John: "No, Mr. Merrick. No. No son as loving as you are could ever be a disappointment." But Merrick is not yet convinced, as he will be later, that he is loved: "If only I could find her. If she could see me with such lovely kind friends, here now, perhaps she could love me as I am. I've tried so hard to be good."

Merrick's finding the unconditional acceptance of a maternal love— the confirmation that others love him as he is—provides much of the psychological action of the film's latter part. Here Anne Treves plays a role in providing Merrick the self-confirmation he needs. Moved by his touching expression of love for his mother, she begins to cry, lapsing into inarticulate emotion just as Merrick had done at the start of the scene. Merrick then reaches toward her with a handkerchief. The gesture is loving but not erotic. It fits in with the idealized mother-child relation just established but also serves as Merrick's first (and only) chance to behave toward a woman as any adult male might.[12]

Merrick is similarly loving but essentially childlike in the film's representation of his relationship to Mrs. Kendal. In his one scene with the actress, Lynch's Merrick displays none of the suggestive verbal facility of his counterpart in Pomerance's play. Instead he remains passive and extraordinarily innocent, asking Mrs. Kendal, for instance, about her involvement in the theater:

> *Merrick:* Mr. Treves tells me that you're in the theater. Do you live there?
> *Kendal:* Oh no, Mr. Merrick. I just work there.

In one of the film's remarkable similarities to Pomerance's play, the scene depends, in part, for its structure on allusion to *Romeo and Juliet*. But here Merrick does not read himself against the text, becoming a true hero of love by renouncing Romeo's self-destructive anger. Instead he remains voiceless, confined to Romeo's words from the "passionate pilgrim" interchange with Juliet. With Mrs. Kendal speaking Juliet's lines, the effect of the scene is to suggest Merrick's sublimation of desire into prayer and her effort to provide him confirmation, the assurance of his worthiness. Opening at random Mrs. Kendal's gift of an exquisite Shakespeare, almost as someone with his evangelical upbringing might open the Bible for a text of special personal application, Merrick begins, saying "I've heard of this" (despite his earlier saying he has not read Shakespeare):

> If I profane with my unworthiest hand,
> This holy shrine, the gentle fine is this:
> My lips, two blushing pilgrims, ready stand,
> To smooth that rough touch with a tender kiss.

Perhaps startled by the implication of these words, Merrick begins to close the book, "embarrassed," as the screenplay puts it. But Mrs.

Kendal picks up the thread, transforming Merrick into pilgrim and holy palmer at once:

> Good pilgrim, you do wrong your hand too much,
> Which mannerly devotion shows in this;
> For saints have hands that pilgrims hands do touch,
> And palm to palm is holy palmer's kiss.

Merrick and Mrs. Kendal play out the rest of the interchange, which turns artfully on the relation between kisses and prayers:

> *Merrick:* O, then, dear saint, let lips do what hands do.
> They pray, grant thou, lest faith turn to despair.
> *Kendal:* Saints do not move though grant for prayer's sake.
> *Merrick:* Then move not while thy prayer's effect I take.
> Thus from my lips by thine my sin is purged.

Whatever erotic potential Mrs. Kendal may have suggested to Merrick has by this point been utterly transformed into a diffuse feeling for the holy. Mrs. Kendal closes their play by placing a chaste kiss on Merrick's cheek and conferring on him a new identity: "Oh, Mr. Merrick, you're not an Elephant Man at all . . . no, you're Romeo." Her line receives a significant echo later in the film when Merrick is cornered by the crowd in the public restroom of the London train station. In facing down the crowd, Merrick repeats the language of Mrs. Kendal: "I am not an elephant! I am not an animal! I am a human being!" Thus the film links Mrs. Kendal's confirmation of Merrick's worth with his own self-affirmation.

And thus Mrs. Kendal plays an essentially maternal role in relation to Merrick, a point the film signals visually through its use of her picture. Her first gift to Merrick is her picture, which he declares "beautiful," using language identical to that he uses to describe his mother. Merrick gives it, in his own words, "a place of honor . . . next to my mother." When Merrick lies down to die, the camera focuses on the pictures of Mrs. Kendal and Merrick's mother together on his bedside table—that of Mrs. Kendal being actually the more prominent and closer to the bed. After the film moves into a final dream sequence, culminating in Merrick's mother's whispering reassuringly "nothing will die," the camera returns to focus on the table, leading our eyes through the picture of Mrs. Kendal to that of the mother. The effect conflates the two women, suggesting that Merrick has found his mother in Mrs. Kendal and that her acceptance of him has been critical to his receiving the ultimate confirmation that closes the film—spoken by his mother in the dream to which we return: "Nothing will die."

Mrs. Kendal orchestrates the climactic moment of Merrick's public recognition when she dedicates the performance at Drury Lane to him, prompting the fashionable audience to rise in applause. The moment would be unendurable (it is nearly so anyway) if it were meant to suggest the gracious bestowal of an acceptance essential to Merrick's self-worth. Merrick would again be on display, his identity conferred by his viewers, his story scripted by his exhibitors. What saves the scene is our already understanding the fullness of Merrick's own self-acceptance, a point clarified by his telling Treves as they dress for the theater: "I am happy every hour of the day—my life is full because I know that I am loved. I've gained myself. I could not say that were it not for you." Nowhere is Montagu's central influence on the film any more apparent. Merrick has arrived at the knowledge Montagu considers necessary for the development of mature, healthy personality, the knowledge that he is loved. Treves—even more than Mrs. Mothershead, Anne, or Mrs. Kendal—has assisted Merrick in completing the search for his mother he has spoken of earlier: "If only I could find her." Although unable to cure his patient, Treves's care has been vitally effective in bringing about Merrick's well-being. Treves has done what Montagu considers the "next best thing" to being a mother: He has behaved like one.

Realizing he is loved sets Merrick free for death. By placing Merrick's death immediately after his night at the theater, the film presents it as the final crescendo of a rising series of triumphs. We learn of Merrick's impending death from a conversation between Mrs. Mothershead and one of her nurses as they dress for the theater. How much Merrick knows of his own prognosis is unclear, but he has long understood that his condition is incurable. In successive scenes, then, Merrick effectively completes his relationship with Treves, thanking his friend for helping him to know that he is loved; fulfills a long-standing desire to visit the theater (a bit badly reminiscent of the "last wish" cliché of dying children nowadays); and receives the applause of the Drury Lane patrons. On returning to the hospital, he bids farewell to Treves and then, alone in his room, signs his model of the cathedral, bringing it to completion with an "it is finished." The film stresses the careful, unhurried deliberation of his preparation for bed. He removes the pillows, stacking them neatly, and then lies down in the bed. Clearly the film is indebted here to the historical Treves's surmise that, on what he recalls as the night of Merrick's death, he had made the "experiment" of trying to sleep like other people. We have been well prepared for Merrick's lying down in bed by the camera's repeated attention to a picture hanging in his room, a picture of a child sleeping peacefully in bed. One cut to this picture has come at an especially noteworthy moment: just before Treves answers negatively to Merrick's asking if he can be cured. The film's handling of this picture, together with the sequencing of events on the last night of Merrick's life, suggests that Merrick is attempting something more intentional than an "experiment" when he lies down in bed. Yet it would be a mistake to call Merrick's act suicide, for here there is no willful rejection of the gift of life. Merrick has lived his life in response to a bodily reality beyond his control; now he simply lets that bodily reality run its course. He can do this because his bodily condition no longer determines who he is; loved by others, he is truly no longer an Elephant Man. Merrick's lying down in bed poses a nice problem for medical ethicists used to distinguishing between extraordinary and ordinary means of treatment. Merrick has always sustained his life by the extraordinary (or in medical parlance "heroic") means of sleeping sitting up; his life comes to an end as he adopts the ordinary means of sleeping lying down like the rest of us.

The film's rendition of Merrick's death is without violence or struggle. The effect is one of peaceful, childlike slumber, an effect accentuated by the rather leisurely pacing of the dream sequence, the loving close-ups of Mrs. Kendal's and Merrick's mother's pictures, and the calm softness of Mrs. Merrick's voice continuing her affirmation of life after the images of elephants have disappeared. In one last visual tribute to the guiding spirit of Montagu, the camera focuses briefly during these last moments on a picture directly above Merrick's bed, the representation of a woman standing next to a sheep, her hand on its neck. The image recalls Merrick's earlier standing by his bed and reciting the Twenty-third Psalm, the act that makes possible his permanent stay in the hospital. The picture above the bed suggests that the Lord who shepherds Merrick through the valley of the shadow, who promises life and acceptance, is a woman, a mother. This is the gospel according to Montagu.

And, lest we miss the allusive good news, Lynch calls our attention to the book (if not the chapter and verse) in a screen following the film's credits: "This has been based upon the true life story of John Merrick, known as the Elephant Man, and not upon the Broadway play of the same title or any other fictional account." This passage is interesting both for what it does and for what it leaves undone. Acknowledgment of indebtedness to Treves and Montagu is one purpose—but in fact that has already been accomplished in the screen following the film's title: "Based on *The Elephant Man and Other Reminiscences* by Sir Frederick Treves and in part on *The Elephant Man: A Study in Human Dignity* by Ashley Montagu." Denial of indebtedness to Pomerance is a more pressing purpose, and here the motive seems to be partly unique and partly typical. Pomerance and the film's producers had engaged in a highly publicized legal battle over proprietary use of *The Elephant Man* as a title, and this dispute may have spurred Lynch's explicit distinction between his film and Pomerance's "fictional account." But the words also imply the privileging of two potential sources over the other one. The assumption seems to be that Montagu and Treves offer fact but that Pomerance offers a rival fictional account—and further that borrowings from the play would signal an undesirable deficiency of imaginative vision rather than a desirable, even necessary, groundwork for imaginative interpretation. As we have seen, though, Treves, Montagu, and Pomerance are all interpreters, all word artists (to different degrees and for different reasons, of course). And thus the framing of Lynch's film in words on a screen is highly appropriate, an enactment of a deep truth about sources. Even this account of Merrick's story— the version where articulated ideas figure least and sights, sounds, and visceral responses figure most—cannot get beyond words and the fictions they inevitably construct. Merrick's bodily reality was one thing; but the physical presence Lynch's camera offers us is something else: something partly made from, and bent by, preexisting words and something that calls forth subsequent words.[13]

Facts Excavated and Fictions Diffused
Merrick in the 1980s

Scholarly and imaginative reflection on the life of Joseph Merrick entered a new phase with the publication in 1980 of *The True History of the Elephant Man*, by physician Michael Howell and free-lance writer Peter Ford. The book's title makes a large claim, promising neither a reminiscence like Treves's nor a study like Montagu's. Instead Howell and Ford's book is to be something like a definitive account, a history of Merrick's life based on objective data rather than subjective impression, on facts rather than fanciful theorizing. Because it makes such a claim, *The True History of the Elephant Man* has become a kind of essential text for all those who find themselves moved to reflect on or write about Joseph Merrick. All the recent treatments we consider in this chapter have approached their subject through Howell and Ford: the biography of Treves by Stephen Trombley, the poetry of Kenneth Sherman, the rediagnosis of Merrick by Drs. J. A. R. Tibbles and M. M. Cohen, Jr., the children's books of Frederick Drimmer and of Howell and Ford themselves. All future work will similarly have to engage Howell and Ford, for they have, in effect, asserted that theirs is a telling of Merrick's story superior to all others.

Howell and Ford do make available a substantial body of factual information about Merrick's life. They correct Treves and Montagu on the important matter of Merrick's Christian name, establishing it, on the basis of a birth certificate, as Joseph Carey Merrick. They definitively establish Merrick's birth date as August 5, 1862, and restore to him his parents, Joseph Rockley Merrick and Mary Jane Merrick, née Potterton, married in the parish church of Thurmaston on December 29, 1861. Possibly important to Joseph's medical history is the fact that Mary Jane Merrick also seems to have been crippled. Joseph Rockley Merrick's family had originally been agricultural laborers before migrating to Leicester for employment in the hosiery industry. Joseph Rockley Merrick worked for a time as the driver of a brougham and described himself on his son's birth certificate as a warehouseman. Later he classified himself as "engine driver at the cotton factory" and became proprietor of a haberdashery shop, managed by his wife. Mary Jane Merrick's parents were also country folk who moved to Thurmaston, a village just north of Leicester, when she was about seven. At the age of twelve, about 1848, she became a servant to a family in Leicester, where she remained in service until her marriage thirteen years later. She and Joseph Rockley Merrick had two children in addition to Joseph. A son, William Arthur, was born on January 8, 1866. He died of scarlet fever on December 21, 1870. The couple's last child was Marion Eliza Merrick, born September 28, 1867.[1]

Especially important is Howell and Ford's redemption of Mary Jane Merrick from Treves's damning portrayal of Merrick's "worthless" and "inhuman" mother. She did not abandon her child to the workhouse; instead she cared for Joseph, as well as for two other children and a haberdashery shop, until her death from bronchopneumonia on May 19, 1873. Thus Joseph was nearly eleven years old when she died, and his memories of her were no doubt quite real. Mary Jane Merrick probably inspired Joseph's interest in the Bible, for she taught in one of the three Baptist Sunday schools in Leicester. Her strong Baptist commitment is reflected in her giving Joseph the middle name of Carey, after Willam Carey (1761–1834), a leading preacher and missionary who was responsible for establishing the strong Baptist ministry in Leicester. Howell and Ford simply do not have enough source material to establish anything like a portrait of Mary Jane's personality, but they do offer one affecting detail. The death certificate for her little son William "bears mute witness to the devastation she felt at losing him." Although Mary Jane Merrick "had signed her name so confidently on her own marriage certificate and on each of the birth certificates of her children," she could "manage no more than a cross" when it came to signing the death certificate of her son (53).

On reading Howell and Ford's account of Merrick's mother, Montagu must have felt at least partially vindicated in his theory of the importance of maternal love to Joseph's mature personality development. Joseph does seem to have received the love of a nurturing mother through much of his childhood, and his later cherishing of her portrait may very well have helped to sustain him. On the other hand, Howell and Ford's work makes some other features of Montagu's theorizing seem even more outlandish. Montagu suggests that the absence of a father may have been a positive benefit to Joseph, for he would thus be free of tyrannical paternal influence and his mother could devote most of her time to him. With her other children and her management of the haberdashery, however, Mary Jane Merrick probably had little available time to give to Joseph. Moreover, Joseph Rockley Merrick was not an absent, but a stubbornly present, father. He lived with Mary Jane Merrick and their children until her death in 1873 and then found care for Joseph and Marion Eliza with their landlady, Mrs. Emma Wood Antill, later marrying Mrs. Antill on December 3, 1874. Under pressure from his new wife, Joseph Rockley Merrick does seem to have rejected young Joseph and perhaps played the role of the tyrannical father in thrashing him. Still he also seems to have gone in search of Joseph on two occasions when the boy ran away, and he sought to help his crippled son to secure employment by obtaining for him a hawker's license and supplying him with goods from the haberdashery to peddle about the streets. Thus the facts of Joseph's relationships with his family are both more ordinary and more complex than either Treves's dismissal of the parents or Montagu's theorizing about gender and love would suggest.[2]

Howell and Ford also provide important correctives to Treves and Montagu on Joseph's work history as an adolescent, his time in the workhouse, and his career as an exhibition. Joseph apparently attended school until the age of twelve, at which time he was expected to contribute to the household economy. He worked for about two years in a cigar factory until the progressive deformation of his right arm made it impossible for him to hand roll the cigars. After an extended period of unemployment, he then took to peddling his father's goods door to door.

His degree of success in this most difficult occupation failed to satisfy his father and stepmother, and, after one particularly painful thrashing, he left home for the streets of Leicester. Soon thereafter Joseph began living with the family of his uncle, Charles Barnabus Merrick, hairdresser, tobacconist, and umbrella repairer. Joseph continued to hawk haberdashery for the next two years but was denied a renewal of his hawker's license when it expired. Late in 1879, Joseph realized he was becoming an excessive burden on his aunt and uncle, who were expecting another child. "On the first Monday after Christmas 1879," Joseph "presented himself to Mr. William Cartwright," one of the relieving officers for the parishes of Leicester Union, "demonstrating his deformities and pleading an inability to work."[3] He was admitted to the Leicester Union Workhouse that day.

Merrick was not in the workhouse from his earliest childhood, as Treves believed; nor was he repeatedly shuttled back and forth from workhouse to hospital by the authorities, as Montagu suggests. Merrick signed himself out on March 22, 1880—after about twelve weeks' residence—in order to look for work, but after two days of unsuccessful effort, he again returned to picking oakum at the mercy of the parish. He also made at least one trip to the Leicester Infirmary, probably in 1882, where he underwent successful surgery for the removal of part of the trunklike growth on his face, an experience he referred to some years later in the autobiographical pamphlet sold at his exhibition.[4] Joseph did, then, venture out of the workhouse on at least two occasions, but there is little in Howell and Ford's account to suggest Joseph's being tossed back and forth by the authorities in the manner Montagu depicts. Indeed, given the grinding reality of the workhouse as Howell and Ford present it, Joseph would probably have welcomed more journeys to the infirmary.

Doubtless simply from lack of evidence, Howell and Ford are somewhat vague about how Joseph first came to have the idea of going on public exhibition as a freak. What they do make clear is that he initiated contact with Mr. Sam Torr, a star of the British music halls who opened in 1883 a Gaiety Palace of Varieties in Leicester. Mr. Torr organized a syndicate with four fellow managers to stage Joseph's exhibition about the country, and on August 29, 1884, Joseph was able to sign himself out of the workhouse forever. Joseph's debut was at Nottingham in The Living, a music hall managed by a Mr. J. Ellis. He then made a couple of appearances, including one in Leicester, before heading to London for the winter season and the management of Tom Norman.[5] Howell and Ford modify substantially the image of Merrick's manager's cruelty created by Treves and developed by Pomerance's play and Lynch's film. Without minimizing the agony of life on exhibition or ignoring the fact "that living in close proximity to Joseph must have imposed its peculiar limitations and tensions" (83), Howell and Ford suggest that Norman and his fellow managers were probably more concerned for Joseph's welfare than other accounts have allowed. On this subject, they quote Norman's unpublished autobiography directly: "I can honestly state as far as his comfort was concerned whilst with us, no parent could have studied their child more than any or all the four of us studied Joseph Meyrick's. . . . The big majority of showmen are in the habit of treating their novelties as human beings, and in a large number of cases, as one of their own, and not like beasts" (83).

It is perhaps impossible to know how much Norman is involved in special pleading. One thing is clear, however: that Joseph's managers at least acted in his financial interest. The fifty pounds he was able to accumulate during twenty-two months of exhibition represented a substantial nest egg in a time when a whole family's income might be no more than a pound a week. Joseph was undoubtedly better off financially than ever before, but social toleration for the freak shops in London was diminishing. As the police and magistrates became more determined in their opposition, Joseph's value as an attraction declined. Thus he set off with his Austrian manager for the tour of Europe that was a failure from the start. Howell and Ford place his abandonment and robbery by the manager at Brussels in early June 1886, and they add interesting speculation to the nature of his journey from Belgium back to London. Howell and Ford suggest that Joseph made his way to Ostend in hopes of taking the packet service to Dover and that it was at Ostend that Joseph was refused passage by the captain of the cross-channel ferry. That Joseph was at Ostend seems certain, for Howell and Ford have unearthed a letter referring to the Elephant Man by a Mr. Wardell Cardew, written to W. H. Kendal, the husband of Mrs. Kendal, and saying, "I have had the most awful case in my care at Ostend" (87). Perhaps Cardew suggested to Joseph that he make his way to Antwerp, where he could use the daily packet service into Har-

wich and take the train from there into Liverpool Station. Such is the
route Howell and Ford believe Joseph took.[6]

Howell and Ford's most significant contribution to Joseph's "true
history" lies in their account of his life from birth until his arrival at
Liverpool Station. They add helpful details about a variety of other
matters that help to fill in the contexts for understanding his life: conditions in the East End of London, the nature of the fairs and freak
shows, the routine of daily existence in the workhouse. At times, however, these contextual details seem excessive or peripheral, as in the
seven pages devoted to a history of George Wombwell's traveling fair,
which, as Howell and Ford are at pains to show, was in Leicester in May
1862. As the fair did include elephants, and these were allowed to
"move ponderously through the streets" at midday as a kind of "impressive walking advertisement" (49), it is possible that a pregnant
Mary Jane Merrick, stumbling perhaps in the crush of the crowd, could
have fallen in the path of one of the great beasts, although, as Howell
and Ford point out, the reports of the local press for May 1862 include
no account of such an incident. What makes Howell and Ford's lavish
attention to the whole matter most curious is that they have already
discounted as "medical folk-belief" and "superstition" (20) Merrick's
attributing his deformity to his pregnant mother's being knocked down
by an elephant.

The mixed nature of Howell and Ford's enterprise becomes apparent in their taking such great pains, on the one hand, to establish the
possibility of an event, while, on the other hand, declaring it to be
without explanatory value for their central subject. Surely such attention to the stuff of legend must seem inconsistent with "true history,"
conceived as a record of objectively established data organized with a
view toward establishing causal relations between events. This does
seem, for the most part, the way Howell and Ford conceive of their own
history. In discussing Treves's reminiscence, for instance, they are
careful to categorize it "as a powerful and unforgettable *literary* achievement" (emphasis ours). Their sense of its literary quality emerges in
the comment that "it may rest a little heavily on melodrama, but it
remains as highly readable as when it was written, and fully deserves
to be read." Here Howell and Ford are implicitly distinguishing their
own work from Treves's. What makes a literary work deserving of con-

tinued reading is its readability, its ability to somehow grasp and involve audiences. What makes history worth reading is its truth. The
distinction between Treves's work and their own becomes even more
obvious as Howell and Ford continue their discussion of Treves's reminiscence: "It raises incidental questions about the relationship between objective truth and the validity of literary creation, and should
not be looked at uncritically" (14). Treves has given us a readable literary creation, Howell and Ford offer objective truth. Yet even the title of
Howell and Ford's book points to the problems inherent in such a naive
version of historical truth. For it proclaims a true history not of Joseph
Merrick, but of the Elephant Man, and what is the Elephant Man if not
a fiction, a legend, an identity created not simply by the suffering individual who assumed it but by all those who have looked at him, thought
about him, and read his and their own experience somehow through his
mysterious presence? What would a true history of such a figure look
like?

What Howell and Ford's book looks like is a mixed creature, a combination of factual detail with elements of melodrama, Victorian novel,
colonial rhetoric, and Shakespearean romance. Despite Howell and
Ford's distinguishing their work from literary creation, the book has a
clear dramatic structure, one taken over from Treves and very much
reminiscent of Pomerance's play. Its first chapter begins with Merrick
installed for viewing at the shop in Whitechapel Road, comments on
the "poverty and deprivation" of the district and its contrast with the
"imposing classical facade" (9) of the London Hospital, and then follows Treves as he makes "his own pilgrimage" (14) to Tom Norman's
shop. A kind of colonial rhetoric is especially evident in Howell and
Ford's description of Tom Norman's "ushering his visitor from the hospital opposite into the dark interior" (16), where he encountered "a
creature supposedly half-human, half-beast—a kind of urban Caliban" (17). Here, too, we get our first glimpse into Treves's character.
Even though only thirty-one, he had ministered to the ills of one of the
"worst slums of Europe" and thus might be supposed "shock-proof"
(17). Nevertheless he is "shaken by his first glimpse of Joseph Merrick;
and perhaps also taken unawares by his revulsion at the sickening
stench given off by Merrick's body" (17). The chapter proceeds with a
physical description of Merrick, based on Treves's reminiscence, and
an initial biography of Treves, "already a figure to be reckoned with in

the medical world" (19). The conclusion focuses on the arranging of Merrick's journey across the road to the hospital, its deft last paragraph stressing, or indeed schematizing, the essential contrast between Treves and Merrick and the first offering of connection on Treves's part: "Treves handed Merrick his visiting card. The first meeting between Frederick Treves, a young surgeon with an ever more ambitious career before him, and Joseph Merrick, the Elephant Man, a humble freak whose hopes for the future were of an altogether more modest character, was over" (21).

This first chapter points distinctly to the limitations of Howell and Ford's book as true history. First, it is based almost exclusively on Treves's reminiscence, as is the whole book's account of Merrick's life from his meeting with Treves until his death. Second, the first chapter tells the story of Treves's meeting with Merrick, not the true story of Merrick's life. Indeed the authors seem unable to conceive of any other shape for Merrick's life, perhaps because Treves's reminiscence exerts such a powerful influence on them or perhaps because there is such a deep mythic structure present in the whole story of Treves and Merrick's encounter and life together. Chapter 2, for instance, presents a biography of Treves, beginning with his origins in Dorsetshire, detailing his education and early career successes at the London, and leaving him again poised—as at the end of chapter 1—at the beginning of a great career: "The world, in a very real sense, was on the verge of opening up as Treves's oyster" (29). Chapter 3 concentrates on Treves's first clinical encounters with Merrick and on the early attempts at a diagnosis of Merrick's affliction. Not until chapter 4 do Howell and Ford provide a basic biographical narrative for their putative subject.

In their treatment of Joseph's life in the London Hospital, Howell and Ford follow the structure of events established by Treves: Joseph's meeting with women, his visit to the theater, his sojourn in the country, his death. The decisive influence of Treves is evident also in Howell and Ford's several attempts to will their narrative closed. They quote two paragraphs from Treves's reminiscence on Joseph's death, arguing that these should be regarded "as the definitive version." Thus Howell and Ford confer the status of true history on Treves's speculations that Joseph had made the "experiment" of lying down to sleep out of "the desire that had dominated his life . . . the pathetic but hopeless desire to be 'like other people' " (148–149). One might expect a narrative of

Joseph's life to end here, but it's not so easy for Howell and Ford to keep the story contained within the note of hopeless determinism supplied by Treves. Joseph's heroism demands to be acknowledged, and thus Howell and Ford reinvoke Treves, who could, of course, never quite keep Joseph's story contained either. Calling Treves "too fine a doctor to mistake the flesh for the man," Howell and Ford cite the words Treves "sought . . . to express what he had learnt of Joseph's internal nobility": "As a specimen of humanity, Merrick was ignoble and repulsive; but the spirit of Merrick, if it could be seen in the form of the living, would assume the figure of an upstanding and heroic man, smooth browed and clean of limb and with eyes that flashed undaunted courage" (149). Noteworthy here is Howell and Ford's echoing of Treves's tendency to divide Merrick into body and spirit. When the accounts seek to say something final, they present Merrick either as a disgusting specimen, the flesh, determined by his bodily reality—which dictates, even while rendering hopeless, his desire to be like others—or as transcendent spirit, in which case his body is but a mask and not his true form. Neither account seems able to rest in an image of Merrick both as bodily being and transcending spirit. Perhaps it would take a different kind of history, one that actively resists the will to closure, to rest with Merrick as truly body and truly spirit.

Treves's words cited above close chapter 11 of Howell and Ford's book, but again the authors seem moved to say something beyond the end. Allusively titled "The Figure in Time's Fabric," chapter 12 (its number recalling both epic and Treves's volume) reads much like the epilogue of a Victorian novel, one of those sprawling yet carefully patterned dramas of human interdependence and competition in the "tangled bank" termed society. The chapter traces out the continuing history of each of the characters, beginning with Treves, of course, but including also such lesser players as Tom Norman, Sam Torr, Mrs. Kendal, Bishop Walsham How, and even Sir Reginald Tuckett, whose sole involvement in Merrick's life is to have "first pressed Treves to go and view the Elephant Man" (162). After a brief review, then, of Treves's many books, and of Montagu's and Pomerance's treatments of Merrick's story, Howell and Ford again attempt to conclude their true history. The "closing and most valid image of Joseph," they argue, is of his walking at night in the garden of the London Hospital:

The freedom to walk there unobserved and take the cool night air into his lungs, together with the scent of the spring flowers, became one with the hard-won freedom and dignity of his spirit under the stars: and so the limits to the span of his existence, the various griefs and injuries which his life sustained, even the hideousness of his flesh, were transformed eventually into matters of small importance. (166–167)

One senses perhaps the effort by Howell and Ford to avoid quoting Treves here, yet the influence of Treves's rhetoric is apparent. Again Joseph is "transformed," converted from one form to his true form as his bodily experience becomes irrelevant, unreal. Perhaps sensing the inadequacy of this conclusion, Howell and Ford allow Joseph to speak in what may be his own voice, helpfully reprinting *The Autobiography of Joseph Carey Merrick* as appendix 1. But by reprinting Treves's reminiscence in its entirety as appendix 2, they opt to allow him to frame Joseph's history once more.

Despite their objections to Treves's melodramatic quality, Howell and Ford themselves often substitute melodrama for history. Their description of Joseph as he returns to London from the Continent provides a case in point. Joseph appears "inexplicably" upon the platform of Liverpool Street Station, "his will . . . gone, his demoralization complete," his only apparent option a return to the Leicester workhouse: "And Leicester lay ninety-eight miles away from London, even supposing he could summon the strength to walk such a distance; and in the knowledge that once the doors of that terrible place closed again behind him it would this time be for ever" (89). The thematic purpose of this description is to establish Merrick's absolute dependence on Treves for his salvation, which seems to occur as Treves "bundles" Joseph into the cab for the ride to the hospital: "The Elephant Man questioned nothing, but sat in a silent daze, seemingly all at once overcome with a great, trusting sense of calm. Then, as the cab turned out of the station, he sagged into a sudden and astonishingly child-like sleep" (90). Howell and Ford are quite explicit in their casting of Treves as savior. In their account, Treves as he rides in the cab is already making up his mind "that the time had come for the [hospital] rules somehow to be broken, and he was prepared to use his own prestige to that end." Treves has made a choice between the options that Howell and Ford have been casting for him since the beginning of their tale: the continuing quest for his own success and glorification, on the one hand, or the opening of himself to the needy and vulnerable on the other. Treves chooses the way of humiliation, of renunciation of invulnerability and opening to finitude: "Having descended in his hansom cab like a *deus ex machina* to rescue a broken life, he intended to see the role through to the end" (91).

An appropriate subtitle for Howell and Ford's book might ask, "What kind of father will Frederick Treves be?" Will he be the omnipotent, controlling, self-contained figure who remains at a distance from the subjects of his skill, or will he be a loving father who enters into the lives of his patients, and most especially, into the life of his lowliest son? Merrick throughout is presented as an alien, the other, a child in need of adoption, and yet one who would bring with him utterly unexpected gifts of his own. He is variously the suffering servant, taunted and humiliated in the workhouse; the Christ child to whom "none would give . . . lodging except in an outhouse, or a stable, as if he were a wild animal" (83); and an angel, as is suggested by Howell and Ford's description of the terrified rejection of Joseph by the woman who, with her husband, was to entertain Merrick at their country cottage: "As with other women who suddenly came face to face with Joseph unawares, the first glimpse proved devastating" (143). Not only is the whole situation reminiscent of the myth of Baucis and Philemon, but the curious use of "unawares" must surely, given the context, recall the injunction of Heb. 13:2: "Be not forgetful to entertain strangers: for thereby some have entertained angels unawares" (King James Version).

Howell and Ford suggest the different possibilities of fatherhood open to Treves through their parable of how Joseph came to leave the home of his natural father and reside with his uncle Charles. Joseph Rockley Merrick had, like some demanding patriarch, established a quota of goods for his deformed son to sell each day. "Inevitably," Howell and Ford tell us, the day came when Joseph failed to "sell the required quantity." Returning home, the boy "received the severest thrashing he ever was given," one that caused him to leave "the house knowing that this time he would never return." Joseph went into the streets: "His father sought for him no more" (58). If Joseph Rockley Merrick appears the unsatisfiable figure of the law, Uncle Charles by contrast seems the loving father of the Gospel, the Good Shepherd who goes endlessly in search of the lost. Reading this section of Howell and

Ford's book as parable helps to make sense of what might otherwise seem to be extraneous details about Uncle Charles. As the "youngest of the three sons born to old Barnabus and his wife Sarah," Charles had declined to "follow his father into the trade of bobbin-turner at the cotton factory," choosing "instead to become a barber's apprentice." In short, as the youngest son, he could break from following his own father, from living up to his father's demand (this parable somewhat modifies that of the Prodigal Son but does, like Jesus' great story, cast the younger son, the one who breaks from the father, as he who can experience unlimited love). In his trade as barber, Charles was able to establish "a stable and well-founded business, bringing security to his family" for the greater part of his working life. But that security was not inviolable, for Charles and his wife Jane "had seen three of their four young children die before reaching the age of eighteen months." For Charles, however, this wounding was not reason for closing up and turning inward, for armoring against further pain. The remedy for suffering was to love more. When Joseph Rockley Merrick cast his son into the streets, and sought for him no more, Uncle Charles "went out into the streets of the city to search until he found the boy, then persuaded him to go back to the house in Churchgate above the hairdressing saloon. He and his wife would take his nephew into their own home to be treated as one of the household" (58–59).

Howell and Ford's search for an appropriate father for Joseph continues with their description of his adoption by Tom Norman, who aids Joseph in his escape from nonbeing and ultimate anonymity, namelessness. In defense of Joseph's exhibition, Howell and Ford remind us that "short of a miracle, there had been for him no other conceivable line of escape from the grinding limbo of workhouse life, which could only spiral ever downwards to end in the unmarked shadow of a pauper's grave." "For the moment," then, "Tom Norman was the nearest Joseph Merrick came to having a fairy godfather" (72). Tom Norman prefigures the appearance of Joseph's true fairy godfather, who works the miracle of saving Joseph from his life of isolation without returning him to the limbo of the workhouse or the shadow of an unmarked grave. That godfather, of course, is the descending *deus ex machina*, Treves, figured in the text also as Prospero to Merrick's Caliban. Howell and Ford first describe Merrick as an "urban Caliban" during their account of Treves's initial encounter with the Elephant Man. On one level, the allusion functions as part of Howell and Ford's colonialist rhetoric. Treves as physician-scientist later attempts to "chart" every feature, every peculiarity of the "chaotic anatomical wilderness" (30) that is Merrick's body. A similar need to order the wilderness motivates the authorities' suppression of the freak shows in the East End. For all their defense of Merrick's English exhibitors, Howell and Ford argue that such suppression "was all part of a long and, it has to be said, civilizing process" (38). Thus the Elephant Man as "urban Caliban" figures the anarchy both of disease and of the East End, a double unruliness being brought under control by the benevolent enlightenment emanating from the authorities and the London Hospital.

More interesting is the significance of Howell and Ford's allusion to *The Tempest* for our understanding of the relationship between Merrick and Treves. Howell and Ford come round to conscious reflection on the allusion near the end of the book, as they note how the story of the Elephant Man and Treves, "like the relationship between Prospero and Caliban in Shakespeare's *The Tempest*," can yield continually shifting meanings as "new social parables are read in or drawn out." Thus "the monstrous whelp Caliban" shades into the "Noble Savage," while the "omnipotent magician Prospero . . . is revealed to have feet of clay" (165–66). But Howell and Ford have alluded even better than they know. Treves, like Prospero, broke his staff, giving up his art, surgery, at the age of fifty. He likewise drowned his book "deeper than did ever plummet sound" (5.1.56), consigning to oblivion the manuscript that would have clinched his reputation as a writer, the manuscript devoted to his famous patients. These acts signify for both Prospero and Treves the renunciation of power, the acceptance of limitation, the decision to give every third thought to the grave. Prospero is a type of the descending god, the role Treves has played throughout Howell and Ford's dramatic version of the Elephant Man's story. As Prospero turns to Caliban near the end of the play, saying, "this thing of darkness I / Acknowledge mine" (5.1.275–76), so Treves has acknowledged Merrick his own. Howell and Ford's semi-intentional allusion offers us the privilege of reading the Merrick-Treves relationship through Shakespeare's insight. Merrick, like Caliban, has been constructed as a "thing of darkness" by Treves's and others' fears: He is thus Treves's own. And he will cease being a "thing of darkness" only when others like Prospero-Treves give up the need for omnipotent control, acknowledging his "darkness"—with all that it suggests about human limitation, wound-edness, finitude—as their own.

We hope it will not seem too farfetched to offer, at this point, what is frankly and obviously a speculation about Treves's persistent habit of misnaming Merrick "John." We have noted in chapter 2 some of the ways in which "John" might seem to Treves a more appropriate name for Merrick than "Joseph," especially given the fatherly associations of the latter. Howell and Ford's casting of Treves as the descending god— a pattern perhaps already evident in the reminiscence—points further to the appropriateness of John as Merrick's name. For in the New Testa-ment, John is the Gospel of divine Sonship, a relationship between the Father and Son characterized by what Arthur McGill has called *"total and mutual self giving."* The relationship is suggested by such pas-sages as 5:26, "Because the Father has life in himself, so he has granted the son also to have life in himself," and 8:28, spoken by the Son, "I do nothing on my own authority, but speak only as the Father has taught me." In such a relationship, McGill argues, "the Father and the Son do not have their identity in terms of the reality that they pos-sess and hold onto within themselves, but in terms of their giving this reality to the other."[7] Sonship so conceived points toward the nature of God's power and response to suffering. God's power is not dominative coercion exercised through force but total self-giving that enters into suffering. So Treves, too, responds to Merrick's suffering not through dominative power but by entering into it as fully as possible. He freely helps to bring Merrick to life, and Merrick offers his own glory back to Treves without resentment. As father and son, they enhance each other through their actions, each giving to the other without being dimin-ished himself. They thus approach a unity of love, that love without which, also according to John, we "remain in death" (1 John 3:14). Certainly our earlier analysis of Treves's reminiscence suggests that his relationship with Merrick was not always free of manipulation or self-aggrandizement; certainly its characteristic feature was not always mu-tual self-giving. But perhaps Treves thought that Merrick had at least pointed him toward the kind of love that the writer of John knew, and perhaps that is the reason Treves so stubbornly, even stupidly, insisted on calling Merrick "John."

One of the many ironies surrounding Joseph Merrick's story is that if Treves's prose remade Merrick, the creative treatments deriving from

Treves's and Montagu's accounts inflict analogous contortions on Treves, diminishing his long, eventful career by focusing so intensely and speculatively on his period of involvement with Merrick. If Howell and Ford's *True History* attempts to bring back some of the lost facts and contexts of Merrick's life, Stephen Trombley's *Sir Frederick Treves: The Extra-Ordinary Edwardian* (1989) sets out to do much the same thing for Treves, as the first sentences of its introduction indicate: "Frederick Treves is best known to a contemporary audience as the surgeon who befriended Joseph Merrick—the unfortunate Elephant Man. Yet, without that distinction, he would justify a biographer's labours."[8] Despite the abundance of published material—Treves's writings on subjects outside himself and the comments of others who knew him—his prospective biographers are handicapped by what is in effect a personal silence comparable to Merrick's. As Trombley explains, Treves in the last years of his life put together materials for an autobiography only to suppress the manuscript, which contained details concerning his royal patients, at the advice of a colleague. After Treves's death, his friend and publisher Newman Flower visited Lady Treves, obtained the manuscript and other key documents, and embarked upon a biography. When the project was well under way, Lady Treves insisted that Flower omit any reference to Treves's medical relations with the royal family, and when told that producing a worthy biography under such constraints would be impossible, she replied that "her husband's memory should survive in history by the work he did" (ix). As heir to her husband's papers, she destroyed the autobiographical manuscript and most other primary materials.

Writing under the constraints imposed when indispensable material has been deliberately obliterated in deference to higher authority is bound to outrage any biographer interested in offering a full and fair account; and it may be that some understandable indignation over royalty's policy of withholding facts and the Treveses' acquiescence in being thus silenced finds its way into Trombley's book, which as a consequence of Trevesian censorship is obliged to be "in some ways a public life" (ix). Such indignation would help to account for certain recurrent biases in the study. Though appreciative of Treves's energy, efficiency, humane values, and intellectual curiosity, Trombley presents the surgeon as willing to sacrifice any and all of these to a competitive urge to be first, whether in winning "the great appendicitis race, " or in discovering the most dramatic cases of deformity, or in retiring while at the top of his profession—or, most prominently, in serving his royal masters. This last objective might involve reticence, as in the matter of the autobiography, or even lying, as in Treves's firsthand testimony on the conduct of the Boer War, where Trombley sees him as following the queen's lead and overlooking obvious medical and administrative incompetence to maintain flagging public morale in wartime. Certainly the name Trombley has chosen for his biographical study stresses Treves's role as tool of royalty. *Sir Frederick Treves*, the title, is by itself unremarkable, though the addition of the honorific does draw attention to the baronetcy Treves received from his king and grateful patient in 1903. But the subtitle, *The Extra-Ordinary Edwardian*, makes sense only in light of Treves's royal connections—for, in fact, Treves is much more accurately characterized by the well-known Lytton Strachey title Trombley echoes. Treves, like Strachey's subjects, is one of the *Eminent Victorians*. Born in 1853, Treves lived more than half of his seventy years under Victoria. He achieved his professional eminence and even gained two royal responsibilities (as surgeon in ordinary to the Duke of York and to Victoria herself) during her reign. Only if one believes, as Trombley claims, that "nothing satisfied Treves more in his professional and social life than the glamour and excitement of his royal appointments," that his "important role at court was as sergeant-surgeon to Edward VII" (124), and that the high point of his career was operating on the king's appendix (vii) is Treves to be seen as preeminently an Edwardian. And only if his connections with royalty matter more than do his scientific studies, surgical innovations, public service in medical reform and Red Cross administration, voluminous writing, and involvement with Merrick is he to be construed as "extra-ordinary" rather than "extraordinary."

Trombley writes that his book does not claim "any kind of methodological sophistication" (ix)—a state of affairs that need not inevitably pose interpretative drawbacks but does so when Trombley takes up Treves's involvement with Merrick in the chapter called "Monsters." The problems with this part of the biography are various—the first being that Trombley has not come to specific terms with Treves's reminiscence "The Elephant Man" and the collection to which it gives a title. In his own introduction, Trombley calls *The Elephant Man and Other Reminiscences* Treves's "last book and arguably his best" (viii), an assessment echoed in the final chapter, which terms the collection "his greatest book" (189). These two vague assertions of excellence are, however, the full extent of critical notice the book receives; far more attention is paid to Treves's medical texts and travel narratives. Consequently Trombley's readers have no way to gauge the nature or extent of what is purported to be Treves's supreme achievement as a writer.

Trombley's understanding of the title piece and how it relates to fact and to Treves's earlier publication on Merrick is equally vague. The "Monsters" chapter is unlike all Trombley's others in that well over half of it (some eleven pages out of seventeen) is extracted verbatim from Treves's writing—and much of the rest is expository bridge building between quoted passages. Because "The Elephant Man" is so fully and uncritically quoted, Treves's reminiscent voice takes over from Trombley's in the Merrick chapter. By default, Treves's "Elephant Man" assumes the status of material examined and found accurate by the biographer. Once only does Trombley differ with Treves's 1923 account: "He [Treves] neglects to mention that in addition to one perfect arm, Merrick's sex organs were also perfect; and he gets Merrick's Christian name wrong" (38). What Trombley in his turn gets wrong is the true nature of the reminiscence as one account among several. In the case of Merrick's unafflicted genitals, for example, the "delicate omission" in the 1923 reminiscence is either an editorial decision or a mistake in recollection—but it is a unique omission rather than a characteristic one, as shown by consulting "A Case of Congenital Deformity," the 1885 clinical description Trombley alludes to without examining in his chapter. Similarly, the 1923 assertion that Treves first supposed Merrick to be an imbecile (quoted without comment by Trombley on page 40) is contradicted by Treves's 1884 acknowledgment of Merrick's intelligence as "by no means of a low order."

Although elsewhere—notably in his discussion of Treves's self-refutations on the competence of the Royal Army Medical Corps in the Boer War—Trombley sharply distinguishes variations in Treves's pronouncements, in the "Monsters" chapter he does not examine and interrogate everything Treves says of Merrick, contemporary descriptions and recollected ones, to obtain the fullest possible understanding of the medical and personal relationship. Because he fails to do so, his book that adds to our fuller understanding of Treves does not enhance our understanding of Merrick—and indeed perpetuates some of the old misconceptions (those mentioned above along with the myths that Tom Norman was a brutal exploiter and that Mrs. Kendal visited Merrick) laid to rest by Howell and Ford. Despite its flaws, though, Trombley's account of Treves's relations with Merrick ends with an appropriate acknowledgment of the complex blend of Christian charity, bourgeois social responsibility, Victorian desire to normalize, and personal sentimentality causing Treves's interest in Merrick. As the chapter on Merrick closes, Trombley recognizes the paradox of the relationship: Treves's kindly intentions did violence to Merrick by idealizing him, but they also saved him from an even worse fate, dying destitute "in the most appalling circumstances" (51).

Among the first to make artistic use of Howell and Ford's *True History* was Kenneth Sherman, whose volume of poetry, *Words for Elephant Man*, appeared in 1983. Sherman responded particularly to a comment that Howell and Ford attribute to Merrick's exhibitor, Tom Norman: "It was not the show, it was the tale that you told." The pitchman's remark—which appears as an epigraph to "Showman," the first section of *Words for Elephant Man*—points to the need to story Merrick, to locate his experience within an explanatory narrative. The ability to create stories is the measure of the showman's art, but it is also one of our primary ways of contending with suffering. As its title indicates, *Words for Elephant Man* seeks to give Merrick the language he needs to give shape to his own experience, to locate his suffering within a story, to create his own tale. At the same time, Sherman's title points to his interest in looking critically at the ways in which Merrick has been cast in language, at the words spoken by others for Elephant Man.

The difficulty Merrick poses for language is explored in "The Only Electric Lady," which treats the experience that made a showman of Tom Norman. "As a young man," he "paid a penny / to see *The Only Electric Lady*," whose body gave off sparks that "flew like inchworms of light" and "bolted" Tom back when he touched her.[9] Later Tom "discovered she was connected . . . to an electric coil," as was "the metal plate under the damp / carpet on which the customer stood." The disillusionment was, "Tom said, / *Like seeing the soiled underpants of God*" (9–15), but the experience caused him to realize that the tale, not the show, was what mattered. Merrick, however, presented a particular problem for Tom, for he was beyond language: "With me he never had to say a word. / I was beyond metaphor, / my stench / cutting through the intricacies of fiction" (22–25). The poem concludes by suggesting that Merrick's resistance to metaphor troubled Norman, whose preference was for a simpler and more controllable, if also more fraudulent, kind of exhibit: "That is why when Treves came to see me / they had to fetch Tom in a pub, / he / was drinking, / he was dreaming / *The Only Electric Lady*" (26–31).

Several of Sherman's poems follow the strategy of allowing Merrick to answer others' descriptions of him. In "First Meeting Treves," Merrick describes his first visit to the hospital, where he is photographed and measured and has his blood tested. What follows is Merrick's own story of why Treves judged him imbecile at this point: "I try talking and my voice / like a caged bird suddenly let loose / bounces off the lab white walls. / Treves writes on his chart / *imbecile*, when really / it's men speaking two / different languages: / he, the words of a man who has everything / me, the words of a man who has words" (6–14). Curious here is Sherman's attribution, much like Pomerance, of verbal facility to a figure so inexpressive as Merrick. Both writers seem to have felt acutely the particular vulnerability caused Merrick by his difficulties in being understood.

Sherman's Merrick answers others' descriptions of him again in "Before the Pathological Society of London," a poem that begins with scientific language: "*Longitudinal sulci / subcutaneous tissue / papillomatous growth*" (1–3). Merrick reflects on the distancing effect of such terms: "That too is language / designed to keep you / five steps away, / explain my pain" (4–7). Reversing the roles in this "medical theatre," Merrick describes his audience as "a row of ventriloquists' puppets" as they thumb back, as if by rote, "through a thousand yellowing texts" in search of the appropriate category for him: "*What is it? / What is it?*" (5–17). In this reversal, Merrick becomes his own exhibitor, his own showman, offering his audience something that will not be distanced, something that breaks the order of all previous texts: "Gentlemen, / do you not know revelation / when you see it, / my figure / naked and hunched / a curdled question mark / that breathes?" (18–24).

In its overall design, *Words for Elephant Man* follows Howell and Ford quite closely, beginning with poems about Merrick's exhibition, then exploring his origins in Leicester, his years in the workhouse, the closing of his show in England, and his failed Continental tour. Sherman's last section, "Dislocations," treats the familiar episodes of Merrick's life after his return to London: his installation at Bedstead Square, his reception of visitors, his trip to the theater, and his building of the model church, which Merrick leaves to perplex posterity:

> God created a creature whose ugliness
> made men wince—a model of imperfection
> who fed on poetry, who moulded such
> architectural beauty
> (only man thinks in the perfect
> > tense). (11–16)

Several of the last, and most original, poems in Sherman's book concern Merrick's attempts to think beyond "the perfect tense," beyond a language of perfection and lapse to one of pure being. In "Tree," one of several poems inspired by Merrick's late trip to the country, he ponders a stark black-and-white photograph of his two arms, "the one I call good because it looks / like other arms / and the one I call bad, / the one that is different" (13–16). He has lived "stretched between" these while always "asking what it would take to / go beyond / to become the gnarled singing tree / upon which / no forbidden fruit is grown / nor any man hanged" (18–24). Merrick, however, is unable to escape self-consciousness or his entanglement in language. In "The Animal Side," he whimsically fantasizes about becoming an animal—his "head / bony and grey / mounted on a wall / miraculously / singing" (20–24)—but he soon recognizes, in "In the Country," that his fate is to be aware of himself and related to both world and self through the fallen medium of language: "The problem here / is that I see, / in ponds / in rivers / my halved image / the problem here is that / I interpret / the flies / that sing / about my temporary flesh" (17–26).

Merrick's nearest approach to a language of being is through analogy. "Incurable" returns Merrick to the hospital, where he "cannot help / but hear the groans / of those above, / those who strive / those for whom there is / a cure" (4–9). Merrick finds an appropriate analogy for his own condition through difference, through his contrast with those who strive: "In vases, / the flowers I brought back / from the

country, / static and dry. / They are / what they are / and aspire to
nothing more, / their shadows / stippling the late afternoon wall" (10–
18). Merrick's aspiration to pure being is suggested, too, by the final
poem of the volume, which gives Merrick a voice beyond death with
which to question those who attempt to encase him in the fixity of his
skeleton's display. "Now you have it all," Merrick begins, "the cap /
and veil, / the cloak, the / slippers like big paper bags / my bones"
(1–6). But the poem's conclusion suggests the futility of trying to find
what one is looking for in Merrick by assembling his bones, by seeking
a final answer to his riddle. For he still questions us, his speech a kind
of music, aspiring to movement, to being, and refusing to be translated
fully into any other code: "Did you hear / what Lady Kendall referred
to / as my *voice so strangely musical* / echoing / in the dark / against
the glass / of the display case / the cold / bronze plaque?" (20–28).

The difficulty of grasping Merrick fully is suggested obliquely by
the most recent diagnosis of his condition, offered by Drs. J. A. R.
Tibbles and M. M. Cohen, Jr., in a 1986 article for the "Medical History" section of the *British Medical Journal*. Tibbles and Cohen contest
the long-standing diagnosis of Merrick as suffering from neurofibromatosis. They argue instead that he exhibited the features of the Proteus
syndrome, named for the old man of the sea in Greek mythology, who,
while given the gift of prophecy, frustrated those who questioned him
by changing shapes and eluding their grasp. Tibbles and Cohen make
significant use of Howell and Ford's factual discoveries about Merrick.
Indeed Howell and Ford supply nearly all the material of the case report on which Merrick's rediagnosis is based. Tibbles and Cohen also
make extremely effective use of one figure from *The True History of the
Elephant Man*, a photograph of a plaster cast of Merrick's foot, showing
its heavily ridged, almost corrugated look, the result of a condition
known as "moccasin foot, a form of plantar hyperplasia." The figure
suggests an extraordinary resemblance between Merrick's foot and that
of a five-and-a-half-year-old child (also represented in the article)
whom Tibbles and Cohen have diagnosed as having the Proteus syndrome. This child appears in the article almost as Merrick's double, as
Case 2 to Merrick's Case 1. The boy's highly enlarged head, severe
facial and cranial asymmetry, and "enlarged and grossly deformed"
right hand are all especially reminiscent of Merrick. Tibbles and Cohen include three photographs of the boy's developing "facial dysmor-

phism": at one month, five months, and five and a half years of age. These must seem somewhat uncanny to those familiar with the photographs of Merrick, for they show dramatically the bulging overenlargement of one side of the child's face, with the consequent pressing of the nose sideways and the forcing upward of the lip on one side of the skewed mouth.[10]

Tibbles and Cohen establish their rediagnosis by showing first that Merrick's condition did not conform in important ways to neurofibromatosis. "In the case of Joseph Merrick," they argue, "there is no evidence of a family history of neurofibromatosis or of cafe au lait spots in adulthood which surely would have been recognised and described by clinicians of the stature of those who examined him, such as the dermatologist H R Crocker" (684–685). These cafe au lait spots are nearly definitive for neurofibromatosis, as they "are present in over 99% of the patients" with the condition. Moreover, despite Montagu's argument that Merrick's tumors were specifically nerve fiber tumors, Tibbles and Cohen point out that "there is no histological evidence of neurofibromas." Finally, the manifestations of the condition in Merrick's case were "much more bizarre than those commonly associated with neurofibromatosis" (685).

On the other hand, Merrick's case does exhibit several features compatible with a diagnosis of the Proteus syndrome, a term coined "by Weidemann *et al* in 1983 to identify a disorder with protean manifestations including partial gigantism of the hands or feet, or both, asymmetry of the arms and legs, plantar hyperplasia, haemangiomas, lipomas, varicosities, linear verrucous epidermal naevi, macrocephaly, cranial hyperostoses, and 'hypertrophy' of long bones" (684). To enumerate the features of the disorder manifested by Merrick is almost to reproduce the list above: "macrocephaly; thickened skin and subcutaneous tissues, particularly of the hands and feet, including plantar hyperplasia, lipomas, and unspecified subcutaneous masses; hypertrophy of long bones; and overgrowth of the skull." "Merrick's normal mentation," Tibbles and Cohen add, "is also compatible with the Proteus syndrome" (685).

Tibbles and Cohen's revision of Merrick's diagnosis gave rise to the remythologizing of Merrick in the popular press. A headline in *Science News* for July 25, 1987, announced, "As of '87, He's Proteus Man." The article noted the appearance of a report on neurofibromatosis by a National Institutes of Health panel but curiously gave nearly all of its space to something not addressed specifically in the report itself: the condition of the Elephant Man. David A. Stumpf, panel chairman, offered the reassuring information that "it was the group's consensus that Merrick actually suffered from an extremely rare disease known as the Proteus syndrome" and not from neurofibromatosis. "The updated diagnosis is of more than historical interest," the *Science News* writer commented, "as it may help to free neurofibromatosis victims from the fear of the severe deformation that is more properly associated with the Proteus syndrome."[11] A piece in *Newsweek* for February 29, 1988, took a similar tack. After briefly summarizing the arguments of Tibbles and Cohen, "What the Elephant Man Really Had" welcomed the rediagnosis of Merrick as a way of calming the fears of parents of children with neurofibromatosis.[12] Surely one can only applaud here the efforts to reduce the fear associated with neurofibromatosis. One would hope that this could be accomplished, however, without re-mythologizing Merrick as a god, as a Proteus—if not an Elephant—Man, as one who is, above all, not like us. Unfortunately Merrick now plays this role of "what we are not" quite regularly in the popular culture—thus Bill Murray in the film *Ghostbusters II* on first seeing Sigourney Weaver's baby: "He's ugly. Not Elephant Man ugly, but ugly"; or Sylvester Stallone in *Sports Illustrated* on the "paralytic sneer" that signified his ubiquitous unpopularity as a child, his sense of exclusion from every community: "I was the original Elephant Man . . . I only learned to smile a couple of years ago."[13] Perhaps the rediagnosis of Merrick was the necessary condition for the proliferation of such references in the popular media, for surely it is easier now to cast him as the other than it was when he was understood to have the relatively common neurofibromatosis.

As we have seen above, one of the factual contributions of Howell and Ford has been to indicate just how the public perception of freak shows changed during the last half of the nineteenth century so that an exhibition such as Merrick's came to be seen as indecency, particularly for a child audience. In the 106 years since the Whitechapel exhibit was closed and Merrick was "moved on," cultural perceptions of childhood and deformity alike have continued to change. Whereas the Victorian ruling class perceived children as fundamentally different from adults, as innocent beings to be sheltered and protected from harsh realities, our own day largely erases the distinctions between generations and insists on informing children about things as they are, however grim the world of AIDS and drugs and nuclear weapons may be. Furthermore, although the present era is no more innately compassionate than was Merrick's, advances in medical science have solved (or at least tackled) the mysteries of disease and disability; and the more physical facts we know about a disorder, the less inclined we are to view it as a moral affliction. Thus, if it was once unthinkable that children should encounter Merrick, it has now become highly desirable, at least in print. The cultural shift is clearly indicated by the recent publication of two children's books on the Elephant Man, one by Howell and Ford themselves and another by Frederick Drimmer.

Howell and Ford's version, *The Elephant Man: Retold for Children* (1984), attractively illustrated by Robert Geary, offers an optimistic account of Merrick's life to a primary-school audience. As in their *True History*, Howell and Ford essentially follow Treves for their version of Merrick's experiences at the London Hospital. Here again are the familiar details of the 1923 reminiscence, from the initial cab ride to the last happy days in Bedstead Square with the notice of society and the visit of royalty, the excursions to Drury Lane and the country. But here also are other kindnesses suggesting, as does the *True History*, that Treves and the people he brought to Merrick's rooms were not alone in offering compassion. Howell and Ford rely on brief flashbacks to reveal glimpses of Merrick's sufferings—the workhouse, the loss of his mother, the cruelty of his stepmother—and their book also acknowledges the treachery of Merrick's Continental exhibitor, who is given a fictive identity that manages at once to perpetuate and to subvert the English xenophobia present in earlier versions: The thieving showman, "Mr. Ferrari," is described by a character within the story, rather than by the narrator, as "not an Italian-born Italian, more your cockney ice-cream version." But though they acknowledge the dark times, Howell and Ford emphasize the comforts and fellowship of Merrick's life in the days before his residence at the London.

As they do in the *True History*, Howell and Ford present Merrick's English exhibitors as promoters, not exploiters. The story begins at the fictive "Sam Roper's Fair" as the proprietor, cozily called "Uncle Sam" by the narrator, instructs his young nephews Harry and Bertram about the new addition to their group: "Sam Roper's Fair, as you know, is a family outfit. We look after our people, and I want you to look after Mr. Merrick."[14] The boys become Merrick's hosts, friends, and protectors; later, when the fairground days end, Merrick's London exhibitor, Tom Norman, proves equally benevolent. The details of the Whitechapel show are true to Treves's account, but Howell and Ford stress the staginess of the showman's harsh demeanor ("If I seem to speak a bit rough it's all a part of the act. The public expect it, you see" [23]) and the fair treatment Merrick received behind the scenes ("Every evening Mr. Norman would count up the takings and carefully pass half of them on to Joseph" [26]). Even when Merrick is established among well-wishers at Bedstead Square, allusions to earlier kindnesses appear: "Yet Joseph had never had any trouble when it came to making friends, either among the fairground folk or in the hospital," observes the narrator just after mentioning Merrick's enjoyment of discussions with Treves. Later, after describing Merrick's death, the narrator reminds the audience that "those who became his friends had included showmen as well as young people, doctors, nurses, famous actresses, and members of the royal family" (63).

Because it emphasizes human kindness rather than monstrous deformity, Howell and Ford's *Elephant Man* is a comforting book for its young audience. It is also a didactic book giving attention to Joseph Merrick's deserving character but prominence to the good conduct of those who truly knew him. The last sentences clearly echo those of Treves's reminiscence; but the young readers of these words are meant to understand that the surgeon was not alone in seeing beneath the disfigured skin and that they too can join the ranks of the humane and discerning: "The crowds who clustered to see him in the freakshows had known him only as the Elephant Man, a dreadful sight to wonder over. His friends knew differently, because they discovered the real Joseph. They knew he was someone of courage and gentleness who had managed to triumph over the worst that fate could do to him. Joseph Merrick had shown how the real person he happened to be was more important than the outward appearance of his poor crippled body" (64).

In Howell and Ford's juvenile book, then, the audience is to identify not primarily with Joseph Merrick but with his friends—a matter made easy through the invention of benevolent juvenile characters, Harry and Bertram, who are introduced before Merrick appears and through whom that first encounter with Merrick is mediated. Merrick remains the Other, and his story is a means by which young readers can develop insightful compassion for others. Frederick Drimmer's version, *The Elephant Man* (1985), written for an older juvenile audience, has a different didactic end, and its rhetorical means are accordingly different. Drimmer's narrative encourages identification with Merrick and through that imaginative act fosters self-esteem among readers facing the ordeals of adolescence.

Audiences familiar with the different renditions of Merrick's story will find it interesting but not surprising that Drimmer's book, like various other accounts, begins with Treves, not Merrick. The narrative starts in 1884, "the year Frederick Treves's great adventure began,"[15] and until chapter 5 we see the medical encounter from his point of view. Only then, in "Parade of the Elephants" (a chapter title identical to one in the *True History*), does the point of view shift from Treves's to Merrick's. The shape of Drimmer's narrative thus indicates the tenacious authority of Treves, not only because the surgeon appears before the title character does, but also because his reminiscence sets the preliminary pattern for this account, as it has done for Montagu and for Howell and Ford in the *True History*. The pattern also enacts in the rhetorical level what is happening on the narrative level: Treves's increase of fellow feeling for Merrick, his steady but never entirely straightforward move from conceiving Merrick as object to accepting him as patient and valuing him as friend. Finally, beginning his story with the surgeon and ending with an afterword that carefully locates it within factual and scientific contexts, Drimmer implicitly demonstrates the sympathetic bond between himself and Treves. Just as Treves's objective in his relations with Merrick was to foster self-esteem in Merrick, so one of Drimmer's goals is to cultivate such a positive attitude in his young readers. The following passage, one of Treves's observations on Merrick, might also be seen as a highly colored version of what Drimmer hopes to offer his audience:

> He is changing, mused the surgeon, just as I hoped he would. He no longer thinks of himself as a freak, a monster more hideous than Victor Hugo's hunchback of Notre Dame. In part that is because there are no mirrors to remind him how unsightly he is. But also it must be because he's found that people don't turn away from him once they've really come

to know him. His goodness and sweetness, like a powerful light, shine
through so brightly, people barely see deformity.

And, because they care for him, at last he can care for himself. (104–
105)

The passage quoted above suggests Treves's benevolence as well as
Merrick's emotional good health, and Drimmer's narrative consistently
offers a more positive view of Treves, Merrick's exhibitors, and Victorian society in general than do the Elephant Man plays or the film. In
Drimmer, the first medical encounter is a highly humane one, with the
surgeon offering Merrick a bun and settling him before the fire (26–
27). Here, Treves acknowledges from the outset that Merrick is no imbecile (32). Even with this knowledge of Merrick's mental competence,
Treves seems neither callous nor remiss in allowing a return to the life
of exhibition, for he keeps track of Merrick during the migrant period
following the London exhibit but preceding the Continental tour—and
anyway, the life Merrick resumes is presented as far from degraded.
Drimmer's narrative highlights Tom Norman's flashy prosperity but
gives no indication of cruelty or exploitation. Indeed, Norman here is
interested enough in his protégé to attend the Pathological Society
meeting and perceptive enough to recognize Merrick's alert hopeful-
ness before the medical men. Later, when in the "Easy Street" chapter
we gain Merrick's own perspective on the days of exhibition, the emphasis is on the managers' fairness and Merrick's comparative prosperity. Even the "Austrian manager" who steals Merrick's nest egg at
least leaves behind other valuables, a silver watch, chain, and cuff-
links that Merrick pawns to pay for his passage to London.

As the afterword carefully explaining his sources indicates, Drimmer attempts to make his story as faithful to fact as possible by following Treves and Howell and Ford with regard to dates, main characters,
and verifiable events, by making the dialogue echo Treves or others
who knew Merrick whenever possible, and by supplying up-to-date
scientific explanations to correct popular Victorian misconceptions
such as the "rampaging elephant" explanation of Merrick's anomaly,
supplemented in Drimmer's book by a footnote on the genetic cause of
such disorders. Drimmer also announces which minor characters and
details he has invented—and these explicit inventions together with
the essentially positive interpretations of Treves and the other real peo-

ple who surrounded Merrick in his adult life paradoxically give a compelling mythic shape to a narrative that follows, as far as possible, the
verifiable facts of Merrick's life. In Drimmer, the growth of Merrick's
self-esteem takes on something of the familiar tale of a deserving outcast attaining the status he deserves (Oliver Twist, Dick Whittington,
or the young master of Puss in Boots) and something of the equally
familiar story of inner worth recognized beneath a repellent exterior
(Beauty and the Beast, the Frog Prince).

A chief element in making Drimmer's mythic rendition, like
Howell and Ford's children's book, a story suitable for a young audience
is how it circumscribes, and thereby weakens, the cumulative force of
the human cruelty suffered by Merrick. Treves, Norman and the other
English exhibitors, Nurse Ireland, Mrs. Kendal, and Mrs. Maturin (the
actual name of the "young and pretty widow" who first visited Merrick
at Bedstead Square) are all unequivocally benevolent—and there is
none of the sense we get from Pomerance, Lynch, and Faudree and to a
lesser extent from Howell and Ford and Trombley that some vague but
potent negativity lies at the patriarchal, or matriarchal, heart of Victorian culture and all its institutions. In Drimmer's narrative, Merrick's
mistreatment comes at the hands of three people marginal to the story
as told: his stepmother, who is made a wicked witch of the first water in
standard folk-tale tradition; the fictive master of the Leicester workhouse, whose very name, "Quigger," suggests sadistic brutality; and
the larcenous Austrian impresario discussed above. Significantly, the
cruel usage Merrick suffers at the hands of these three characters occurs before his establishment at the London Hospital. When Merrick
enters there, he comes into that special place of mythic convention, the
garden or room or cottage or palace where nothing harmful or even ambiguous seems able to enter. In Drimmer we encounter no sinister
night porters or sniggering socialites or Faustian healers. Ensconced in
what a chapter title alluding to a London Hospital witticism terms the
"Elephant House," Merrick develops self-esteem, not just from the
visits of ladies and royals alike but also from his growth as a creative
being who designs, rather than merely assembles, cardboard castles
and churches. Merrick's definitive validation as a prince of the spirit
comes in blatantly fairy tale form: Along with the Christmas gift of the
dressing case (pure Treves), he receives a kiss under the mistletoe from
the beautiful Nurse Ireland (pure Drimmer).

Although Drimmer draws on the power of myth to pattern his account of Merrick's life, the previously mentioned need to keep his readers close to the facts is equally strong. Something of this sense is discernible in Drimmer's choice of illustrations: Instead of an artist's supplementary interpretation of the story, the strategy adopted in Howell and Ford's children's book, Drimmer provides a photographic record of the visual documents in the case, as do Montagu and Howell and Ford in their *True History* — Merrick's birth registration, the Fildes portrait of Treves, pictures of Merrick in 1884 and 1886, casts of various body parts, the skeleton, the "yachting cap" and mask, the entrance to the rooms in Bedstead Square, the cardboard church, front and back covers of the *Autobiography*, likenesses of Mrs. Kendal, Princess Alexandra, and her family. Similarly, Drimmer's presentation of Merrick's death carefully balances a respect for the circumstances as they are known and for psychological plausibility with a concern for the generic conventions of children's literature. Drimmer neither falsifies the death scene nor puts it in the most starkly factual manner. In the last chapter, "To Sleep Like Other People," Merrick is especially tired and cozy, conscious of the actions preceding his death without exactly intending them:

> He became aware he was moving down the bed and the pillows were moving down with him, his head resting on one of them.
>
> He knew he shouldn't be doing it.
>
> But he wanted to. It felt so good.
>
> His heavy head sank deeper into the soft pillow.
>
> For an instant he felt a pain in his neck. Somehow he didn't mind it. He almost enjoyed the sensation.
>
> Joseph became drowsier and drowsier. He drifted off to sleep. (135)

Thanks to this tactful conclusion, Merrick need not shrink to a mere victim whose life, having at last become emotionally gratifying, ends by a pathetic accident. Nor need he seem a suicidal sufferer whose last act would seem to undercut the self-esteem Treves, and Drimmer, wish to cultivate. Here, the emotionally healthy Merrick called into being by the kindness of Treves and others has been saved by Drimmer for the story's young audience. In this account, Merrick's is a good death — an unsought but unresisted release from physical pain.

Drimmer's portrayal of Merrick as a figure with whom adolescents can identify suggests a decisive change in his understanding of Merrick from that informing his earlier book, *Very Special People: The Struggles, Loves, and Triumphs of Human Oddities*, published in 1973. A collection of anecdotal material on carnival and circus freaks, *Very Special People* is unquestionably sympathetic to its subjects: As its subtitle suggests, its purpose is to insist that they have struggles, loves, and triumphs like those of normal people. Nevertheless Drimmer's subjects remain "human oddities," and the volume enshrines Merrick as the oddest of the odd, setting him apart even from all other freaks by reprinting Treves's reminiscence as the last piece in the book and labeling him a "Very Very Special" person. While it is perhaps impossible to know exactly what accounts for the change in Drimmer's view of Merrick, it seems reasonable to attribute it to the appearance of Howell and Ford's *True History* between the time of *Very Special People* and Drimmer's *Elephant Man*. With the appearance of Howell and Ford's book, Merrick gained for the first time real, identifiable parents, who more or less loved him. He gained siblings, a youthful family tragedy in the death of his brother, and an aunt and uncle who cared enough for him to take him in when his father and stepmother rejected him. His aspirations and purposes also came to seem more real, less "special": to roll cigars or hawk haberdashery about the streets, to avoid becoming too great a burden to his aunt and uncle when their economic and family situation became more difficult, to escape the workhouse, even if it meant going on exhibition. In short, the effect of Howell and Ford's book has been, on one level, to significantly demythicize Merrick. Yet, as we have shown in this chapter, their *True History* itself also significantly remythicizes Merrick, especially in his relationship to Treves. That process of remythicizing is continued by others as well: from Trombley—who gathers all Treves's contacts with deformed patients under the chapter heading "Monsters"—to the medical writer of *Science News*—who, following the lead of Drs. Tibbles and Cohen, designates Merrick "Proteus Man"—to Drimmer himself, who casts his version of Merrick's story for adolescents in the pattern of Dick Whittington or the Frog Prince. All these tellings testify to the strong pressure toward myth somehow inherent in Merrick's story. Or perhaps the strong pressure is in us, as we seek to cast Merrick either as "thing of darkness" or prince of the spirit, in order to avoid acknowledging him as one of our own.

9

Afterword

During the 1980s, Merrick's story saturated the public consciousness in diverse forms, through various genres, at all cultural levels. The Elephant Man became a commonplace, a personage seriously discussed in a *PMLA* essay that compares the Pomerance play and the Lynch film and humorously portrayed in Gary Larson's cartoon *The Far Side*, where the Elephant Man and the Buffalo Gal strike up an acquaintance at a bar. Newspapers and tabloids routinely and loosely used the epithet "Elephant Man" in their headlines, whether sensational (claiming that Cher would adopt a child with the "Elephant Man disease") or scientific (announcing discovery of the genetic location of neurofibromatosis).[1] Cinematic reflections of Merrick's story continued to appear: lingering traces of Elephant Man themes, preoccupations, and images in the subsequent film work of David Lynch, comparable stories of radical deformity bravely endured (*Mask*, among others), explicitly reflexive treatments taking fictive versions of the story, not facts, as a point of departure (*The Tall Guy*, a British farce whose protagonist is a gawky American actor, in love with a nurse and playing the Elephant Man in a camp Lloyd-Webberesque musical called *Elephant*, with a chorus line of quasi Babars and such songs as "He's Packing His Trunk").

Because facts and fictions about Merrick have proliferated and have permeated the culture, reconstructing a genealogy for contemporary narratives would be a much murkier matter than it was in earlier times. There are simply too many major and minor potential influences to take into account. Our intent here at the end is not to continue the discussion of who begot what. Nor do we attempt a summing up. Any sort of "last word" would be a false gesture, for the one thing that can be said of Merrick's story in its diverse forms is that it does not close and they do not stop appearing. Thus, we end as we began, with an auto-biography—that of popular entertainer Michael Jackson, one of the many contemporary artists who have shown interest in the Elephant Man. We have selected this example for several reasons. Jackson's celebrity would inevitably make any presumed interest in the Elephant Man an enhancement to Merrick's myth—however unsubstantiated or superficial that interest might be. There is, however, evidence of significant interest. Reports of Jackson offering half a million dollars for Merrick's skeleton made the newspapers and a popular magazine in 1987; though the story of an offer seems to have been a hoax, the interest in Merrick appears genuine.[2] In his highly publicized rock video *Moonwalking* (1988) Jackson dances with an animator's rendition of those bones—a superimposition of an elephant skull on a human body, the very effect that would result if one could strip the fictive flesh from the fictive bones of the crude painted depiction announcing the Elephant Man's exhibition to Treves and the other Londoners who came and looked. Most important, Michael Jackson is, like Joseph Merrick, a fascinating real-life Proteus. The deliberate agency of cosmetic surgery has changed the one, whereas an intractable, progressive disorder remade the other; but despite these differences in the causes and effects of their physical mutability, the two are remarkably similar in their respective demonstrations of how a person is partly innate, partly made, and partly reflected, a blend of existing material, individual will, and public perception.

In his autobiography, *Moonwalk*, Jackson does not mention his interest in Merrick or his alleged efforts to obtain the Elephant Man's skeleton, but the narrative offers anyone familiar with Merrick's story a remarkable sequence of parallels to consider. Whether the resemblances are conscious allusions, unconscious echoes, or just coincidental affinities, they are a striking indication of how much common ground exists between the rich American celebrity and the poor British freak, of how effectively the man denied a mirror can serve as "The

Man in the Mirror" for Jackson. Even before the narrative of *Moonwalk* begins, two pictures evoke Merrick's world as much as they do Jackson's. The inside front cover presents a still life of elaborate personal accessories comparable to those from the Elephant Man's dressing case. Pictured are a case itself, a glittering red tie and single silver glove, scissors, a rhinestone-headed silver cane, various pieces of jewelry, sunglasses, a passport, framed photographs, and a little bust: the accessories of a late twentieth-century dandy, all reflected in a looking glass. The picture preceding chapter 1 is yet more reminiscent of Merrick. Here, Michael Jackson appears in silhouette. His hat, curls, and contorted profile with puffed-out upper lip suggest Merrick's large, lumpy head. The twist of the torso and partial bend to the legs give an impression of spinal curvature and hip misalignment. One arm and hand appear normal, with the thumb sharply distinct from the closed fingers. The other arm is mostly hidden behind the torso; and because the fingers were moving while photographed, the hand has a blurred, flipperlike quality. An important point to keep in mind here is that although Jackson's shadow resembles Merrick, the man casting the shadow would not. Furthermore, this resemblance fixed in black and white is only a pose—a quicksilver moment among many for Jackson. Much the same effect derives from the trademark Michael Jackson legs that dance across each page's bottom margin border. Easily recognizable from their black trousers, white socks, and black shoes, the legs are frozen in an awkward, nearly clubfooted posture evocative of Merrick's stance. But the slim shoes are a far cry from Merrick's loose slippers, and motion-implying lines to the side of the legs suggest that the pose is both deliberate and ephemeral—an awkward stasis that punctuates and emphasizes the graceful movements framing it. Dandiacal self-deformity is as piquant a sauce for Jackson as high-life fantasies were for Merrick.

If these visual images are suggestive, the autobiography Jackson offers has its own resemblances to Merrick's story. Like Merrick's two-shilling pamphlet, Jackson's narrative begins with a fairy tale formula emphasizing the metamorphic power of words: "I've always wanted to be able to tell stories, you know, stories that came from my soul. I'd like to sit by a fire and tell people stories—make them see pictures, make them cry and laugh, take them *anywhere* emotionally with something as deceptively simple as words. I'd like to tell stories to move their

souls and transform them."[3] The story Jackson proceeds to tell is like
Merrick's in many ways. Jackson's parents appear like Merrick's in that
the father is emotionally distant, the mother beautiful, adored, and
crippled in youth. Like Merrick, Jackson has lived a life of exhibition.
He has experienced the ferocity of crowds and the two paradoxical consequences: isolation ("I believe I'm one of the loneliest people in the
world" [162]) and lack of privacy ("You can't do anything unless special
arrangements are made" [270]).

Perhaps because of unflinching public scrutiny, perhaps because
of his minority status in a predominantly white culture, Jackson seems
to have developed a dissatisfaction with his appearance that might
seem more appropriate for someone with Merrick's afflictions. Jackson's autobiography stresses the adolescent skin troubles that made
him enjoy transforming himself, by means of a five-hour makeup job,
into the Scarecrow in *The Wiz* (96, 135). He is also defensive about the
much-publicized plastic surgery that has, over the years, changed his
appearance so radically that his waxwork image in a Hollywood gallery
of stars had to be redone. Admitting to two nose jobs and the addition of
a chin cleft, Jackson denies having undergone processes of eye widen-
ing and skin lightening (229). If Merrick's many interpreters, from
Treves on, have conceived of him as a presexual being, Jackson, who
first gained fame as a child star, has in adult years presented a public
persona suggesting androgyny or never-grow-up boyishness. More than
once the media have alluded to him as Peter Pan, and the autobiography does nothing to dispel this impression. Female celebrities parade—but chastely—through Jackson's life as here chronicled: Elizabeth Taylor, Brooke Shields, Liza Minnelli, and Katharine Hepburn
are mentioned by name. Jackson's first "real date" was with another
famous woman, Tatum O'Neal. Jackson's innocent comment on that experience, *"She touched me"* (165), suggests that he, like the Merrick
presented by Treves and many of his successors, must have deeply required the recognition implied by that private gesture, so different from
being grabbed, mobbed, and exploited by the crowds. Pomerance's
Merrick and Mrs. Kendal feel strongly for each other because they both
know what it is to exist as object of the public gaze. Jackson's affinity
for famous women (those mentioned as well as his editor, Jacqueline
Kennedy Onassis, who provides an introductory statement for the autobiography) must rise in great part out of much the same empathy. Cer-

tainly for Jackson, as for these women and for Merrick, all the world ends up being a stage—indeed, Jackson's mention of being applauded when he attends plays (249) precisely parallels the blend of triumph and violation that Lynch's Merrick experiences at Drury Lane.

What might Michael Jackson see in Joseph Merrick, the man whose initials mirror his own and the myth so fascinating to the very culture that has half- perceived and half-created his own persona? A fellow self-exhibitor, one who started out, as Jackson did, with an impresario? A fellow sufferer existing in limbo between celebrity and freak—gazed at, appropriated, and reduced to the role he plays, colonized by the dominant values of his culture? Might an enormously successful black entertainer consider the Elephant Man his Victorian counterpart? Or, more positively, might Jackson sense that Merrick is his counterpart in achieving the triumph of grace over awkwardness? Jackson, as a dancer, can convert an ungainly pose to a beautiful move in the world of the flesh. For Merrick, the accomplishment had to be spiritual, but it was apparent all the same. As to the matter of wanting to buy Merrick's skeleton: Was it nothing but an idly considered publicity stunt? Or did Jackson the master of moves and the person easily touched by pictures (220) understand the eloquence of those bones? How might he see the significance of such a purchase—as appropriating Merrick's bones, or as protecting them from exhibition? An aspect of Merrick emphasized by more than one of his interpreters is that of church builder—might Jackson in his turn think to enshrine the saintly relics? Or could there be for Jackson a third alternative, neither appropriation nor the protection of sanctified bones? Do Jackson's autobiography and the *Moonwalking* video perhaps represent his own way, a dancer's way, of re-membering Merrick, of metaphorically laying flesh and movement back on those bones frozen in the stillness of the exhibition cabinet? Merrick thus remembered would be again a living being, one moving in time and in relation to others, one partly graspable in story but always eluding final formulation and hence inviting fresh articulation.

We hope to have remembered Joseph Merrick in something of that spirit here.

Notes

Chapter 1.
Introduction

1. Murray M. Schwartz, "Shakespeare through Contemporary Psychoanalysis," in *Representing Shakespeare: New Psychoanalytic Essays*, ed. Murray M. Schwartz and Coppélia Kahn (Baltimore: Johns Hopkins University Press, 1980), 24.

Chapter 2.
Merrick at First Hand: Miscellaneous Accounts

1. Michael Howell and Peter Ford, *The True History of the Elephant Man* (London: Allison & Busby, 1980), 81. Future citations will be given parenthetically.

2. The *Autobiography* is included as an appendix in Howell and Ford, 168–69.

3. The tales of the Brothers Grimm were a staple of Victorian childhood, as affirmed by a number of the writers collected in Lance Salway's *Peculiar Gift: Nineteenth-Century Writings on Books for Children* (London: Kestrel, 1976). In 1855, William Caldwell Roscoe characterized Edgar Taylor's *German Popular Stories* (1823–26), a selection of Grimm tales with Cruikshank illustrations, as a translation "which has ever since [its English publication] been one of the first favourites in every household" (28). Writing in 1887, the time of Merrick's residence at the London Hospital, Edward Salmon speaks of Grimm as being, along with Aesop and Andersen, a basic choice of all classes of parents: "in the houses of rich and poor alike," "among the first books placed in the hands of their children" (47). Interestingly, Salmon sees the Grimm tales as crucially concerned with inculcating two qualities that all Merrick's acquaintances discerned as pre-eminent in him: contentment and modesty. As Salmon puts it, a persistent moral of the tales is that "by being dissatisfied with what we have, we risk even that" (47).

4. Although we have read the next eight texts—those from the *British Medical*

Journal, the *Transactions of the Pathological Society of London,* and the London *Times*—in their original sources, the page citations refer to the single source where readers will find them most conveniently: Ashley Montagu's *Elephant Man: A Study in Human Dignity* (1971; reprint, New York: E. P. Dutton, 1979), 101–125, appendices 1–8.

5. In a chapter on fibromas, under the section dealing with pendulous tumors, Crocker gave the following description of Merrick:

> An extraordinary case of the kind was brought to the Pathological Society by Treves. I had an opportunity of examining the patient there and at a show, where he was exhibited as an "elephant man." The bulk of the disease was on the right side; there was enormous hypertrophy of the skin of the whole right arm, measuring twelve inches round the wrist and five round one of the fingers, a lax mass of pendulous skin, etc., depending from the right pectoral region. The right side of the face was enormously thickened, and in addition there were huge, unsymmetrical exostoses on the forehead and occiput. There were also tumors affecting the right side of the gums and palate, on both legs, but chiefly the right, and over nearly the whole of the back and buttocks; the skin was immensely thickened, with irregular lobulated masses of confluent tumours, presenting the ordinary molluscous characters. The left arm and hand were small and well formed. The man was twenty-five years old, of stunted growth, and had a right talipes equinus, but was fairly intelligent. The disease was not perceived much at birth, but began to develop when five years old, and had gradually increased since; it was, of course, ascribed to maternal fright during pregnancy.

From H. Radcliffe Crocker, M.D., *Diseases of the Skin: Their Description, Pathology, Diagnosis, and Treatment* (Philadelphia: P. Blakiston, Son & Co., 1893), 631–632.

6. In the *Autobiography* Merrick mentions having "to undergo an operation on my face, having three or four ounces of flesh cut away" (Howell and Ford, 169), a mass that was responsible for the trunklike effect. Howell and Ford date this operation in 1882 (66–67), punctuating Merrick's period of residence at the Leicester workhouse.

7. Sir Wilfred Grenfell, *A Labrador Doctor: The Autobiography of Wilfred Thomason Grenfell* (1919; reprint, London: Hodder & Stoughton, 1929). Howell and Ford make their suggestion on p. 158.

8. John Berger, *About Looking* (New York: Pantheon, 1980), 4.

9. Berger, 18–19.

10. For an extended discussion of the connection between the British project of empire and the development of zoos, see Harriet Ritvo, *The Animal Estate: The English and Other Creatures in the Victorian Age* (Cambridge: Harvard University Press, 1987), especially 205–42.

11. Sir John Bland-Sutton, *The Story of a Surgeon* (London: Methuen & Co., 1930). Citations will be given parenthetically.

12. D. G. Halsted, *Doctor in the Nineties* (London: Christopher Johnson, 1959). Citations will be given parenthetically.

Chapter 3.
Frederick Treves and the Art of Reminiscence

1. See Montagu, 13–38; Howell and Ford, 170–187; Frederick Drimmer, *Very Special People: The Struggles, Loves, and Triumphs of Human Oddities* (New York: Amjon Publishers, 1973), 379–404.

2. For concise biographical details on Treves, consult *Plarr's Lives of the Fellows of the Royal College of Surgeons of England*, rev. Sir D'Arcy Power et al. (London: Simpkin Marshall, 1930), 2: 430; "Frederick Treves," *Dictionary of National Biography* (London: Oxford University Press, 1937), 856–58. Dr. Stephen Trombley has written a book-length biographical account: *Sir Frederick Treves: The Extra-Ordinary Edwardian* (London: Routledge, 1989).

3. Thomas Hardy, "In the Evening," in *The Complete Poems of Thomas Hardy*, ed. James Gibson (London: Macmillan Co., 1981), 802. The five-stanza poem is a dialogue—questions from the deceased Treves in his "chalky bed" and vague answers from a "spirit attending."

4. Sir Newman Flower, *Just As It Happened* (London: Cassell & Co., 1950), 118–21.

5. Thomas Hardy's *Autobiography* is a classic crux for students of the form in that its details and commentary often ring true, yet ultimately they are arranged and articulated not by Hardy but by his wife, Florence.

6. According to Halsted, Treves was fond of recounting this true "moral tale" to the young doctors at the London. Halsted offers his version of the story in *Doctor in the Nineties*, 41–42, adding to Treves's anecdote the following ironic coda:

> The curious thing about this story is that something very like it was to befall Treves himself, in the most tragic manner. His own daughter became ill with an abdominal pain, and for some time he was not sure what was the matter with her. Only when it was too late did he realise that she had appendicitis—on which he was such an acknowledged expert. By this time it had developed into an advance [sic] stage of peritonitis, and the poison was working into her system. Treves attempted to operate, but without success. At the eleventh hour he called in two of his surgeon colleagues, but they refused to take any responsibility for the case, pointing out that if he could not save her, no one could. Her death was a terrible blow to him. (42)

7. On the matter of Merrick's passage from the exhibition to the London Hospital, cf. Grenfell, 86.

8. *The Ring and the Book*, published in 1868–69, is Browning's twelve-book poem based on the murder of Pompilia Francheschini, a case reported in the Old Yellow Book he happened upon at a Florentine bookseller's. Taking the factual account as his source, Browning enters via dramatic monologues into various minds to approximate, in palimpsest fashion, the complex and incremental thing that is the "truth" of the affair. Among the viewpoints expressed are the diverse popular opinions, the arguments advanced by principals in the affair and their advocates, and the overarching reflections of the pope, whose judgment determines the sentence.

Treves's *Country of "The Ring and the Book"* presents the factual background of Browning's story, with particular emphasis upon the Italian places where the actions of the narrative took place. Scrupulous accuracy was, according to Treves, the *modus operandi* of Browning, who followed his original "with as much exactness as the limner of a missal copies a passage of Holy Writ" (xi)—and a comparable precision is Treves's concern in his own book. It seems especially telling that Treves went so far as to take the photographs illustrating his text "for the most part, at or about the actual date in the calendar on which occurred the episode with which the particular scene is associated" (xiii). Given such extraordinarily painstaking attention to detail, Treves's subsequent inaccuracies in the specifics of Merrick's story are striking, whether these errors rise out of failing memory in the last year of the ailing writer's life or out of his wish to shape Merrick's story, an impulse strong enough to override even Treves's habitual attentiveness to factual accuracy. See Sir Frederick Treves, *The Country of "The Ring and the Book"* (London: Cassell & Co., 1913).

9. Howell and Ford discuss changing public opinion as to the decency of exhibiting freaks on 38–39.

10. For an anecdote illustrating Treves's decisiveness, see Howell and Ford, 28.

11. On this point see, for example, Stella Bingham, *Ministering Angels* (Oradell, N.J.: Medical Economics Co., 1979), 75.

12. All contemporary accounts of Merrick's death state that it occurred in the afternoon. Treves's reference to Merrick's "last night" is, like others of his inaccuracies, an artistic misremembering. Whether or not Treves intended to do so, the effect of his revision of the facts as they stood is to enhance the allegory he is making of Merrick's life.

13. Howell and Ford, 53–54.

14. Treves's awareness of the connection between a change of hat and a change of identity is comically suggested by his attempts at disguise during the illness of the Prince of Wales just before his coronation. At that time a number of measures were taken to maintain secrecy about the prince's condition. When Treves was summoned to go to Windsor to attend the prince, he "went down in an old suit and overcoat, and an ancient tweed cap so as not to be recognised." As his biographer Stephen Trombley suggests, simply wearing a tweed cap was unlikely to prevent Treves, with his "well-known face" and "distinctive walrus moustache," from being identified. Nevertheless, Treves here seems clearly sensitive to the possible transformation implicit in a change of hat. See Trombley, 127.

Chapter 4.
Merrick as Exemplar: Ashley Montagu on Maternal Love

1. Montagu, *The Elephant Man: A Study in Human Dignity* (New York: E. P. Dutton, 1979), xiii. Further references are to this edition; they will be cited parenthetically.

2. Howell and Ford, 40.

3. Merrick, born in 1862, lived with his mother and father until her death in May 1873. His father then moved the family into lodgings, where their landlady was a twenty-nine-year-old widow, Mrs. Emma Wood Antill. In December 1874, Merrick's father and Mrs. Antill married, and Joseph continued to live with them until he was cast out into the streets, apparently in 1877. See Howell and Ford, 40–59.

4. See Montagu, 39, 40, 120.

5. Howell and Ford, 40.

6. Merrick lived with his uncle Charles Merrick, a hairdresser, and his family from 1877 until just after Christmas 1879, at which time he presented himself to the relieving officer in Leicester, "demonstrating his deformities and pleading an inability to work." He was admitted immediately to the Leicester Union Workhouse. See Howell and Ford, 60.

7. The quote is from Laurens Van der Post, *Flamingo Feather* (New York: William Morrow & Co., 1955), 93.

8. Sir Frederick Treves, *The Elephant Man and Other Reminiscences* (London: Cassell & Co., 1923), 15–16.

9. The Pope quotation consists of lines 196–200 of "Eloisa to Abelard." See *Pope: Poetical Works*, ed. Herbert Davis (London: Oxford University Press, 1966), 115.

10. Ashley Montagu, ed. *The Meaning of Love* (1953; reprint, Westport, Conn.: Greenwood Press, 1974), 17.

11. Montagu, *The Meaning of Love*, 18–19.

12. Ashley Montagu, *The Direction of Human Development* (1955; reprint, New York: Hawthorn Books, 1970), 307.

13. Montagu, *The Meaning of Love*, 20. See also Ashley Montagu, *Immortality, Religion, and Morals* (New York: Hawthorn Books, 1971), 76.

14. Montagu, *The Meaning of Love*, 21.

15. Ashley Montagu, ed. *Man and Aggression* (New York: Oxford University Press, 1973), xix, 3–18.

16. Montagu, *Man and Aggression*, 16.

17. Ashley Montagu and Floyd Matson, *The Dehumanization of Man* (New York: McGraw-Hill, 1983), 219–20.

18. Howell and Ford, 95.

19. Montagu, *The Meaning of Love*, 21–22; Montagu, *The Direction of Human Development*, 311–12.

20. Montagu, *Immortality, Religion, and Morals*, 63.

21. Montagu, *Immortality, Religion, and Morals*, 63. Quoted are lines 2–3 of George Eliot's poem "O May I Join the Choir Invisible." For the complete poem, see Eliot, *Poems, Essays, and Leaves from a Note Book* (New York: Doubleday, Page & Co., 1901–4), 362.

22. Mrs. Kendal wrote of her connection with Merrick in chapter 15 of *Dame Madge Kendal by Herself* (London: John Murray, 1933), 281–87.

23. Susan Sontag, *Illness as Metaphor* (New York: Farrar, Straus & Giroux, 1978).

24. Howell and Ford, 136.

25. J. A. R. Tibbles and M. M. Cohen, Jr., "The Proteus Syndrome: The Elephant Man Diagnosed," *British Medical Journal* 293 (September 13, 1986): 685.

26. Tibbles and Cohen, 683.

Chapter 5.
Merrick at Center Stage: Bernard Pomerance's *Elephant Man*

1. " 'Elephant' Men Stampede Legit; Pomerance Work Set for B'way," *Variety*, March 7, 1979, 174.

2. Jed Harris and Ric Gruczynski collaborated on a production of a play about the Elephant Man in Milwaukee in 1975. Apparently no script of this play has survived (Jed Harris, conversation with the authors, July 28, 1989). An opera, to be called "Hopi Prophecies," was written in the late 1970s by composer Michael Roth and librettist Dan Schreier. It merged the story of the Elephant Man with that of Lincoln and Grant. As far as we have been able to determine, it was not performed (Michael Roth, conversation with the authors, October 3, 1989).

3. " 'Elephant' Men Stampede Legit," 174.

4. Bernard Pomerance, *The Elephant Man* (New York: Grove Press, 1979), v. Future citations are to this edition; they will be cited parenthetically.

5. Stanley Kauffmann, "Arts and Lives," *New Republic* 180, no. 7 (February 17, 1979): 25.

6. Gerald Weales, "Show and Tell: An Elephant for All Seasons," *Commonweal* 106, no. 6 (March 30, 1979): 181.

7. Steve Lawson, "Beauty of the Beast: The Elephant Man," *Horizon* 22, no. 6 (June 1979): 21.

8. Martha Bayles, "Deformation of Character," *Harper's* 262 (May 1981): 67–68. William E. Holladay and Stephen Watt argue that Pomerance "implicates modern audiences in the smugness they despise in his Victorians." To what degree this "implication" is a matter of Pomerance's conscious intention, however, remains vague. Like Bayles, we remain unconvinced; Pomerance allows his audience to exempt themselves from his social critique by focusing that critique on a doctor, a figure with whom contemporary audiences are unlikely to identify. See "Viewing the Elephant Man," *PMLA* 104 (1989): 880.

9. Weales, "Show and Tell," 181; John Simon, "Clouded Emerald," *New York* 13, no. 40 (October 13, 1980): 55; Jack Richardson, "Freak Shows," *Commentary* 68, no. 1 (July 1979): 63.

10. Dean Valentine, "On Stage: The Parable Maker," *New Leader* 63, no. 10 (May 7, 1979): 23; Walter Kerr, "Theatergoers Were Asked to Help Make Magic," *New York Times*, December 30, 1979, sec. 2: 1, 3; Simon, " 'An Angel' Comes to Huntington . . . ," *New York* 12, no. 5 (January 29, 1979): 121.

11. Lawson, "Beauty of the Beast," 16.

12. Stanley Kauffmann, "Books and the Arts," *New Republic* 180, no. 19 (May 12, 1979): 24–25; John Simon, "Quip, Quip against the Dying of the Light," *New York* 12, no. 19 (May 7, 1979): 84–85; and Richardson, "Freak Shows," 62–63.

13. Janet Karsten Larson, "Poetry of Religion on Broadway: 'The Elephant Man,'" *Christian Century* 97, no. 1 (January 2–9, 1980), 14.

14. Arthur C. McGill, *Death and Life: An American Theology* (Philadelphia: Fortress Press, 1987), 50.

15. David Willbern, "Shakespeare's Nothing," in *Representing Shakespeare: New Psychoanalytic Essays*, ed. Murray M. Schwartz and Coppélia Kahn (Baltimore: Johns Hopkins University Press, 1980), 255.

16. *Romeo and Juliet*, 5.3.45–48.

17. Plato, *The Republic*, in *Great Dialogues of Plato*, trans. W. H. D. Rouse, ed. Eric H. Warmington and Philip G. Rouse (New York: New American Library, 1956), 403.

18. 1 Corinthians 3:10–11. (King James Version).

19. Stanley Hauerwas, *Suffering Presence: Theological Reflections on Medicine, the Mentally Handicapped, and the Church* (Notre Dame: University of Notre Dame Press, 1986), 6.

20. Hauerwas, 81.

21. This is perhaps as good a place as any to indicate the difference between our treatment of Pomerance's play (and of Merrick's story more generally) and that of Holladay and Watt in "Viewing the Elephant Man." Whereas their tendency throughout is to resolve such relationships into such polarities as master-slave, subject-object, and domination-victimization, we stress Pomerance's efforts to create, both in the theater and the church, a space of interplay, of true meeting, where such polarities can be overcome. Content central to our study is marginal in theirs. Despite Pomerance's placing the building of the church firmly at the center of his play, the church receives only one brief mention by Holladay and Watt near the end of their article, where we are told that Treves rejects "mere consolation" and that the play's offered "salvation" is "not religious but political" (879). Also marginalized in their investigation of "the social origins of Merrick's victimization," (870) is the physical reality of Merrick's condition. The fullest description of his disorder is relegated to a footnote, and the article communicates very little sense of his bodily experience. This double marginalization of church and body should not be surprising, for it is the church that is formed around the Incarnation and insists on being a community of embodied persons living specific histories. For Holladay and Watt, Merrick is essentially like all others; the article glances at the problem of the individual and the typical (869) and, in keeping with its loosely Marxist spirit, presses him toward the typical. This is quite apparent in their epigraph and the transformation they ring on it near the end of the article. "Man stands amaz'd to see his deformity / In any other creature but himself," they begin, quoting John Webster's *The Duchess of Malfi*, but their conclusion denies Merrick any otherness: "So, regardless of John Webster's observation, men do stand amazed to see their own deformity." One telling fact suggests the degree to which

Holladay and Watt are engaged by what Merrick can represent rather than by his individual, bodily, and historical existence: Despite their knowledge of Howell and Ford's *True History of the Elephant Man*, they consistently get Merrick's Christian name wrong, referring to him as John.

22. Hauerwas, 52.

23. Ernest Becker, *The Denial of Death* (New York: The Free Press, 1973), 47–66. See especially p. 51, where Becker comments, "And so the core of psychodynamics, the formation of the human character, is a study in human self-limitation and in the terrifying costs of that limitation."

24. Luke 6:24 (King James Version).

25. Treves, *The Elephant Man*, 25: "Other ladies followed the Queen's gracious example and sent their photographs to the delighted creature who had been all his life despised and rejected of men." Cf. Isaiah 53:3: "He is despised and rejected of men; a man of sorrows, and acquainted with grief: and we hid as it were *our* faces from him; he was despised, and we esteemed him not" (King James Version).

26. Cf. Isaiah 40:4: "Every valley shall be exalted, and every mountain and hill shall be made low: and the crooked shall be made straight, and the rough places plain" (King James Version).

Chapter 6.
Merrick on the Fringe: Plays by Thomas Gibbons, William Turner, and Roy Faudree

1. On the Frankenstein melodramas that followed in the wake of Mary Shelley's novel, see "Melodrama and Burlesque: 1823–1832," chapter 1 of Steven Earl Forry, *Hideous Progenies* (Philadelphia: University of Pennsylvania Press, 1990), 3–42.

2. Production information from " 'Elephant' Men Stampede Legit," 174. Citations of the play will refer to Thomas Gibbons, *The Exhibition: Scenes from the Life of John Merrick* (New York: Dramatists Play Service, n.d.) and will be given parenthetically.

3. Jed Harris, letter to the authors, August 2, 1989. All quotations are from the typescript of the original workshop production.

4. Quoted in John Righetti, "Turner Discusses Staging of 'Elephant Man,' " *Pitt News* (Pittsburgh), December 1, 1978, 9.

5. Righetti, "Turner Discusses Staging of 'Elephant Man,' " 9.

6. " 'Elephant' Man Stampede Legit," 174. For the play's revival in 1987, see " 'The Elephant Man' Returns," *Daily Hampshire Gazette* (Northampton, Mass.), May 13, 1987, 32.

7. C. Hugh Holman, *A Handbook to Literature* (Indianapolis: Odyssey Press, 1978), 216.

8. Quoted in Chris Rohmann, "An Avant-garde 'The Elephant Man,' " *Valley Advocate* (Amherst, Mass.), May 11, 1987, 8.

9. All quotations are from *The Elephant Man*, copyrighted Roy Faudree, 1975.

We thank Mr. Faudree for his kindness in providing us a copy of the play.

10. Rohmann, "An Avant-garde 'The Elephant Man,' " 8.

11. Gibbons, 24.

Chapter 7.
"If Only I Could Find Her": David Lynch and Merrick's Search for the Lost Mother

1. Bayles, "Deformation of Character," 66–68; Bruce Kawin, "The Elephant Man," *Film Quarterly* 34, no. 4 (Summer 1981): 21–25; Holladay and Watt, "Viewing the Elephant Man," 868–81.

2. The word screen reads "Based on *The Elephant Man and Other Reminiscences* by Sir Frederick Treves and in part on *The Elephant Man: A Study in Human Dignity* by Ashley Montagu."

3. Quotations are directly from the film, *The Elephant Man* (1980), directed by David Lynch, unless otherwise identified. A screenplay of the film, written by Christopher De Vore, Eric Bergren, and David Lynch has been published (Paramount, 1980). When we cite the screenplay, indication is given in the text itself with page numbers in the notes.

4. *Variety*, May 16, 1979, 52.

5. Cf. De Vore, Bergren, and Lynch, *The Elephant Man* (Paramount, 1980), 13–14.

6. Leslie Fiedler, *Freaks: Myths and Images of the Secret Self* (New York: Simon & Schuster, 1978). See especially his pages on the Elephant Man, 170–77.

7. J. Hillis Miller, Introduction to Charles Dickens, *Oliver Twist* (New York: Holt Rinehart, 1962), xvi–xix. George Orwell makes much the same point in his essay on Dickens in *Dickens, Dali, and Others* (New York: Harcourt, Brace & World, 1946). Holladay and Watt also stress the narrative shape of melodrama in the accounts of Merrick's life by Treves, Pomerance, and Lynch; their specific focus, however, is on the way Merrick's experience is shaped by the patterns of domestic melodrama, with Merrick cast as the innocent heroine. See "Viewing the Elephant Man," 870–74.

8. William Tilbury Fox (1836–79), specialist in diseases of the skin, was the teacher of H. Radcliffe Crocker (1845–1909), author of *Diseases of the Skin* (originally published in 1888).

9. De Vore, Bergren, and Lynch, 1.

10. De Vore, Bergren, and Lynch, 7–8.

11. De Vore, Bergren, and Lynch, 39.

12. In the screenplay, the scene ends with Anne and Merrick "locked together in the communication of intense sympathy," while Treves, as if from the outside, looks on "in wonder." The effect is to emphasize even more strongly than the film does the childlike and presexual quality that has been part of Merrick's story since Treves's reminiscence. Merrick plays the child's role here as he and Anne Treves enact a moment of silent sympathy reminiscent of the preverbal, mutually loving

gaze of child and mother. De Vore, Bergren, and Lynch, 84.

13. As is often the case with films, David Lynch's *Elephant Man* generated an identically titled "book version," written by Christine Sparks (New York: Ballantine, 1980) but copyrighted by Brooksfilms Inc., the film's production company. The book's primary fidelity is clearly indicated by a page listing the major film credits opposite the title page—and below the credits, the same disclaimer that appears at the end of the film: "Based on the life of John Merrick the Elephant Man, and not upon the Broadway play or any other fictional account." As one would expect, this novel is, for the most part, a prose rendition of what goes on in Lynch's film version. The novel's innovations are of two basic sorts—amplification of things stated less fully on the screen and articulation of things not stated, either because saying them would be impossible (the camera may show a haggard Treves, but there is no plausible way of saying that a "premature pallor" makes him look older than his years) or awkward (Mothershead's thoughts on mothers who have abandoned their deformed children could be put into dialogue on the screen, but the result would be undue talkiness, whereas the novel can quite naturally contain a long paragraph in her consciousness, as it does on p. 69).

Many of the details supplied by the novel serve as glosses to the film's characterizations. These supplementary bits of information are sometimes factual: the family backgrounds of Frederick and Anne Treves and of Carr Gomm, for instance. At other times, when they refer to invented characters, such glosses are inevitably fictive. For example, the novel invents a past for Mothershead, who is said to have been one of Florence Nightingale's first nurses. Occasionally, however, the novel offers fictions where facts are available. For instance, Treves's actual daughters, Hetty and Enid, are given more fashionable 1980 names, Jenny and Kate, and their respective presentations as a plain, intelligent girl with "the chilly hard-bitten mind a scientist needed. What on earth would a woman do with such a mind?" (8) and as a pretty, shallow creature of convention tell us less about the real children than about 1980s perceptions of repressive Victorian stereotypes. But in factual and fictive moments alike, the Sparks novel remains a supplement to the Lynch film, not an alternative to it. What is worth noting about this situation is that congruence can seem a good deal like confirmation to an unreflective mind. If two accounts agree with each other, they must be true—and thus for some people, at least, the narrative offered in the Sparks novel will validate the Lynch version of Merrick's story.

Chapter 8.
Facts Excavated and Fictions Diffused: Merrick in the 1980s

1. For details on Merrick's early years, see Howell and Ford, *True History*, 40—54. All quotations are from this edition; they will be given parenthetically.

2. For details in this section, see Howell and Ford, 55—56.

3. For Joseph's early working life and admission to the workhouse, see Howell and Ford, especially 56—60.

4. Howell and Ford, 60—69.

5. Howell and Ford, 71—72.

6. For Joseph's career on exhibition and his difficult journey back to London, see Howell and Ford, 69—91.

7. Arthur C. McGill, *Suffering: A Test of Theological Method* (Philadelphia: Geneva Press, 1968), 69—70.

8. Trombley, *Frederick Treves,* vii. Future page references are to this edition; they will be given parenthetically.

9. Kenneth Sherman, *Words for Elephant Man* (Oakville, Ont.: Mosaic Press, 1983), 22, lines 1—8. Future citations are from this edition; line numbers will be given in the text.

10. Tibbles and Cohen, "The Proteus Syndrome," 684—85. Future citations will be given parenthetically.

11. "As of '87, He's Proteus Man," *Science News* 132 (July 25, 1987): 55.

12. "What the Elephant Man Really Had," *Newsweek* 111 (February 29, 1988): 64.

13. Franz Lidz, "Rocky: The Article," *Sports Illustrated* 73 (November 12, 1990): 83.

14. Michael Howell and Peter Ford, *The Elephant Man: Retold for Children* (London: Allison & Busby, 1984), 9—10. Future page references will be given parenthetically.

15. Frederick Drimmer, *The Elephant Man* (New York: G. P. Putnam's Sons, 1985), 14. Future references will be given parenthetically.

Chapter 9.
Afterword

1. Now that the medical consensus is that Merrick suffered from the Proteus syndrome rather than neurofibromatosis, his being associated with the latter— typically a far milder disorder—is troubling, especially to clinical specialists studying neurofibromatosis and to patients identified as having it. Nonetheless, as Peter R. W. Bellerman, president of the National Neurofibromatosis Foundation, has stated in a letter to us, "even the most responsible media organizations, while recognizing the false connection, still make references such as 'Neurofibromatosis, incorrectly known as the Elephant Man's disease,' or 'formerly known as the Elephant Man's disease.' " Ironically, Bellerman's observation serves as implicit confirmation of the belief on which Tom Norman based his exhibition of Merrick as the Elephant Man: A compelling story does indeed hold the public mind more tenaciously than truths and facts will do.

2. J. Randy Taraborrelli's unauthorized biography *Michael Jackson: The Magic and the Madness* (New York: Birch Lane Press, 1991) discusses Merrick on pp. 438—40. According to Taraborrelli, the much-publicized purchase attempt was essentially a hoax. Taraborrelli reports that Jackson, having been deeply moved by the Lynch film, became keenly interested in reading about the details of Mer-

rick's medical history after suffering burns in a 1984 accident but that the bone-buying story was something Jackson thought up as a publicity stunt. The tale of a $500,000 offer, disseminated by Jackson's manager Frank Dileo and denied by the London Hospital, did succeed in attracting public notice of a crude and rather negative sort. Even so, our sense is that a serious sympathy must have preceded, and may have coexisted with, the idea of gaining publicity through an apparent attempt to acquire Merrick's bones—and our objective here is to speculate on the nature of that sympathy rather than on the circumstances of the purchase story.

3. Michael Jackson, *Moonwalk* (New York: Doubleday, 1988), 5. Subsequent citations will appear parenthetically in the text.

Select Bibliography

"As of '87, He's Proteus Man." *Science News* 132 (July 25, 1987): 55.

The Autobiography of Joseph Carey Merrick. In Michael Howell and Peter Ford, *The True History of the Elephant Man.* London: Allison & Busby, 1980, 168–169.

Bayles, Martha. "Deformation of Character." *Harper's* 262 (May 1981): 66–68.

Becker, Ernest. *The Denial of Death.* New York: Free Press, 1973.

Berger, John. *About Looking.* New York: Pantheon, 1980.

Bingham, Stella. *Ministering Angels.* Oradell, N.J.: Medical Economics Co., 1979.

Bland-Sutton, Sir John. *The Story of a Surgeon.* London: Methuen & Co., 1930.

Carr Gomm, F. C. "Death of 'The Elephant Man.'" *Times* (London), April 16, 1890, 6.

Carr Gomm, F. C. Letter to the Editor "The Elephant Man." *Times* (London), December 4, 1886, 6.

Clark, Brian. *Whose Life Is It, Anyway?* Chicago: Dramatic Publishing Co., 1974.

Cristofer, Michael. *The Shadow Box.* New York: Drama Book Specialists, 1977.

Crocker, H. Radcliffe, M.D. *Diseases of the Skin: Their Description, Pathology, Diagnosis, and Treatment.* Philadelphia: P. Blakiston, Son & Co., 1893.

"Death of the 'Elephant Man.'" *British Medical Journal* 1 (April 19, 1890): 916–17.

De Vore, Christopher, Eric Bergren, and David Lynch. *The Elephant Man.* Paramount, 1980.

Drimmer, Frederick. *The Elephant Man.* New York: G. P. Putnam's Sons, 1985.

Drimmer, Frederick. *Very Special People: The Struggles, Loves, and Triumphs of Human Oddities.* New York: Amjon Publishers, 1973.

"The Elephant Man." *British Medical Journal* 2 (December 11, 1886): 1188–89.

"'The Elephant Man' Returns." *Daily Hampshire Gazette* (Northampton, Mass.), May 13, 1987, 32.

"'Elephant' Men Stampede Legit; Pomerance Work Set for B'way." *Variety*, March 7, 1979, 174.

Eliot, George. *Poems, Essays, and Leaves from a Note Book*. New York: Doubleday, Page & Co., 1901–4.

Faudree, Roy. *The Elephant Man*. Copyright: Roy Faudree, 1975.

Fiedler, Leslie. *Freaks: Myths and Images of the Secret Self*. New York: Simon & Schuster, 1978.

Flower, Sir Newman. *Just As It Happened*. London: Cassell & Co., 1950.

Forry, Steven Earl. *Hideous Progenies*. Philadelphia: University of Pennsylvania Press, 1990.

Gibbons, Thomas. *The Exhibition: Scenes from the Life of John Merrick*. New York: Dramatists Play Service, n.d.

Grenfell, Sir Wilfred. *A Labrador Doctor: The Autobiography of Wilfred Thomason Grenfell*. London: Hodder & Stoughton, 1929. Reprint of 1919 edition.

Halsted, D. G. *Doctor in the Nineties*. London: Christopher Johnson, 1959.

Hardy, Thomas. *The Complete Poems of Thomas Hardy*. Edited by James Gibson. London: Macmillan Co., 1981.

Hauerwas, Stanley. *Suffering Presence: Theological Reflections on Medicine, the Mentally Handicapped, and the Church*. Notre Dame: University of Notre Dame Press, 1986.

Holladay, William E., and Stephen Watt. "Viewing the Elephant Man." *PMLA* 104 (1989): 868–81.

Holman, C. Hugh. *A Handbook to Literature*. Indianapolis: Odyssey Press, 1978.

Howell, Michael, and Peter Ford. *The Elephant Man: Retold for Children*. London: Allison & Busby, 1984.

Howell, Michael, and Peter Ford. *The True History of the Elephant Man*. London: Allison & Busby, 1980.

Jackson, Michael. *Moonwalk*. New York: Doubleday, 1988.

Kauffmann, Stanley. "Arts and Lives." *New Republic* 180, no. 7 (February 17, 1979): 24–26.

Kauffmann, Stanley. "Books and the Arts." *New Republic* 180, no. 19 (May 12, 1979): 24–25.

Kawin, Bruce. "The Elephant Man." *Film Quarterly* 34, no. 4 (Summer 1981): 21–25.

Kempinski, Tom. *Duet for One*. New York: S. French, 1981.

Kendal, Dame Madge. *Dame Madge Kendal by Herself*. London: John Murray, 1933.

Kerr, Walter. "Theatergoers Were Asked to Help Make Magic." *New York Times*, December 30, 1979, sec. 2: 1, 3.

Kopit, Arthur. *Wings: A Play*. New York: Hill & Wang, 1978.

Larson, Janet Karsten. "Poetry of Religion on Broadway: 'The Elephant Man,'" *Christian Century* 97, no. 1 (January 2–9, 1980): 14–18.

Lawson, Steve. "Beauty of the Beast: The Elephant Man." *Horizon* 22, no. 6 (June 1979): 16–24.

Lidz, Franz. "Rocky: The Article." *Sports Illustrated* 73 (November 12, 1990): 83.

McGill, Arthur C. *Death and Life: An American Theology.* Philadelphia: Fortress Press, 1987.

McGill, Arthur C. *Suffering: A Test of Theological Method.* Philadelphia: Geneva Press, 1968.

Medoff, Mark. *Children of a Lesser God.* Clifton, N.J.: J. T. White, 1980.

Miller, J. Hillis. Introduction to Charles Dickens, *Oliver Twist.* New York: Holt Rinehart, 1962.

Montagu, Ashley. *The Direction of Human Development.* New York: Hawthorn Books, 1970. Reprint of 1955 edition.

Montagu, Ashley. *The Elephant Man: A Study in Human Dignity.* New York: E. P. Dutton, 1979. Reprint of 1971 edition.

Montagu, Ashley. *Immortality, Religion, and Morals.* New York: Hawthorn Books, 1971.

Montagu, Ashley, and Floyd Matson. *The Dehumanization of Man.* New York: McGraw-Hill, 1983.

Montagu, Ashley, ed. *Man and Aggression.* New York: Oxford University Press, 1973.

Montagu, Ashley, ed. *The Meaning of Love.* Westport, Conn.: Greenwood Press, 1974. Reprint of 1953 edition.

Orwell, George. *Dickens, Dali, and Others.* New York: Harcourt, Brace & World, 1946.

Plarr's Lives of the Fellows of the Royal College of Surgeons of England. Rev. Sir D'Arcy Power et al. London: Simpkin Marshall, 1930. 2: 430–36.

Plato. *The Republic.* In *Great Dialogues of Plato,* translated by W. H. D. Rouse, edited by Eric H. Warmington and Philip G. Rouse. New York: New American Library, 1956.

Plato. *Timaeus.* Translated by H. D. P. Lee. Baltimore: Penguin, 1965.

Pomerance, Bernard. *The Elephant Man.* New York: Grove Press, 1979.

Pope: Poetical Works. Edited by Herbert Davis. London: Oxford University Press, 1966.

"Reports of Societies. Pathological Society of London, Tuesday 2 December 1884." *British Medical Journal* 2 (December 6, 1884): 1140.

"Reports of Societies. Pathological Society of London, Tuesday 17 March 1885." *British Medical Journal* 1 (March 21, 1885): 595.

Richardson, Jack. "Freak Shows," *Commentary* 68, no. 1 (July 1979): 62–64.

Righetti, John. "Turner Discusses Staging of 'Elephant Man,'" *Pitt News* (Pittsburgh), December 1, 1978, 9.

Ritvo, Harriet. *The Animal Estate: The English and Other Creatures in the Victorian Age.* Cambridge: Harvard University Press, 1987.

Rohmann, Chris. "An Avant-garde 'The Elephant Man,'" *Valley Advocate* (Amherst, Mass.), May 11, 1987, 8.

Salway, Lance. *A Peculiar Gift: Nineteenth-Century Writings on Books for Children.* London: Kestrel, 1976.

Schwartz, Murray M. "Shakespeare through Contemporary Psychoanalysis." In

Representing Shakespeare: New Psychoanalytic Essays, edited by Murray M. Schwartz and Coppélia Kahn, 21–32. Baltimore: Johns Hopkins University Press, 1980.

Shaffer, Peter. *Equus.* New York: S. French, 1973.

Sherman, Kenneth. *Words for Elephant Man.* Oakville, Ont.: Mosaic Press, 1983.

Simon, John. "'An Angel' Comes to Huntington, 'The Grand Tour' Comes to Nothing." *New York* 12, no. 5 (January 29, 1979): 119–21.

Simon, John. "Clouded Emerald." *New York* 13, no. 40 (October 13, 1980): 54–56.

Simon, John. "Quip, Quip against the Dying of the Light," *New York* 12, no. 19 (May 7, 1979): 84–85.

Sontag, Susan. *Illness as Metaphor.* New York: Farrar, Straus & Giroux, 1978.

Sparks, Christine. *The Elephant Man.* New York: Ballantine, 1980.

Taraborrelli, J. Randy. *Michael Jackson: The Magic and the Madness.* New York: Birch Lane Press, 1991.

Tibbles, J. A. R., and M. M. Cohen, Jr. "The Proteus Syndrome: The Elephant Man Diagnosed." *British Medical Journal* 293 (September 13, 1986): 683–85.

Treves, Sir Frederick. "A Case of Congenital Deformity." *Transactions of the Pathological Society of London* 36 (1885): 494–98.

Treves, Sir Frederick. *The Country of "The Ring and the Book."* London: Cassell & Co., 1913.

Treves, Sir Frederick. *The Cradle of the Deep: An Account of a Voyage to the West Indies.* London: Smith, Elder & Co., 1908.

Treves, Sir Frederick. *The Elephant Man and Other Reminiscences.* London: Cassell & Co., 1923.

Treves, Sir Frederick. *Highways and Byways in Dorset.* London: Macmillan Co., 1906.

Treves, Sir Frederick. *The Influence of Clothing on Health.* London: Cassell & Co., 1886.

Treves, Sir Frederick. *The Lake of Geneva.* London: Cassell & Co., 1922.

Treves, Sir Frederick. *The Land That Is Desolate: An Account of a Tour in Palestine.* London: John Murray, 1912.

Treves, Sir Frederick. *The Other Side of the Lantern: An Account of a Commonplace Tour round the World.* London: Cassell & Co., 1905.

Treves, Sir Frederick. *The Riviera of the Corniche Road.* London: Cassell & Co., 1921.

Treves, Sir Frederick. *Surgical Applied Anatomy.* London: Cassell & Co.; Philadelphia: H. C. Lea's Son & Co., 1883.

Treves, Sir Frederick. *The Tale of a Field Hospital.* London: Cassell & Co., 1900.

Treves, Sir Frederick. *Uganda for a Holiday.* London: Smith, Elder & Co., 1910.

Trombley, Stephen. *Sir Frederick Treves: The Extra-Ordinary Edwardian.* London: Routledge, 1989.

Turner, William. "The Elephant Man." Manuscript.

Valentine, Dean. "On Stage: The Parable Maker." *New Leader* 63, no. 10 (May 7, 1979): 23–24.

Van der Post, Laurens. *Flamingo Feather.* New York: William Morrow & Co., 1955.

Weales, Gerald. "Show and Tell: An Elephant for All Seasons." *Commonweal* 106, no. 6 (March 30, 1979): 180–81.

"What the Elephant Man Really Had." *Newsweek* 111 (February 29, 1988): 64.

Willbern, David. "Shakespeare's Nothing." In *Representing Shakespeare: New Psychoanalytic Essays*, edited by Murray M. Schwartz and Coppélia Kahn, 244–63. Baltimore: Johns Hopkins University Press, 1980.

Index

Articulating the Elephant Man

Designed by Ann Walston

Composed by Brushwood Graphics, Inc.,
in Bodoni Book with Poster Bodoni display

Printed by R. R. Donnelley & Sons Company
on 50-lb. S. D. Warren's Cream White Sebago,
and bound in Holliston Aqualite
with James River Papan endsheets